The Gardener's Guide to Growing

DAYLILIES

The Gardener's Guide to Growing
DAYLILIES

Diana Grenfell

David & Charles
Newton Abbot

TIMBER PRESS
Portland, Oregon

PICTURE CREDITS

Karl Adamson: 24, 32, 35, 39, 48, 88, 103; Scott Alexander: 136, 138, 139; Derek Carver: 130, 131, 151; Pam Erikson: 62; Roger Grounds: 58, 69, 84; Jack Hobbs: 85, 143; Marc King: 1, 14, 17, 18, 20, 23, 27, 36, 38, 40, 43, 45, 51, 53, 65, 75, 77, 78, 80, 83, 92, 109, 111 (top), 115, 116, 118, 126, 132, 134, 140, 144, 148; David Kirchhoff: 64, 68, 73, 95, 106, 110, 111 (bottom); Lynn Purse: 7, 98, 101; Werner Reinerman: 55; Karl Rupp: 135; Doris; Simpson: 61; Matthias Thomsen-Stork: 10, 114; Bob Schwarz: 2, 120; Kevin Walek: 94; Justyn Willsmore: 3, 8, 44, 47, 56, 57, 66, 70, 74, 91, 100, 104, 112, 122, 125, 142.

Illustrations on pages 13, 26–31, 119 and 122 by Coral Mula

NOTE: Throughout the book the time of year is given as a season to make the reference applicable to readers all over the world. In the northern hemisphere the seasons may be translated into months as follows:

Early winter	December	*Early spring*	March	*Early summer*	June	*Early autumn*	September
Midwinter	January	*Mid-spring*	April	*Midsummer*	July	*Mid-autumn*	October
Late winter	February	*Late spring*	May	*Late summer*	August	*Late autumn*	November

First published in the UK in 1998 by David & Charles Publishers,
Brunel House, Newton Abbot, Devon
ISBN 0 7153 0695 2

First published in North America in 1998 by Timber Press Inc.,
133 SW Second Avenue, Suite 450, Portland, Oregon 97204, USA
ISBN 0-88192-461-X

A catalog record of this book is available from the Library of Congress.

Designed by Sue Michniewicz
Printed in Italy by Lego SpA

Acknowledgements

Daylilies are grown worldwide under very different conditions, so in the preparation of this book I have been reliant on the help of growers in many countries. I would like to thank everyone who has contributed, and in particular, in no special order:

Marc King who was a most valuable source of information. He supplied sketches for some of the illustrations and many superb photographs; he also checked much of the text. Kevin Walek for his overview of 'Growing Daylilies in North America' and for checking text, suppling and tracking down photographs and answering numerous queries; he also introduced me to all the daylily people in Florida. Matthias Thomsen-Stork who, along with his other invaluable help, put me in contact with European daylily breeders and growers. The other contributors: David Kirchhoff, Eve Lytton, Scott

Alexander and Ian Gear, who gave so freely of their time and expertise, and provided photographs.

François Verhaert for allowing his house and garden to be used as a photographic studio. Cor Govaerts, Juliane Kraut, Hanne and Karl Rupp, Werner Reinerman and Tomas Tamberg for information and photographs.

Lynn Purse for sharing her ideas and artistic flair for growing daylilies and for her photographs. Pat Bennett for helpful suggestions about worthwhile cultivars. Bob Schwarz for supplying up-to-date information on the categories of Spiders, Spider Variants and Unusual-form daylilies, and for photographs. Jean Norris and her Committee of the Central Florida Hemerocallis Society.

The American Hemerocallis Society's e-mail Robin for sharing their rich seam of knowledge,

including Jim Shields, Gus Guzkinski, Jo Halinar, Bill Watson, Melanie Mason, Melanie Vlasso, Lyn Stoll, Beth Creveling, Pat Crooks Henley, Matt Reyna, Don Jerabek and Greg McMullen, Roger Mercer, Peter Brandt-Sorheim, Patricia Loveland, Betts Daume, Dianne Taylor, Pam Erikson, Lisette Brisebois, Phil Brockington, Chris Darrow, Donald Spencer, Charlotte Chamitoff and many others.

Other American colleagues, including Dr Darrel Apps, Roswitha Waterman, Bob Clary, John Harris, Dr Lyn Batdorf, Margo Reed, Don Marvin.

British colleagues, including Jan and Andy Wyers, John Newbold, Chris Searle, Ted and Mary Czaicki, Gerald Sinclair, Valerie Anderson.

Ra Hansen and John Benz for information and cultural hints in their nursery catalogues.

Photographs: page 1 'Condilla', one of the best golden-yellow, double daylilies; page 2 'Ghost Dancer', an elegant reflexed, spatulate, Unusual daylily in pale, otherworldly tints; page 3 The vigorous and prolific, small-flowered daylily 'Cranberry Baby'.

CONTENTS

FOREWORD

There can be few, if any, perennials which have, in the twentieth century, received so much attention from and been so popular with gardeners, growers and breeders than the daylilies, or *Hemerocallis*. The variety now on offer is enormous, and, to all except the collector or specialist, often bewildering.

In the United States, for instance, several hundred daylily cultivars are introduced each year and, at the last count, the American Hemerocallis Society had registered 40,000 different named selections. Not all will be widely offered, but one might well ask 'Why so many?' The short answer is because most daylilies are adaptable and showy plants, able to withstand extremes of cold, heat and humidity, and, along with the *Hosta*, a genus that also originated in Asia, have become the most popular perennials in North America. This popularity has led to the development of an almost insatiable, mostly collector's, appetite for new flower forms, which the breeders are more than fulfilling. From triangular, circular, star- or spider-shaped to frilled, doubled, miniature or small-flowered, fragrant and deciduous or evergreen, there are any number of diverse types from which the gardener can choose.

So how do you choose the best plants for your garden from the multitude available? Well, we are lucky to have someone of Diana Grenfell's authority to provide us with this clear, factual and well-researched guide to a fascinating and now somewhat complex genus. Diana has written this book in terms that we can all understand. Beginning with the species and their introduction to cultivation, it gives information about the start of selective breeding and includes details on the most recent hybridization work in the United States and elsewhere. Although Diana herself has a wealth of experience of growing daylilies at Apple Court in Hampshire and regularly visits daylily growers in North America, she has added to the value of this book by inviting contributions from experts in North America, Europe and Australasia, giving us a genuine world view from which to assess the importance and role of these plants for present day gardeners.

Not just a treatise on the genus *Hemerocallis*, this book is also a practical guide to how to use daylilies in gardens and how to grow them well. The successes of breeders mean that there are now daylilies that will fit almost any garden situation, but we need to be given the confidence that what we choose will grow, thrive and flower well in our particular climate. Most of us want to grow daylilies in association with other plants in our gardens, such as grasses, shrubs or conifers: this has not been overlooked. Diana gives some first class suggestions on planting companions and schemes. This is, indeed, a valuable book for all gardeners and one which will, I feel sure, be dipped into constantly for reference and inspiration.

Ruffled pink 'Vi Simmons' with the rose 'Sommerwind' and *Ammi majus*.

INTRODUCTION

Twenty-five years ago daylilies were scarcely known in Britain but today they are rapidly heading towards becoming as popular here as they are in America. This growing enthusiasm is reflected in the numbers now available.

I have known and loved the early scented species and cultivars since childhood, but when, some twenty years ago, I started seriously looking for a wider choice I was surprised to find just how few there were obtainable. I remember visiting the famous Beth Chatto Gardens in Essex in the late 1970s and seeing a deep lustrous purple daylily in what was then considered a very modern form: round, ruffled and wide-petalled. On enquiring as to availability I learned that there would be none for at least ten years!

Thinking to bridge this seemingly interminable gulf of disappointment I set out to see whether I could find it, or others almost as desirable, anywhere else. My searches took me first to Germany and Switzerland, and later to America, where I discovered daylilies more marvellous than my wildest dreams. Well and truly hooked, I have been collecting them ever since.

In this book I hope to share some of my passion for these sumptuously exotic plants, and to encourage other gardeners to grow them. There is now an enormous range of daylilies to choose from, with flowers in a once unimaginable spectrum of colours and great diversity of form, bred in climates varying from the sub-tropical luxuriance of Florida to the cooler conditions of Canada with its icy win-ters. Clearly, not all daylilies will grow in all climates, and there are other limitations on which can be grown in any particular garden, but it is possible to have an extraordinarily wide range in most gardens. It is my aim to point the way to choosing those daylilies that will give you the highest performance in your particular garden and to give some insight into the many varieties and how they came into being.

The choice of daylilies in the chapter entitled A Selection of the Best Daylilies (p.40) is personal insofar as I have grown and cherished a great many of them in our garden at Apple Court. Others I have seen, often over several years, in the gardens of enthusiasts in different parts of the United States from Florida to Pennsylvania, in gardens in New Zealand, South Africa and several countries in Europe; yet others are included because they are the favourites of experienced growers from all over the world, whose knowledge of these plants I greatly respect. This selection is, nevertheless, just a taster for the feast yet to come. My aim is that this book will be a sufficient incentive to encourage others, both gardeners who have not grown daylilies before and keen collectors, to venture still further into the world of daylilies.

This book is vastly enriched by the contributions of respected breeders and growers from all over the world: I sincerely thank them for so generously sharing their wealth of knowledge and experience of growing daylilies.

'Moonlight Mist' is a charming, ruffled miniature in soft shades of ivory cream and pink. An early-morning-opener, it has rain-resistant blooms.

1

EARLY HISTORY & BOTANY

aylilies have been known and grown for thousands of years. Natives of Asia, they are featured in paintings and folk legends dating back to Confucius (551–479BC). They were originally grown as food or medicinal plants. The Chinese name for *H. fulva* is "hsuan-sao" meaning the forgetting bush, alluding to its tranquillizing and hallucinatory properties: the young, boiled shoots were often given to those who were in mourning.

Daylilies first reached Europe via the trade routes: *H. lilioasphodelus* (syn. *H. flava*) probably arriving in Hungary, and *H. fulva* in the sea ports of Lisbon or Venice. References to both first appeared in the works of the European herbalists Clusius (1525–1609) and Lobel (1538–1616) in the sixteenth century and in Gerard's (1545–1612) *Herball or Historie of Plantes* (1597). Daylilies, along with peonies and lilacs, were among the very few ornamental plants taken to America by the early settlers and used in their homestead gardens.

During the last two hundred years other species have reached Europe from Asia, including *H. minor*, which was described by Philip Miller, Curator of the Chelsea Physic Garden (1722–71), although his description is rather vague. In the nineteenth century, plant hunters such as Wilson, Forrest and Kingdon-Ward, found important species, mainly in the Yangtze River Gorge country in western China. Living plants of *H. dumortieri* were shipped by Phillip von Siebold to the botanic garden in Ghent. *H. middendorffii* was first collected by Alexander von Middendorf and described by him after it had flowered in the botanic garden in St. Petersburg. *H. fulva* 'Flore Pleno' arrived in Europe in 1869, and later *H. citrina* and *H. fulva* 'Maculata' were received by Charles Sprenger and Willy Muller (in Italy), who disseminated them, and other species, around Europe.

A brick-red Unusual seedling makes a wonderful foil to *Sambucus racemosa* 'Aurea' in this garden.

The first recorded daylily hybrid 'Apricot' was introduced in 1893 and given the Award of Merit from the Royal Horticultural Society in the same year. A cross between *H. lilioasphodelus* × *H. middendorffii*, it was one of many crosses introduced by the pioneer hybridizer, George Yeld (1845–1953). He and Amos Perry (1871–1953) were the only British breeders of daylilies in the early part of the twentieth century. Perry's output was prodigious although a large proportion of his introductions are now lost. Of those remaining, 'Thelma Perry', a strongly scented yellow, and 'Lady Fermoy Hesketh' are treasured by those gardeners whose preference is for the older sorts.

In the mid-1950s two iris growers started their own daylily hybridizing programmes. Harry Randall's 'Amersham' and 'Missenden', both early red tetraploids, were awarded First Class Certificates by the Royal Horticultural Society. Leonard Brummitt's introductions in the 1960s and 1970s, bearing the 'Banbury' prefix, were highly regarded in their time but were soon superseded by the work of Robert Coe (p.126). For the next thirty years British gardeners looked to the United States and, in a small way, to European breeders, for new daylilies.

Classification

The genus *Hemerocallis* (from the Greek *hemera* a day and *kallos* beauty) was so named by Linnaeus in the eighteenth century and placed by him in the Liliaceae (lily family), along with hostas, kniphofias, aloes and the true lilies. It has long been recognized that Linnaeus' lily family was far too large to be meaningful. Under the modern classification of the monocotyledons proposed by Dahlgren, Clifford and Yeo (1985) and now widely used, daylilies are placed in their own family, the Hemerocallidaceae. However, more recent molecular DNA studies show that daylilies are most closely related to phormium, which would place them in the family Phormiaceae, in the order Asparagles.

Habitat

The genus *Hemerocallis* contains (at most recent estimates) approximately 30 species of evergreen, semi-evergreen or herbaceous (winter dormant or dormant) perennials, natives of meadowlands, marshy river valleys and deep, rich soils at forest margins. It is endemic in eastern Asia, according to Chung and Kang (1994) and is found in China (north of the Yangtze river), Mongolia, north-eastern Siberia, North Korea, South Korea (except for its southern tip), and the Japanese islands of Honshu (central spine and northern half), Hokkaido and Sakhalin. *H. fulva* and *H. lilioasphodelus* can be found wild in parts of Europe, but it is unlikely that they are natives. Where daylilies are indigenous, the climate is characterized by monsoonal, humid summers, with the rainfall decreasing from south to north, and dry winters.

BOTANY

Daylilies are monocotyledons and mostly clump-forming, sometimes rhizomatous perennials, making mounds of leaves, from which arise usually branched scapes bearing trumpet-shaped, lily-like flowers. Produced over a long period from early to late summer, each flower only lasts about a single day. The species flower colours are limited to yellow, orange and fulvous shades, although the range has been vastly extended by hybridizers over the past 75 years.

The Crown

The junction point from which the leaves, flowers and roots begin to grow is called the crown. If it becomes damaged, part or all of the plant will die. It should be planted to lie approximately 1cm (½in) below soil level. It is the crown, and the growth buds overwintering on it, that determine the frost hardiness of a daylily.

The Root System

The roots of daylilies spring directly from the crown and are generally pale tan-brown and thick, often with fleshy swellings, though some also have fibrous roots. Springing from the sides of the crown and growing outwards and downwards, they may taper and be forked, like the claws of a crab. They can be cylindrical as in *H. dumortieri* or spindle-shaped as in *H. fulva*, although those of *H. lilioasphodelus* and *H. middendorffii* are relatively fibrous. Generally the roots form dense, compact clumps, although *H. lilioasphodelus* and *H. fulva* increase freely by rhizomes. Hybrids may be intermediate in root character.

The swollen organs on the roots act as food reservoirs, carrying the plants through dormancy and enabling them to grow away vigorously rather earlier in the spring than competing plants.

The Foliage

The leaves of daylilies are strap-shaped, smooth to finely ribbed, usually somewhat folded inwards along the midrib and arise from the crown in two ranks, arching upwards and outwards as they ascend to form a fan. Varying in colour from pale to dark green, they may possess a glaucous bloom and are often yellowish to very pale green in spring, sometimes assuming rich yellows and ochres in autumn.

H. aurantiaca, a warm climate plant, is the only evergreen, the others being more or less winter dormant.

The Flower Scapes

The flowers of daylilies are borne on erect or oblique, usually rigid, scapes (leafless stems) that arise directly from the leaf fan. Hollow and smooth, they range in colour from pale green to almost black, as in 'Sir Blackstem'. In width they can be as much as 5cm (2in) thick, as in 'Scapes from Hell', or delicately slender, as in 'Kindly Light'.

Scapes vary in height from as little as 4cm (1½ in), as in *H. darrowiana* (p.16), to over 2m (6ft), as in *H. altissima* (p.15). The scapes of the hybrids range from 22–115cm (9–45in), averaging between 45–75cm (18–30in), but reaching 1.2m (4ft) in some of those of Unusual Form.

They are more or less round in section and more or less branched in their upper third. *H. multiflora* is notably free-branching while *H. dumortieri* and *H. middendorffii* branch only towards the tips. *H. nana*, by contrast, has unbranched scapes and bears solitary flowers. If the plant is transplanted or divided, the scapes are normally considerably lower than the registered height the following season.

Proliferations (see also p.151) can sometimes produce scapes up to 10–12cm (4–5in) long and their own flowers while still attached to the parent plant, as in 'Yesterday's Memories' and 'Double Cutie'. This is more likely to apply to daylilies growing in hot climates.

The Bracts

The bracts, situated on the upper third of the scape, are usually held below the base of each branch, although they occasionally appear at slight node-like swellings on the scape. Resembling small, thin leaves, they are elongated-oval, extending to a point, raised along the midrib and vary from pale green to dark brownish-black. They usually shrivel after flowering.

The Flower Buds

The buds first appear small and almost round, gradually elongating until they reach their maximum length on opening. They also gradually swell above the tube, the tip still pinched together, and are lightly ridged on the outer surfaces. Ranging from light green to mahogany-brown, as

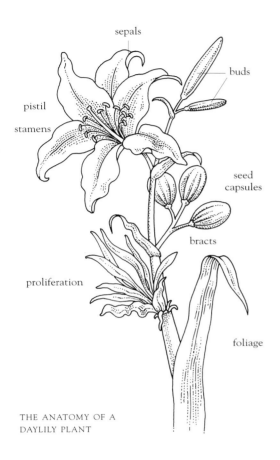

sepals

buds

pistil

stamens

seed capsules

bracts

proliferation

foliage

THE ANATOMY OF A
DAYLILY PLANT

DAYLILY FLOWER CROSS SECTION

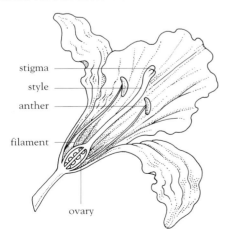

stigma

style

anther

filament

ovary

in *H. dumortieri*, as anthesis approaches the buds assume the final colour of the sepals although they are flushed green until fully open, particularly towards the tip.

The Flowers

The flowers of daylilies are large and colourful. The flower is attached to the scape by a short pedicel and is made up of six petal-like segments, known collectively as tepals. These are arranged in two sets of three, the outer ones (initially forming the casing of the flower bud) being called sepals, the inner ones, petals. The sepals are usually narrower and more pointed than the petals. The petals and sepals are usually united towards the base, forming a short tube. The perianth is more or less trumpet-shaped in outline, flaring only slightly in the species and early hybrids, but usually recurving sharply or rolling back in the modern hybrids.

The reproductive organs arise from the throat or tube. There are six slender stamens at the tips of which dangle the anthers which produce pollen, the male reproductive agent. The pistil, the female organ, is a single tube, rather thicker and protruding further than the stamens, and arising from their midst. The end attached to the flower is swollen and contains the ovules; the other end has the slightly swollen stigma. When receptive, the stigma becomes sticky so any pollen that touches it will adhere. Fertilization takes place when the pollen grows down the tube inside the pistil to reach the ovules. After fertilization the flower falls away, leaving the ovary capsule to ripen.

Fragrance

Several species of daylily are noted for their fragrance, classified as musk or heavy and smelling like honeysuckle. The fragrance of *H. lilioasphodelus* is considered the most powerful, closely followed by *H. citrina* and *H. thunbergii*. A slight fragrance may also be detected in *H. altissima*, *H. dumortieri*, *H. middendorffi* and *H. minor*. Humidity and soil moisture are critical factors in the expression of fragrance in daylilies. In fragrant nocturnal daylilies the scent is apparent upon opening, but in fragrant diurnals it does not develop until the day has warmed up. In cooler climates far less fragrance is apparent in most daylilies.

The Seeds

The seeds develop in the roughly egg-shaped, dark green ovary capsules, which consist of six segments, separated by six ribs. When ripe (60–80 days after fertilization), the segments spring open in pairs revealing three rows of round or ovoid seeds, each with a slightly raised point at one end. They are usually black and shiny if fertile, almost white if sterile. The number of seeds in the capsule varies with the species or cultivar, and is always fewer with tetraploids.

2
HEMEROCALLIS SPECIES

Apart from the fragrant yellow, early flowering *H. lilioasphodelus*, *H. dumortieri* and *H. middendorffi*, species daylilies are not grown in gardens as much as the modern hybrids, which on the whole have greater ornamental value. Nonetheless, the species are valuable because it is from them that all the characters found in hybrid daylilies have been derived.

The definition of a species is open to various interpretations but in principle a species should be a clear and distinct entity. The problem with daylilies is that there are relatively few characters by which the species can be distinguished, and this makes it harder, rather than simpler, to tell one from another. Consequently, opinions differ on how many daylily species there are in existence – some botanists putting the number as low as 12, others putting it as high as 30. A number of new species have been named by botanists working in the field in China, Korea and elsewhere, but as these have not yet reached the West and have not been verified by Western botanists they are not discussed here. The genus may well undergo considerable revision in the future. (Z = Hardiness zone rating.)

H. altissima Stout (1943) The Tsu-kin-shan Daylily, Purple Mountain Daylily This species has fully dormant, coarse, spreading leaves, up to 1.2m (4ft) or more. The erect, stiff scapes, up to 2.2m (7ft), are the tallest of any species. They branch in the upper quarter, bearing occasional leaf-like bracts up to 10cm (4in) long. The nocturnal flowers, produced from late summer to early autumn, are 7.5cm (3in) across, trumpet-shaped, pale yellow and slightly fragrant on warm evenings. The seed capsules are widest at the summit. The roots are coarse with spindle-shaped swellings and erect fan bases.

A native of China, this species was introduced to

H. altissima is a tall-growing species that has been much used in the breeding of Spider daylilies.

America in both seed and plant form by Dr Albert Steward in about 1930. His material came from the Purple Mountain, Nangking Province, but was thought originally to be from the Lower Yangtze Valley. However, the Chinese expert Dr Hu questions this locality as, from her experience, daylilies were not native to this region. She presumes that Steward obtained his plants from local farmers.

H. altissima is unique among daylilies for its height; the genes for this factor are being used by certain breeders to produce taller daylilies. It is also valued for its fragrance and its nocturnality. Where temperatures are warm, it is a perfect nocturnal, opening its flowers at around dusk and having them fully closed by dawn. However, where temperatures are lower it will take longer to open and may remain half-open all the following day. Typically, it flowers later in the season than most daylilies, from midsummer into the autumn, and is now being used to raise later flowering daylilies. A famous plant, raised from the original seed, grew for some years at New York Botanic Garden and was over 2m (6ft) tall. The plant itself has been lost but its genes live on in hybrids such as 'Autumn Minaret'. The New York Botanic Garden plant was also remarkable for the narrowness of its floral segments and these genes gave rise to spider daylilies (see p.116). Z6

H. aurantiaca Baker (1890) Orange-Fulvous Daylily The rather coarse, strongly two-ranked, glaucous and evergreen leaves of this species reach 80cm (32in). The thick scapes, up to 90cm (36in), are arching. They branch near the top, bearing a few leafy bracts in the upper third. The flowers are borne on notably short pedicels (stalks) or with no stalks at all. There are up to 20 per scape, up to 13cm (5in) across, funnel-shaped and less open than all other species except for *H. dumortieri*. Their colouring is an intense burnt orange with yellow midribs and slightly fulvous flushing. The capsules are oblong. The roots, with tuberous swellings, are stoloniferous and far-reaching. A native of southern China, it was introduced to Kew Gardens about 1870 from where clones have been distributed. It is not by any means certain that *H. aurantiaca* is a true species. Z6

Although a rarity in gardens, perhaps on account of the brashness of the flower colour and because of its reputation for tenderness, *H. aurantiaca* has several qualities that breeders prize. It is evergreen and the genes for this are dominant over the genes for dormancy, so that when it is used as a parent the offspring are invariably evergreen. It also has the longest flowering season of any daylily species. It was also used by hybridizers to produce wider petals.

H. aurantiaca 'Major' Baker (1895) Differs from the foregoing species in its lesser stature, the scapes only rising to 60cm (24in), and in its larger, though less widely opening flowers, which are 12cm (5in) across. The flowers, borne in midsummer, sometimes with a few in early autumn, are a more even orange, lacking the reddish-brown overtones of *H. aurantiaca*. Again, the botanical status of this plant is not clear. It is much more tender than *H. aurantiaca*. Z8

H. citrina Baroni (1897) Citron Daylily, Long Yellow Daylily Vigorous, hardy and drought tolerant, this species has arching, coarse, broad leaves, up to 110cm (42in). They are deep green but assume a distinctly blue-green sheen in sunlight, the bases flushed purple. Forming a compact clump, the foliage dies down unattractively towards late summer, being the most profoundly dormant of the species. The scapes are stiffly erect, to 114cm (45in), and branch in the upper quarter. The nocturnal flowers, up to 65 per scape, are 12cm (5in) wide and 17cm (7in) long, and narrow and stiff. They are very fragrant and pale citron-yellow, with the sepals greenish on the reverse with purple tips. The black capsules are obovoid to subspherical. The roots form compact clumps. Many have club-like swellings, others are long and slender. The younger roots are orange, the older, main ones are brown. Thought to be self-infertile. Z4

Introduced from Shen-Shi, southern China in 1895 by Giraldi, this species has long been treasured for its sweet fragrance, its soft colouring and above all because it opens in the early evening. It is much used in hybridizing for its fragrance. Its nocturnality is also a useful quality. It was unsurpassed in the early days of hybridizing, particularly when crossed with *H. thunbergii*. Widely cultivated in parts of China as a source of dried flower buds for culinary use.

H. citrina 'Baroni' is a hybrid between *H. citrina* and *H. thunbergii*. It differs from *H. citrina* in small details.

H. citrina var. vespertina (Hara) Erhardt (1988) Originally considered a species, the botanical status of this plant is still not clear. It is certainly not the same as typical

H. citrina, nor is it the same as *H. thunbergii*, as suggested by Dr Hu. In character it seems to be intermediate between *H. citrina* and *H. altissima*, and may have specific standing somewhere between the two. It produces very tall scapes, up to 1.8m (6ft), which may branch as much as seven times, some forking again at the tips. The many scapes produce up to 75 buds, ensuring a very long flowering season: recorded by one grower as lasting from July until October. The flowers are a clear light yellow, about 7.5cm (3in) across, and slightly fragrant.

H. coreana Nakai (1932) This species has leaves up to 45cm (18in) long and scapes to 80cm (32in), with numerous branches towards the tips. It produces up to 80 flowers per scape. Borne on short pedicels, they are 12cm by 13cm (5in) with wax-like, greenish-yellow floral segments. The capsules are apical and the roots 'roughly rugose' (Nakai).

Introduced from Korea to the United States by Dorsett and Morse in 1929, there is still confusion as to the true identity of this species since it contains features in common with *H. lilioasphodelus* and *H. minor*. Zone rating not yet determined.

This species is as yet unknown in Europe and is little known in America.

H. darrowiana Hu (1969) Named for Dr Darrow of the American Hemerocallis Society, this is a miniature species with leaves no more than 8cm (3in) long. It forms dense clumps, the inner leaves erect, the outer ones arching. The scapes, up to 4cm (1½in), each bear 2 yellow flowers, to 6cm (2½in) across, somewhat resembling those of *Zephyranthes* in shape. Zone rating not yet determined.

Found on Sakhalin Island in 1969; has not yet reached the West.

H. dumortieri Morren (1834) Dumortier's Daylily Named in honour of B.C. Dumortier of Belgium (1797–1878), this species forms a dense clump. The 35cm (14in) leaves become lax after blooming. The scapes, which are the same length as the leaves or a little taller, are unbranched and lean towards the ground. They bear up to 4 barely fragrant flowers which are reddish-brown in bud, opening rich deep yellow and up to 7cm (3in) across. The short flower stalks are hidden by two, attenuate, overlapping bracts. The capsules are subglobose.

Native to Japan, Korea, Manchuria and eastern Siberia, this species was introduced by von Siebold into Holland in 1830, from whence it was spread around Europe by seed, giving rise to several clones. *H. dumortieri* var. *rutilans* Perry (1929) and *H. dumortieri* var. *altaica* Pearce (1952) are not genuine botanical varieties but garden cultivars.

H. dumortieri, a deep yellow flowered species daylily still grown in many gardens.

The spelling *dumortierii*, adopted by Bailey, is now deemed incorrect. Prized for its early flowering. Z4

H. esculenta Koidzumi (1925) The arching leaves of this species are up to 80cm (32in) long, with up to 13 per fan. They have minute papillae along their margins. The erect scape, up to 90cm (36in), branches only near the tip and bears bracts only above the first branching. Each scape bears 5–6, orange, trumpet-shaped flowers, 10cm by 11cm (4in by 4½in), on notably short pedicels. Capsules oblong; seeds ovoid. The roots spread out from the crown rather than growing down, and lack swellings. Z5

Native to meadows in the mountains of Japan and on Sakhalin Island, this plant was introduced by Nakai in 1935. It is doubtful whether it is a true species. It is now in the Homburger Staudengarten.

H. exaltata Stout (1934) This species has leaves up to 90cm (36in) long and strongly folded along the midrib. It forms a compact clump but the leaves are brown and nearly dormant towards late summer. The 1.2m (4ft) scape branches only at the tip and holds the flowers in a tight cluster well clear of the foliage. The flowers, 12cm (5in) across, are bright orange, opening during the day in early to midsummer. The petals are spathulate (widest past their midway point). Capsules ellipsoid; seeds rounded. Roots are thickened, slightly enlarged and spindle-shaped. Z4

Native to Tobishima, a small island west of Japan. Seeds were sent to New York in about 1930. Its botanical status is unclear. Stout regarded it as a variety of *H. middendorffi* while Kitamura thought it was a form of *H. dumortieri*. In 1970 several variants were found on Tobishima.

H. forrestii Diels (1912) *H. forrestii* has husky, mid-green leaves, up to 30cm (12in) with erect scapes, up to 30–60cm (12–24in) long, branching repeatedly towards the tip and bearing a few short (1cm/½in) bracts as well as some longer (6cm/2½in) conspicuous ones. There are up to 8 flowers on each scape. Up to 7cm (3in) across, they are funnel-shaped and yellow or orange-red, and borne on pedicels up to 2cm (¾in) long. Capsules oblong. Roots fleshy. Z5

A native of Yunnan, south-west China, where, unlike other species, it grows in dry conditions, on rocky ridges and banks. Introduced from Yunnan in 1906. Similar to *H. nana* and very tender.

H. fulva Linnaeus (1762) This species, which tolerates shade better than other daylilies, has broad leaves, 90cm (36in) long, strongly folded along the midrib. The leaves become dormant at low temperatures, resuming growth when soil temperature reaches 10–13°C (50–55°F). The scapes are taller than the foliage and branch in the upper quarter. They each bear up to 20 funnel-shaped flowers with segments that are reflexed and wavy at the edges, 10cm (4in) wide. The flowers vary from rusty orange-red to red and pink, often with a brownish eye. Several varieties have been named. Most have darker, distinctly coloured midribs on the petals. The capsules are oblong and the seeds obovoid. *H. fulva* is stoloniferous with one of the most extensive roots systems among the species; the roots often have spindle-like enlargements.

Its origins are uncertain but it seems to have been long cultivated in China and Japan where it has become widespread. Introduced some time before 1576. Z4

H. fulva is one of the most important species in the story of daylily hybrids since it was from its forms that the first breaks in breeding were made, though many of the varieties are sterile, having a triploid chromosome count. Pink daylilies were first raised from *H. fulva* var. *rosea*, and it was from a cross between *H. fulva* var. *rosea* and *H. aurantiaca* that the first red daylilies were produced.

H. fulva 'Europa' is the most commonly grown form with well-formed flowers of fulvous-red, with darker veins, a broad brownish eye and apricot midrib. Its roots are quite different from those of the typical plant, producing long rhizomes and, unlike most daylilies, most parts of them will produce new plants. Although a triploid, and therefore sterile, its pollen is fertile. It was much used as a pollen parent for many of the early hybrids and, through them, has played an important role in the development of the modern hybrids.

H. fulva 'Flore Pleno' is one of the two double forms of *H. fulva* closely related to *H. fulva* 'Europa'. These forms are often confused, although they are distinct enough.

'Flore Pleno' has beautifully symmetrical hose-in-hose, orange flowers, 15cm (6in) across, with a conspicuous red eye and strongly recurved outer floral segments. This plant was received by the nurseryman Veitch and exhibited at the Royal Horticultural Society in 1860. An original plant from Sichuan is growing in the Homburger Staudengarten.

H. fulva **'Kwanso Variegata'** was introduced prior to 1864 from Japan as *Kwanso foliis variegatis*. The flowers are also double, but quite distinct from 'Flore Pleno' and of poorer form. They are fulvous-reddish and their eyes, though as dark as those of 'Flore Pleno', do not appear so because the ground colouring is darker. The leaves are variably longitudinally striped white, and range from wholly white to wholly green. It is triploid and sterile. *H. fulva* 'Kwanso' is the green form. Kwanso is the Japanese name for daylily.

H. fulva **'Vieux Carre'** is the only evergreen form of *H. fulva*. It played a part in the early hybrids almost by accident simply because it arrived in America with early settlers from Europe, and was there-fore to hand. It is now widespread in Louisiana and the Southern States.

H. fulva **var. rosea** Stout (1930) is a dark-eyed variant; its clones, without the deeper-coloured eye, are distinct among the forms of *H. fulva* for their rosy-pink flowers. A native of Kuhling, it was sent to Dr Stout in 1924 and he named it var. *rosea* 'Rosalind', intending it to be the only clone released. However, because of its unique colouring, the other clones were immediately seized upon by breeders such as Elizabeth Nesmith, L. Ernest Plouf, who named his clone (which did not have a deeper-coloured eye) 'Pastel-rose', and Ophelia Taylor in Florida. It is the main source of pink and red genes in daylilies.

H. **graminea** Andrews (1802) This species has straight, strongly keeled leaves, like grass, up to 75cm (30in) long. The scape, also 75cm (30in), is erect but curving towards the top, and carries up to 3 flowers. Brown-tinted green buds open to orange flowers, 12cm (5in) across, with a yellow throat, which remain open for 2–3 days. Floral segments are wavy and brown on the outside. Z5/6

A native of Amur and the region round Lake Baikal. A plant Maximowicz named *H. graminea* forma *graminea* is now *H. minor*. Stout received a third plant called *H. graminea*, which he regarded as a dwarf form of *H. dumortieri*. Authenticated material of this plant has not yet reached Europe.

H. **lilioasphodelus (syn.** *H.* **flava)** Linnaeus (1753) Lemon Daylily, Tall Yellow Daylily, Custard Lily The abundant upright leaves of this rhizomatous species

H. fulva var. *rosea* 'Rosalind', an early parent in the development of pink and red daylilies.

form loose clumps. Medium to dark green, they are up to 90cm (36in) long. They are dormant at low temperatures, resuming growth when soil temperatures reach 10–13°C (50–55°F). The scapes are taller than the foliage, but weak. They branch towards the top and bear up to 12 lemon-chrome, strongly fragrant flowers, up to 10cm (4in) across. The capsules are ovoid-ellipsoid; the seeds obovoid, black and shiny. The roots are more fibrous than those of other species, occasionally swelling to form spindle-like storage organs. Z4

From Manchuria across northern China, as far west as Gansu province and parts of Siberia. In cultivation in Europe since 1570. *H. lilioasphodelus* is tolerant of damp ground and in the 1980s was seen in such situations in the mountainous areas of Shandong province.

This is by far the most popular species and is treasured by gardeners for the earliness of its flowering, the clear colouring of the flowers, and for their exquisite fragrance. Although diurnal, it is known for its extended flowering period, its flowers lasting well into the night and sometimes into a second day. It was one of the first species to be used by hybridizers, to develop early-blooming, fragrant, comparatively long-lasting flowers.

H. **middendorffii** Trautvetter & Meyer (1856) The Amur Daylily, The Middendorff Daylily This species produces flat, smooth leaves, up to 30cm (12in) over-topped by unbranched scapes, up to 90cm (36in). In early summer it bears barely fragrant, pale orange, unmarked flowers, up to 10cm (4in) across, up to 10 opening in succession. The pedicels are largely hidden by broadly oval bracts. The distinctly ridged buds are green without any brown colouring; the capsules are broadly ellipsoid. The roots are cylindrical, and do not extend far. Z5

A native of northern China, Korea, Japan and eastern Russia, and introduced by Maximowicz in 1860, this species has played an important role in the development of modern hybrids and is a good garden plant in its own right, but has the disadvantage of holding onto its flowers when they are over, instead of shedding them. Often confused with *H. dumortieri*.

H. minor (Miller 1768) The Grass-leaved Daylily Lax, grass-like leaves, up to 60cm (24in), form a compact clump, which dies to the ground in early autumn. The slender scapes, also up to 60cm (24in) tall, branch at the tips and bear not more than 5 flowers in late spring. These are nocturnal, somewhat fragrant, funnel-shaped, 7cm (3in) across, and near lemon-chrome. They last 2–3 days. It is similar in some ways to *H. lilioasphodelus* although easily distinguished by the sepals, which are faintly tinged brownish-red. Capsules ellipsoid. The seeds of *H. minor* are the smallest of the genus. The long, thin roots have bulbous swellings towards the tips. Z4

Native to the steppes of northern China, Mongolia, Siberia and of Korea, this species was seen by Roy Lancaster growing with *Lilium pumilum* along part of the Great Wall, the pale yellow of the daylily making an attractive combination with the orange-flowered Turk's-cap lily.

H. multiflora Stout (1929) Many-flowered Daylily *H. multiflora* has narrow leaves, up to 75cm (30in), shorter than the scapes and turning brown in mid-autumn at the approach of freezing temperatures. The numerous, somewhat leaning and somewhat glaucous scapes, up to 1m (3ft), are abundantly branched in the upper half. Each bears up to 100 flowers with sharply reflexed petals, soft orange-yellow on the inside, reddish-brown on the outside. Up to 7.5cm (3in) across, they are the smallest of all the species. Capsules obovoid. It is the last of the species to flower, starting in late midsummer and continuing into autumn even after the leaves have become dormant. Roots fleshy. Z4

Dr Albert Steward sent specimens collected at the bottom of a rocky gorge near a mountain stream at Ki Kung Shan, Honan, China, to Dr Stout at the New York Botanical Gardens in 1925. Although having little value as a garden plant *H. multiflora* is an important species for breeders because of its multiple top-branching habit. *H. multiflora* is one of the most used species daylilies in breeding, especially for the Small-flowered and Miniature classes, although it is not an early-morning-opener.

H. nana Smith & Forrest (1916) Sword-like leaves, up to 35cm (14in), form compact clumps. The slender scapes lean outwards and are up to 25cm (10in), scarcely overtopping the foliage. They are usually unbranched and bear a solitary flower with inconspicuous bracts just below it. The flowers have narrow reddish-orange segments, which can be fulvous on the reverse. The roots are cord-like to spindle-shaped; the fleshy brown part is some way from the crown. Z9

A native of Yunnan, south-west China, and introduced by Forrest after 1913, this species is closely related to *H. forrestii* and comes from much the same part of the world.

H. plicata Stapf (1923) The leaves of *H. plicata* are up to 40cm (16in) and strongly folded. Its scapes up to 55cm (22in), are irregularly branched, with up to 11 trumpet-shaped, orange-yellow flowers on 2cm (¾in) pedicels. Capsules oblong. The roots are string-like with spindle-shaped swellings towards the tips. Z5

A native of subalpine and alpine regions in south-west and west China, it is very similar to *H. forrestii* and, with *H. forrestii* and *H. nana*, quite distinct from all other species. It is closely related to *H. multiflora*, from which it is distinguished by the lesser stature of the scapes and the smaller number of flowers. The strong folding of the leaves, sometimes cited as a diagnostic character, tends to disappear with good cultivation.

H. thunbergii Barr ex Baker (1890) Thunberg's Daylily, Late Yellow Daylily This robust, compact species produces semi-evergreen, medium to dark green leaves, up to 60cm (24in), bending downwards at the tips. Slender, erect, rigid scapes branch in the upper quarter and are up to 115cm (45in). They bear up to 15 yellow, funnel-shaped, sweetly fragrant flowers, with green throats. Capsules are small and broadly blunt. Compact roots. Z4

Native to northern China, Japan and Korea, and introduced to Kew Gardens in 1873, *H. thunbergii* has been much used in breeding because its flowers are fragrant and remain open for a long time. It is also a very healthy plant: it and its progeny produce plentiful seed.

H. yezoensis Hara (1937) The broad leaves, up to 75cm (30in), of this species are erect but bent over at the tip. Up to 90cm (36in) high the scapes bear up to 12 lemon-yellow, slightly fragrant flowers, up to 10cm (4in) across. Capsules oblong. Roots cord-like and thick. Z5

This native of Hokkaido, Japan is closely related to both *H. thunbergii* and *H. lilioasphodelus*. It is in cultivation in America and Europe.

3

MODERN HYBRIDS & THEIR TERMINOLOGY

Since their first introduction to the West, breeders have sought to improve the performance and effectiveness of daylilies as garden plants. So successful have they been, and so far have modern hybrid daylilies come from the simple, trumpet-shaped flowers and the relatively plain colours of the original species, that specialized terminology has grown up to describe them. The following is a survey of the various terms involved (for an explanation of ploidy see p.37).

FOLIAGE

The foliage of daylilies is generally classifed as dormant, evergreen and semi-evergreen (see Macrodefinitions, below). For those growing daylilies in cold-winter or subtropical regions, it is useful to have more detailed information on the seasonal changes in foliage. The American Hemerocallis Society has further defined the major foliage types by breaking them down as follows: hard dormant, semi-dormant, semi-evergreen, evergreen, soft evergreen (see Microdefinitions below). It is not always easy to tell which category of foliage a daylily has if the weather is either unusually cold or unusually mild. Daylilies perform differently in different climates and may even perform differently in different parts of the same garden. However, most will acclimatize within about two growing seasons to regions other than those in which they were raised.

Macrodefinitions

Dormant daylilies are those whose leaves die back in winter. However, they may not lose their leaves completely.

Dormancy is initiated when, under conditions of shortening days and gradually cooling temperatures in late summer and autumn, abscisic acid (ABA) moves from the stems and leaves to the rhizomes, where it initiates the formation of the dormant buds for next year's growth and is stored both for winter respiration and to fuel the first new growth of spring. The termination of dormancy is controlled by another plant hormone, gibberellin, which becomes active as temperatures slowly rise and day-length increases.

The condition known as 'summer dormancy' affects some daylilies, such as 'Frans Hals' and 'Fairy Tale Pink', as well as other groups of plants, especially those endemic to hot climates. This is when the cycle of growth is completed in late summer and if the ground is particularly dry the leaves start to die away. New growth will soon appear after feeding and watering the ground well.

Evergreen daylilies are those whose foliage is green throughout the year, implying that they are continuous growers, albeit growing at a slower pace during the winter. However, in cold-winter regions, especially in areas of frequent freeze/thaw cycles, the foliage will be frozen and become mushy once there is a thaw. Evergreenness in daylilies is often associated with frost-tenderness but the two are controlled by different mechanisms and do not necessarily coincide.

Semi-evergreen is a term of dubious definition, some authors even disputing whether there is such a category. The best definition seems to be that semi-evergreens are temperature-controlled dormants that are not necessarily deciduous. They may grow continuously and appear evergreen in hot climates, but behave as dormants in colder areas.

Microdefinitions

Hard-dormant daylilies are those whose foliage dies down completely early in the autumn, often after the first frost, remaining dormant until late spring. They need at least 29 days of dormancy to remain vigorous, and in hot climates, where they often cannot get this rest, tend to perform less well, developing grass-like foliage and refusing to bloom,

A sculptured daylily of heavy substance, 'Pear Ornament' sometimes has ruffling deep into the heart.

often dying out completely after a few years. It can take several years to assess whether or not a hard-dormant will perform well in a hot climate.

Semi-dormant daylilies go dormant in very late autumn and winter, only after prolonged cold weather, and reappear again in early spring. They appear to die down only to ground level, rather than below ground as do hard-dormants. In hot climates they can resume growth almost immediately, without a period of chilling.

Semi-evergreen is a category highly dependent on temperature conditions and the most difficult to define. The tips of the foliage die, with about 7–10cm (3–4in) of green remaining above ground. This growth looks like that of a dormant daylily when it begins growing in spring. These daylilies seem to suffer little damage even in the coldest weather, generally performing well throughout a very wide temperature range, although many perform better with a period of chilling in the winter.

Evergreen daylilies are those that remain green all the year round. When frosts occur the foliage will freeze and fall over but a few centimetres will remain above ground and generally this is not affected by the coldest weather. In regions of freeze/thaw cycles there is a danger that the part of the foliage nearest the crown will freeze and then rot when the weather turns warm. A good mulch should prevent any damage. Evergreens need to be watched closely (every day if possible) if further freezing weather strikes after spring regrowth has begun. Mushy leaves can fuse together and prevent the growing point emerging, which would result in the death of the plant. It is advisable to cut off this damaged foliage as a precaution.

Soft-evergreen or tender daylilies are those that remain green all the year round but whose foliage will freeze all the way to the ground and become mushy when frosts strike, often freezing into the ground. Most of these daylilies are bred in hot climates and are the least hardy; they freeze deep into the crown and will dwindle and lose vigour or die if not well mulched. They are most vulnerable in regions of freeze/thaw cycles; the next most vulnerable areas are those where the ground freezes for the whole winter, followed by those that have a permanent winter snow cover.

THE HARDINESS FACTOR
In a mild climate, such as that of most of Britain, many daylilies are wholly frost hardy but in northern continental Europe one species (*H. aurantiaca*) and some Southern-bred varieties may not survive winters unless mulched.

Tenderness and evergreenness both come from *H. aurantiaca*, which is somewhat frost-tender, and *H. aurantiaca* 'Major', which is even more tender. Evergreenness is controlled by one set of genes, tenderness by another set: they do not necessarily occur together. However, the genes for evergreenness are dominant, so whenever evergreens are crossed with dormants the evergreen trait will dominate; the dormant trait will be masked but not absent. This balance between the genes means that many modern hybrid daylilies, which are plants of complex parentage, can adapt the amount of foliage they carry through their resting period in different climates.

Although tenderness has been bred out of some daylilies by the incorporation of genes for hardiness, it is still very prevalent in certain popular, Southern-bred American evergreen diploid lines. Some breeders are converting the very same tender-evergreen diploids to use in their tetraploid lines, so tenderness can also enter many Southern tetraploid lines, for example the tetraploid form of 'Monica Marie'.

SCAPES
Scape height is more subject to climatic and soil variation than the size of the blooms. Daylilies raised in Florida and the Deep South of America often have lowish scapes, which is due to the selection, by breeders, of lower and lower scapes and the intensity of the sun. Many cultivars grown and registered as very short scaped in the Deep South ('Barbary Corsair' and 'Jolyene Nichole') grow much taller in cooler climates.

In certain daylilies the length of the scape is such that the flowers are held among the leaves or only just above them. For garden use it is much more desirable to have scapes that are tall enough to hold the flowers well clear of the foliage and much has been done to ensure that this is now the norm. It is also important that the daylily produces enough scapes and that the flowers are well spaced on the scape.

Height
Scape height is defined by the American Hemerocallis Society as follows:

Dwarf	under 30cm (12in) (Most Dwarfs are also Miniatures, see p.113)
Low	15–60cm (6–24in)
Medium	60–90cm (24–36in)
Tall	over 90cm (36in)

Husky scapes are those that are rather fat or thick.

Branching
Branching enables each scape to carry many more flowers

'Farmer's Daughter' is a sumptuous satin-textured daylily with superb branching. A wonderful performer.

than it would were it unbranched, so hybridizers strive to raise daylilies not only with an adequate number of branches, but also with branches in a well-spaced arrangement known as candelabra branching.

Top-branching is where the branching occurs only at the top of the scape. Some of the older Spiders and many of the low-growing Southern-raised cultivars suffer from this fault and breeders are beginning to address the problem. Descendants from *H. multiflora,* including 'Golden Chimes', 'Corky' and 'Lemon Bells', are multiple top-branched, making very graceful sprays of small flowers coming off the scape just below the top.

Well-branched (candelabra, show-branched) applies to those daylilies with the branches disposed along the scape in a well-spaced arrangement, from the top of the foliage mound to the terminal branch, so that the flower buds are

not crowded. Good examples of this trait are 'Farmer's Daughter' and 'Second Thoughts'. Numbers of branches are often noted, for example 4–5-way branching means that a scape has four lateral branches and one terminal branch.

Low-branched daylilies are those whose scapes start branching within the foliage mound as in 'Scarlet Orbit'.

Pre-scapes

These are scapes that appear very early in the year having been formed as latent rebloom or late-bloom scapes too late the previous season to develop properly. Most pre-scapes do not reach to the foliage tips and are sometimes not even discovered until their blooms are already spent. They are not usually representative of the cultivar's true bloom sequence and are also often not as fully developed or richly pigmented as their normal-season counterparts. These pre-scape blooms, however, can allow hybridizers to glean an early pollen harvest, and also perhaps gain a pod parent from an otherwise later-blooming plant.

PLATE I
HERITAGE – pre 1970

H. 'Sampson'

H. 'Stafford'

H. 'Lilac Chiffon'

H. 'Frans Hals'

H. 'Pink Damask'

H. 'Cartwheels'

H. 'Luxury Lace'

All flowers are shown at approximately ¼ size

H. 'Red Precious'

H. 'Nob Hill'

H. 'Elaine Strutt'

H. 'Frances Fay'

H. 'Fairy Rings'

H. 'Ava Michelle'

BUD COUNT

Bud count refers to the number of buds on each scape, which can vary from less than ten to over fifty, depending on the genetics of the daylily and the amount of sun, water and food available. Traditionally, daylilies formed all their buds before the first flower opened and these continued to open at intervals until all the buds were gone. Nowadays many daylilies are what are known as bud builders, that is they continue to form buds through the flowering period, thus extending the season of bloom.

A high bud count is rated as between 30 and 50 per scape, medium between 20 and 30 and low under 20. Ten scapes of 50 buds is ideal. Cooler climates generally give a lower bud count than hot climates. It is useful to know what constitutes a good bud count locally and to ensure that your future introductions, or purchases, are at least equal to those cultivars that are already performing well. In areas where there is frequent rebloom, a high bud count is not essential, but it is prized in cooler regions where there is only one season of bloom. An overabundance of buds that are tightly clustered together is not a good trait as many flowers will be distorted on opening and the dying flowers will spoil those about to open.

Equally as important as bud count is the number of scapes per clump. A daylily such as 'Pearl Lewis', with a just-adequate bud count of up to 15 per scape, has so many scapes in the clump that it appears as a bouquet of flowers for over three weeks.

FLOWERS

Size

The diameter of the open flowers of daylilies can vary from 3.5cm to over 27cm (1½–11in). The American Hemerocallis Society has placed flower sizes into the following categories, measured across the face:

Miniatures	less than 7cm (3in)
Small-flowered	from 7–11cm (3–4½in)
Large-flowered	from 11–27cm (4½–11in) and above

In general flower size should be proportional to height. The most accurate method of measuring the size of a daylily flower is to use a set of wire rings. The flower size is the diameter of the smallest ring that will encircle the outer edges of the flower in its normal open position. The blooms are at their maximum size during the first half of the bloom season and subsequent batches of scapes invariably have smaller blooms than the size registered.

Shape

The daylily species mostly have trumpet-shaped flowers, but in hybrids these have been greatly modified and a number of new flower shapes have been recognized. The terms describing these new shapes refer either to the side view of the flower or to the face view.

Side View Terms

Trumpet-shaped flowers resemble those of Regal or Madonna lilies where it is only just possible to see the interior of the flower, as in 'Dorothy McDade'.

Flaring flowers are those with segments arching out over the throat, which is shorter than with trumpet-shaped flowers. A flared profile often goes with a triangular front view as in 'Goodnight Gracie'.

Flat describes flowers that open flat except for the throat, which is very short. Flat-faced flowers show their true colouring only from the front.

Oscie Whatley is known particularly for his full, flat-formed daylilies such as 'Molokai'.

FLOWER SHAPES

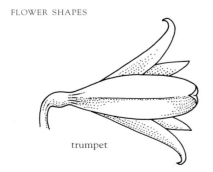

trumpet

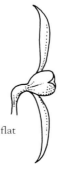

flat

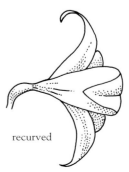

recurved

FLOWER SHAPES

triangular   circular

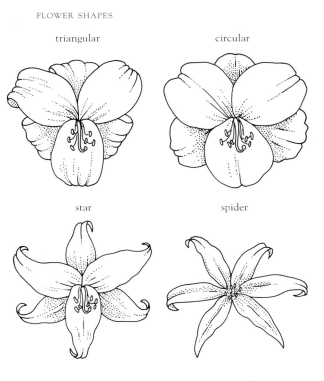

star   spider

Recurved flowers are those whose floral segments roll back so that far more of the flower is seen in profile than in a flat-faced or trumpet-shaped form. Many daylilies require a hot climate in order to recurve fully; 'Neal Berry' is one such.

Front View Terms

Circular flowers appear round in outline and come about as a result of exaggerated overlapping of the usually short, blunt segments so that only a small portion of the sepals can be seen. Many of the Siloam daylilies are circular, a trait inherited from the Spalding and Guidry lines.

Triangular flowers occur when the sepals recurve more than the petals, as in 'Claudine' and 'Emperor's Dragon'.

Star-shaped flowers are closed in the throat and have long-pointed, sometimes pinched petals and narrow sepals that recurve, as in 'Ruby Spider'.

Spider/Spider Variant floral segments are much longer in proportion to their width than the normal flower and the segments do not overlap. When determining the ratio of a

'Country Pride', a floriferous, pale orange, full, fluffy double which flowers well in many regions.

Spider or Spider Variant, measure the longest petal at its widest point as naturally standing (without uncurling, unfolding, or flattening any portion of the petal). For length, stretch out the longest petal to its fullest and measure the length from its tip to the V-shaped notch formed where the adjacent petals separate at the neck of the flower. **Spiderers** are slender-tepalled cultivars that can produce very slender-tepalled offspring, such as 'Garden Portrait' and 'Kindly Light'.

Exotic and Unusual Form is applied to daylily flowers not having narrow enough segments to class as Spiders but having long segments that twist, curl and pinch attractively.

FLOWER SHAPES

double
(layer-on-layer)

double
(hose-in-hose)

ruffled

Informal is a catch-all term for flowers that are untidy in shape, not matching any of the descriptions given above, as in 'Frank Gladney', and which may have other qualities.

Throat and Heart

The throat is the portion of the segments up to the point where the inner surface achieves a right-angle in relation to the stem-pistil line. By this definition, the trumpet-shaped daylilies are all throat except, possibly, at the very ends of the segments. At the other end of the scale, daylilies like 'Lights of Detroit', in which the segments flare quickly from the centre, where they are joined to form the perianth tube, have practically no throat at all. The heart is the very small area at the base of the throat, separating the throat from the perianth tube.

Floral Segments

The general appearance of the flowers may also be affected by the addition of extra floral segments or by the conversion of the stamens into organs that look like floral segments.

Polytepal A polytepalous daylily is one that has more than the usual complement of three sepals, three petals and six stamens. Typically a polytepalous flower will have eight or ten floral segments and a similar number of stamens, as in 'I'm Different'.

Edges The outer margins of the floral segments may be flat, tailored (symmetrical), widely ruffled or looped, evenly ruffled or tightly crimped. Most double daylilies have more or less ruffled edges.

Double Flowers

Double-flowered daylilies invariably have more than the basic complement of six floral segments. The number of extra tepals may be anything from two to eighteen. There are two basic types of doubleness in daylilies, those that form an extra layer, or layers, of petals, leaving the stamens intact, and those in which some or all of the stamens have been converted into petaloids. The petaloids may be formed by the addition of petal-like segments to the stamens, sometimes on only one side of a stamen, sometimes on both sides. Usually the remnants of an anther are visible; sometimes it becomes rudimentary or non-existent, so that the petaloid looks like a normal petal. Some doubles appear very full and fluffy, as in 'Country Pride', while others are only slightly double, as in 'Sometimes Maybe'.

Double daylilies are temperature sensitive and perform magnificently in hot climates but in cooler regions may only produce double flowers during exceptionally hot periods. Some flowers may open fully and some hardly at all. It is quite usual for registered doubles to open as singles at the beginning of their flowering season and as doubles later. Because there is so much extra floral tissue, double daylilies may need pampering to keep them flowering freely and opening fully. Single-flowered daylilies such as 'Fairy Tale Pink' may produce a few double flowers in very hot weather.

Full double has six petaloids and no intact stamens. Also known as a peony or cockatoo form, as in 'Betty Woods'. A full double can also have additional petals that may vary from two to six, plus petaloids formed from the stamens. While the true petals are layered, the petaloids give the flower an overall appearance of a cockatoo or peony double, as in 'Frances Joiner'.

Semi-double has petaloids but fewer normal stamens; some flowers may contain floral tissue that is halfway between stamen and petaloid, as in 'Scatterbrain'.

Crested or Midrib-double is where there are only three true petals, but each has formed petaloid tissue fused to the midrib. This usually projects outwards giving the appearance of even more petals, as in 'Siloam Double Classic'. Extreme forms exhibit more prominent petaloid tissue giving a more fully double appearance as in 'Virginia Franklin Miller'.

Hose-in-hose is a double flower with additional layers of usually six, but sometimes more or less, true petals with the six stamens intact, as in 'Condilla' and 'Layers of Gold'.

Popcorn double is a new term coined for the tightly clustered tetraploid mini-doubles such as 'You Angel You', 'Bubbly' and 'Roswitha'.

Flower Substance

Substance refers to the thickness of the floral segments. These can vary from thin to quite thick and leathery, depending upon the number of layers of pigment that make up the structure of the floral segments. There are two pigment systems, located in different regions within the cellular structure of the tepals (see Colour below). The tepals are covered on both surfaces by the epidermis or skin, composed of a single layer of protective cells. Sandwiched between the two epidermal layers is the mesophyll consisting of tiers of irregularly shaped living cells. It is the number of these tiers and the size of the cells that determines the thickness of the tepals, and this is governed by genetic inheritance. Daylilies with thin tepals have 1–3 layers of cells, those with thick tepals (good substance), up to fourteen. Tetraploid cells are invariably larger than diploid cells. Embedded within the mesophyll is a network of vascular cells that conduct food and water. These are what we recognize as the veins.

COLOUR PATTERNING

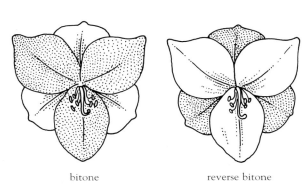

bitone   reverse bitone

Surface Texture

Texture is a quality of the surface of a daylily flower depending upon the single-layered epidermis. The surface may appear smooth as in 'Kate Carpenter', waxy as in 'Pear Ornament', crêped as in 'Brocaded Gown', seersuckered as in 'Gentle Shepherd', corduroy-ribbed as in 'Fairy Tale Pink', leathery as in 'Mary Frances Ragain' or with a pile-like, velvet finish of varying degrees of depth as in 'Kent's Favourite Two'; 'Anastasia' is among those with the densest pile. Crêped or rough-textured flowers absorb light, enriching the colours and, in the case of darker colours, giving them a sultry glow. Daylilies with smooth flowers reflect light, making the colours seem brighter and clearer.

Colour

The pigments that determine the colour of daylily flowers are located in different layers of the tepals. The underlying yellows, oranges and fulvous tints are produced by plastids containing carotenoids situated in the mesophyll, the middle layers of the tepals. The red, pink and purple pigments (which are water soluble) are produced by anthocyanadins concentrated in the vacuoles of the epidermal cells. Thus the pink, red and purple pigments are only surface deep. On the whole yellow-influenced, rusty-red colouring is easier to achieve, and better tolerates hot sun and heavy rain, than the blue-reds whose pigments are superficial and can run off the surface.

The flowers may be evenly of a single colour or may be made up of two or more different colours or shades, combined in various ways. The throat is not included in the definitions below.

Self describes a flower in which the petals and sepals are all the same shade of the same colour; the colour of the throat or filaments may be different.

Blends occur when an amalgam of two colours is distributed evenly across the floral segments, eg salmon and rose-pink as in 'Frank Gladney'.

Polychrome refers to a flower in which several colours may be intermingled across all the floral segments. These are normally pastel shades of cream, yellow, melon, pink, rose and lavender, as in 'Little Rainbow'. Polychrome daylilies were made popular by the late Brother Charles Reckamp. Many so-called polychromes are only melon, blushed pink and lavender.

Bicolor is when the petals and sepals are of different colours, the sepals being the lighter colour, eg red and yellow, as in 'Frans Hals'. Many bicolors display some of the petal colour at the sepal bases but the best examples are those having two distinctly separated colours.

Reverse bicolor is the situation reversed, with the petals being lighter as in 'Something Different', 'Tiny Tiki' and 'Upper Crust Society'.

Bitone occurs if the petals and sepals differ in shade or intensity. Typically the petals are saturated with colour while the sepals are a paler shade, as in 'Blessing' and 'China Bride'.

Reverse bitone has sepals that are a darker shade than the petals as in 'Chocolate Dude'.

Throat Colour

Since the throat can vary from relatively small to quite large, the impact its colouring can make on the overall effect of the flower can be considerable or insignificant. Throat colours are limited to shades of yellow, orange, melon or green. Where the throat is large and the colour a contrast with the main flower colour, the effect can be dramatic, as in 'Open Hearth'. But where a yellow flower also has a yellow throat, the impact is negligible, as in 'Beauty to Behold'. Green throats in daylilies were first seen in diploids in early crosses using the nocturnals and fully developed in certain breeding lines by the early 1950s but did not reach perfection until the 1980s, as exemplified by 'Rose Emily' and 'Sharon Voye'. The earliest green throats faded to yellow but many nowadays stay green all day, such as in 'Kimmswick' and 'Satan's Curls'.

Sunburst throat describes a throat area flowing out onto the floral segments, ranging in colour from yellow to chartreuse-green. It occurs most often in red daylilies such as 'Christmas Is' and 'Dragon King'.

Midrib Colour

The midrib is a stripe dividing the petal into two halves. It runs from the throat to the petal tip. It may be conspicuous or scarcely noticeable, raised (prominent) or flat, and can be a lighter shade or lighter contrasting colour to the petal colour. Most often it is pale yellow or cream but can have a pearl-like appearance. Flowers with floral segments which are long in proportion to their width often have midribs that are pinched towards the tip.

Eyes, Banding and other Markings

A distinguishing pattern on many daylilies is a band of a different or darker shade at the juncture of the segments and the throat. If the darker shade appears on both petals and sepals, it is called an **Eye**. If the darker colour is on the petals only it is called a **Band** as in many of the Siloam small and miniature daylilies. 'Cherry-eyed Pumpkin' is narrow-eyed; 'Queensland' is medium-eyed; 'Paige's Pinnata' is an example of an eye covering most of the visible petal area. The eye or band on a triangular flower will also assume a triangular shape, as in 'Forsyth Ridge Top'.

Halo describes a band or colour that is faint or lightly visible, as in 'Graceful Eye' and 'Russian Easter'.

Watermark or negative eye is a wide strip of a lighter shade where the segment colour meets the throat, as in 'Magic Carpet Ride' and 'Respighi'. Watermarks are a genetically determined lack of pigmentation in the eye-zone, revealing a lighter clearer colour that harmonizes with the usually darker outer tepal colour. Sometimes these watermarks have a chalky appearance as in 'Malaysian Monarch'. The first notable watermarked eyes were produced by Bill Munson using 'Tet Catherine Woodbery'.

COLOUR PATTERNING

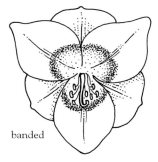

banded

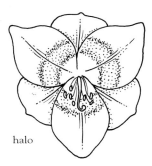

halo

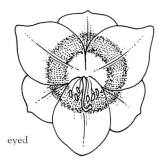

eyed

COLOUR PATTERNING

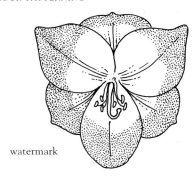

watermark

Washed and Pencil-etched Eyes are produced where the colour of the eye bleeds into the throat, but is bordered on the outer edge with a narrow band, resembling fine pencil etching, as in 'Dragon Dreams' and 'Siloam David Kirchhoff'. 'Exotic Echo' was the first daylily to exhibit this trait. The latest innovation is frosted 'thumbprints', as in 'Devil's Footprint', and a double row of white lines in the eyezone, as in 'Dark Mosaic'.

Veined eyes occur when the eyezone pigmentation, instead of being generally applied to the eyezone, is expressed in subtle veining running through the eyezone. This phenomenon is found in 'Chinese Cloisonne'.

Chevron-shaped eyes are usually present when the floral segments are elongated as in Spider Variants and Unusual-form daylilies, eg 'Mountain Top Experience'. There are examples of rounded full-formed daylilies with this type of eye pattern, eg 'Navajo Princess' and 'Someplace Special'.

Stippling is a breaking up of the top layer of pigment so that lighter colour shows through on to the surface as small dashes, as in 'China Veil'.

Dotting is a concentration of a stippled type of pigmentation resembling the work of the pointillist painter George Seurat. It is usually confined to plum-purple and maroon-purplish colours, as in 'Kaleidoscope' and 'Seurat', which is temperature sensitive. Dr J Halinar has also been working extensively with and for this trait, which he first discovered in 'Dots a Plenty', a near-species seedling.

Borders and edges Darker borders, light centres occur in certain diploid daylilies that have denser layers of pigment towards their flower edges. The thicker pigment means that, in hot sunshine, the edges hold their colour longer than the centre, producing the bordered effect as seen in 'Beautiful Edgings' and 'Fama'.

Lighter borders, darker centres is the reverse effect, although it is not weather sensitive but comes about through a lack of pigment and substance around the flower edges. Distinctly lighter borders are usually seen on richly pigmented flowers such as 'Avant Garde' and 'Street Urchin'.

Shark's tooth edging is also caused by a build-up of cell layers along the edges of the tepals, the cells being thinner than normal. They are often lacking in pigment, hence are nearly white in colour. This particular trait shows up as pointed or notched edges as seen in 'Fortune's Dearest', or the earlier, ground-breaking 'Shark's Tooth'. Shark's tooth edging can make the opening of the flower more difficult in cooler climates.

Picotee edges are caused by thick ropes of cells in darker, contrasting colours to the ground colour (usually purple) in tetraploid daylilies. This effect is produced through continuous selection in breeding. 'Canadian Border Patrol' is an example. Picotee edges were first seen and extensively promoted by the Griesbach Klehm breeding programmes in the 1980s.

Gold-wire edges and Braids The phenomenon of gold edges appeared in the tetraploid introductions of Brother Charles Reckamp, such as 'Heavenly Crown', and were little more than a hint of gold thread running through the ruffled edging. Intensive modern breeding has produced more dramatic effects so that in 'Ida's Magic' for example, the edges look like gold-wire embroidered onto the ground pigment. Gold is the colour most frequently seen in these edges, but in 'Regal Braid' the effect is rather of silver wire entwined into a purple picotee edge, no doubt the first of many of this type. Gold-braided edges, as in 'Admiral's Braid' are wider than mere edges, measuring up to 6mm (¼in).

Braided edges, fashioned at a right angle to the plane of the flower are one of the most recent developments as in John Kinnebrew's 'Spacecoast Starburst'. Even greater edge embellishments are now becoming more commonplace and these are appearing in the forms of knobs, hooks and tentacles. These edges add extra weight to the already heavier tetraploid tepals, sometimes making the flower more difficult to open, especially in cooler climates. Significant gold-wire edges are just starting to appear in diploids, but this trend is very much something for the future.

PLATE II
ORANGE, BRONZE AND BROWN DAYLILIES

H. 'Outrageous'

H. 'Cherry Smoke'

H. 'Duke of Durham'

H. 'Double Coffee'

H. 'Country Pride'

H. 'Mauna Loa'

H. 'Show Amber'

H. 'Little Deeke'

H. 'Judah'

H. 'Berlin Tallboy'

H. 'Cajun Gambler'

All flowers are shown at approximately ¼ size

Tipped flowers are those with only the tips of the floral segments, and usually only the petals, in a contrasting colour, as in 'Lights of Detroit'.

Diamond dusting is a phenomenon whereby the surface texture of the tepals of many daylilies, usually those of light colour, is covered with what appears to be a dusting of silver dots. These are caused by sugar crystals produced by the plant to protect the pigment from sun damage and are much more obvious on daylilies growing in hot, sunny climates. Gold dusting can appear on the surface of some darker daylilies, usually reds and oranges. This attribute does not show up in photographs.

Veining on some daylily flowers is very noticeable, particularly on those of lighter colour. Noted introductions exhibiting this feature are 'Little Deeke' and 'China Bride'.

Filaments of daylily flowers are usually yellow, but may also be ivory to chartreuse. They are often tipped, where they correspond to the base colour, in the same shade as the base colour and are now seen in pink, red, mauve, purple and near-black.

Anther colours change during the day as the pollen sacs open; the pollen grains are usually red, brown, yellow, grey or black. Some daylilies have large black anthers, which are an attractive contrasting feature, as in 'Arctic Snow'.

FLOWERING HABITS

Daylilies have three types of blooming habit:

Diurnal daylilies flower during the day, opening between dawn and noon, and closing early in the evening.

Nocturnal daylilies open late in the afternoon or early evening and remain open all night, closing sometime during the following day.

Extended bloom daylilies remain open for at least sixteen hours. Both diurnal and nocturnal blooming daylilies can be extended bloomers.

Rebloom

Rebloom occurs when further scapes arise from a fan that has already bloomed, as distinct from a different fan putting up a scape immediately after flowering has finished on the first scapes. There is no rebloom in a daylily that is not genetically a rebloomer. Some daylilies with a strong rebloom factor should rebloom wherever they are grown, provided there is a long season to ensure high enough temperatures in late summer and early autumn. Where the rebloom factor is less pronounced, rebloom can be encouraged by an ample, continuing supply of food and water.

Instant rebloom occurs when the daylily sends up a new set of scapes before the first set finshes. 'Scarlet Orbit' does this, extending its season of bloom to nearly 5 weeks.

Secondary bloom is when the daylily takes a break before producing the next set of scapes as in 'Bill Norris' and 'Video'. In colder regions, growers prefer instant rebloom as an early onset of autumn frequently means that latecomers will not open.

Continuous bloom is when just as the first scape blooms out, another scape appears. What really counts is how many good blooms there are per season from one fan. Some daylilies, such as 'Stella de Oro' have almost continuous bloom cycles but should be given fresh soil every other year, as well as ample and regular food and water, to keep up the high output.

SEASON OF BLOOM

Daylilies of one sort or another can be in flower from early spring until the first frost, depending on the coldness of the climate. The following terms and abbreviations are generally used to indicate the different seasons of bloom. All are relative to the area in which the daylily is being grown.

EE – Extra Early The first daylilies to bloom: early spring in the hottest regions, early summer in cooler regions.

E – Early These bloom from 3–5 weeks prior to the peak bloom season.

EM – Early Midseason These bloom from 1–3 weeks before the peak bloom season.

M – Midseason Flower at peak bloom time in one's own garden.

ML – Late Midseason These bloom from 1–3 weeks after the peak bloom.

L – Late These open when most others have finished blooming, usually 4–6 weeks after peak bloom time.

VL – Very Late These are the last daylilies to bloom, usually in late summer in the hottest regions and autumn in cooler regions.

MARKER DAYLILIES

Certain daylilies have been nominated as Marker Daylilies by the American Hemerocallis Society – their date of opening marks the start of a bloom season. Examples are: **E** 'Stella de Oro', **EM** 'Mary Todd', **M** (not recorded), **ML** 'Frandean', **L** 'Autumn Shadows', **VL** 'Sandra Elizabeth'.

PLATE III
BOLD-EYED DAYLILIES

H. 'Svengali'

H. 'Daring Dilemma'

H. 'Dragon King'

H. 'Sweet Sugar Candy'

H. 'Oceanside'

H. 'Ben Lee'

H. 'Tigerling'

H. 'Real Wind'

H. 'Tiger Kitten'

H. 'Fooled Me'

H. 'Winter Mint Candy'

All flowers are shown at approximately ¼ size

4
DIPLOIDS VERSUS TETRAPLOIDS

The listing of Tet or Dip next to the name of a daylily in a book or catalogue means tetraploid or diploid and relates to the chromosome count. This may be puzzling to those new to daylilies. Indeed, many gardeners would not be able to tell from looking at a daylily flower whether it is a diploid or a tetraploid. Nor would it matter. But it matters to hybridizers, who must be sure of the pollen they are using, partly because tetraploids and diploids cannot be crossed, but also because great claims are made for tetraploids. They are said to have flowers up to one third larger than their diploid counterparts, with heavier substance and brighter or more intense colouring, sometimes embellished with picotee or gold-wire edges, moreover, they are also said to be better able to withstand hot sunshine and heavy rain. Tetraploids also have greater vigour, stronger scapes, greater winter hardiness and more resistance to insect damage and disease.

On close inspection, other less desirable differences may be evident. The thicker floral tissue of the tetraploid can act to muddy the flower colour. The outline of the daylily may be more rigid without the graceful habit of the diploid. The foliage appears ridged, the upper surface becoming warty, and the sepal tips are thicker and may open prematurely.

Colchicine and Chromosomes

Chromosomes are small bodies within the cell nucleus that carry the genes which determine all hereditary traits. During the course of normal cell division, they are duplicated then drawn apart and separated from each other by a new nuclear membrane. Two identical nuclei emerge, each surrounded by a new cell wall. Colchicine prevents the formation of this new cell wall so that, instead of divid-

ing, the chromosomes remain together in the cell nucleus, which results in the cell having twice the normal number of chromosomes. In daylilies the normal number of chromosomes, known as the diploid number, is 22 (2n=22), in tetraploids the chromosome count is doubled to 4n=44.

Tetraploidy can occur naturally in both plants and animals. It can be induced artificially in daylilies. In 1937 scientists discovered that colchicine, a highly poisonous chemical alkaloid, isolated from the crocus-like, autumn-flowering *Colchicum autumnale*, could be used as a mutagen through a reaction with the protein tubulin, for altering the chromosome complement.

Early attempts at converting dormant daylilies to tetraploids were, in the eyes of many daylily enthusiasts, a retrograde step since the results were ugly, stiff plants with vertically cracking scapes, lacking the refinement of the diploids, which by that time were beginning to acquire a sumptuous beauty with their striking eye patterns and ruffled edges. It was only due to the foresight of a few dedicated daylily breeders like Orville Fay, Bill Munson, Dr Virginia Peck and Brother Charles Reckamp, that tetraploid daylilies have reached their current dizzy heights.

Although more and more amateurs are beginning their own conversion programmes, only the work of a handful of breeders is, as yet, commercially available. Patrick Stamile's 'Candy Series', from 'Siloam Virginia Henson' which perform well over a broad climatic range, are the best known.

The 'Candys'

The tetraploid conversion of 'Siloam Virginia Henson' was chosen by Patrick Stamile as the basis for his Candy Series, many of which fall into the small-flowered category. 'Strawberry Candy', whose other parent is 'Panache', is the most well known: its flowers, which are of thick substance, need warm days and nights to open to their full extent; however,

'Queensland' is one of the excellent daylilies raised from 'Tet Siloam Virginia Henson' and is similar in appearance to 'Winter Mint Candy'.

'Barabara Mitchell' is an opulently ruffled and recurved, pale pink daylily, which performs well in most climates.

programmes, although flower form in these darker colours cannot on the whole yet be compared with diploids.

Diploid daylilies still capture the market in pinks, the exquisite shape and ruffling, exemplified by the Spalding and Guidry lines, not yet being surpassed in form and grace. However, the conversion of 'Barbara Mitchell' (itself a double grandmother of Guidry's 'Janet Gayle'), brought pink tetraploids to a new level of refinement with introductions such as 'Seminole Wind', 'True Grit' and 'Pink Ambrosia'.

Daylily growers and breeders with an interest in the development of Spiders and Unusual Forms (see Chapter 9) are busy converting many older sorts to tetraploid, thus putting strength into weak stems and giving substance to floppy floral segments. In fact, breeders looking for material to convert are reviving interest in a wide variety of long-forgotten, older daylilies that were once considered superseded, but may just possess a particular attribute; 'Trahlyta' being a case in point.

Not only are hybridizers striving to make a good diploid daylily even better in its own right, they want to use its potential attributes, such as a distinctive eye pattern, clear, true colour or a refined flower shape, in a converted form for future tetraploid breeding programmes.

The majority of daylily conversions are inherently unstable and this means that the ploidy needs to be checked when buying tetraploid daylilies for breeding purposes, especially if the plant has been converted for less than two years. Points to check are: that the pollen size is at least 40% larger than the pollen of its diploid counterpart, that the pollen has been at least 40% larger for at least two seasons, and that the seedlings show an obvious affinity to the pollen parent.

Recently, substances other than colchicine have been found even more effective in converting daylilies. These include Surflan and Treflan, which are weedkillers.

Tetraploid Conversion
Details of the methods of converting diploids to tetraploids, either by crown meristem treatment, seedling treatment or tissue culture treatment, are available from all daylily societies.

once in flowering mode it does not stop until cut down by the autumn frosts. 'Custard Candy' and 'Wintermint Candy' having no such difficulties in opening, are a perfect shape with excellent growth habits and pleasing combinations of colour. All the Candys are instantly recognizable due to their similar characteristics such as their roundness and distinctive bold eye. There are now many other daylilies with 'Tet Siloam Virginia Henson' as a parent, these include the beautiful 'Tigerling' and 'Queensland'.

Bill Munson and Steve Moldovan have raised the quality of purple tetraploid daylilies, with intricate eyes and watermarks, to new heights with their tetraploid breeding

PLATE IV
PURPLE DAYLILES

H. 'Swirling Water'

H. 'Malaysian Monarch'

H. 'China Lake'

H. 'Regent Street'

H. 'Grand Masterpiece'

H. 'Tuxedo'

H. 'Gloucester Calling'

All flowers are shown at approximately ¾ size

5

A SELECTION OF THE BEST DAYLILIES

The hybrids listed in this chapter are arranged by flower colour or other distinctive flower characteristics. Use the index to find particular named hybrids.

A number of abbreviations are used to list the key characteristics of daylilies and their flowers. These are listed below. Chapter 3 Modern Hybrids and Their Terminology explains the more technical terms. Details of the awards listed after the breeder's name are given in Chapter 11 (p.131).

Tet = tetraploid; Dip = diploid
Dor = dormant; SEv = semi-evergreen; Ev = evergreen
H = height of scape (as registered by breeder)
F = size of flower (width); Mini = miniature flowers;
   Sm = small-flowered; Dd = double-flowered;
   Her = heritage (bred prior to 1970)
E = early summer blooming; M = midsummer blooming;
   L = late summer blooming
Re = reblooming; Ext = extended flowering
Noc = nocturnal flowering; SNoc = semi-nocturnal
Fra = fragrant; SlFra = slightly fragrant;
   Very Fra = very fragrant

WHITE TO IVORY

Absolute Zero (Millikan 87) Dip, SEv, H50cm (20in), F11cm (4¼in), M, Noc Charming, slightly recurved, ruffled and pleated, near-white to creamy ivory-lemon, matching filaments, green throat. Medium substance and crêped texture. Excellent foliage all summer. Floriferous with good rebloom in many areas but the first flowers to open can be too near the foliage.

'Roman Toga', a pristine near-white daylily suitable for colder gardens; one of many raised by Bryant Millikan.

Arctic Snow (Stamile 85) AM Tet, Dor (most areas), H60cm (24in), F15cm (6in), M, Ext Full-formed, flat, delicately ruffled, somewhat translucent ivory-cream to near-yellow (in some regions) with pink highlights, green throat, black anthers, good substance. Reasonable to only moderate bud count, good branching, vigorous and can proliferate. A superb parent. Very popular in Europe.

Gentle Shepherd (Yancey 80) AM Dip, SEv, H50cm (20in), F12cm (5in), ML, Fra Lightly ruffled, diamond-dusted, translucent, near-white, thin substance and crêped texture, clear green throat. The first breakthrough in breeding for white daylilies, and probably still the whitest daylily available, but has a slightly old-fashioned shape and rather poor foliage; somewhat slow to increase. Suffers from thrip and aphid damage and can pass on leaf streak to its progeny. Can be tender in severe winters. Still very white in its converted tetraploid form.

Give Me Eight (Reinke 93) Dip, SEv, H1.2m (4ft), F20cm (8in), ML, Fra Wide-open, polytepal (eight tepals 80 per cent of the time), near-white, yellow throat and matching filaments, contrasting black anthers, small green heart. The petals have ruffled edges and somewhat pinched midribs, the sepals are narrower, with more pointed tips. Graceful, slender scapes.

Joan Senior (Durio 77) AM, LAA Dip, Ev, H63cm (25in), F15cm (6in), M, Re, Ext Lightly ruffled, diamond-dusted, somewhat translucent, near-white with lemon-green throat, ivory filaments, near black anthers. Full, rounded form; recurved petals and sepals. Bud count of about 25, 2–3-way branching. Reblooms in many areas, proliferates, can remain open for part of a second day in cool weather. Although it needs winter protection in severe cold-winter climates, it performs well in nearly all locations but can be a martyr to thrips and aphids. Excellent pollen or pod parent. Also a tetraploid conversion. Sets a standard for near-white daylilies and still the most popular in the British Isles and Europe. Ian Gear regards it as the best 'white' he has trialled in New Zealand, where it produces an abundance of flower, occasionally reblooming.

Kasuq (Jinkerson 86) Dip, SEv, H65cm (26in), F12cm (5in), ML Lightly ruffled, smooth, diamond-dusted, opaque, near-white to cream self with cream filaments, lemon-green throat. Heavy substance and smooth texture, rain-resistant, early morning opener. Average bud count, a bud builder, so blooms over a long period, slightly too top-branched. An even better performer than its sibling 'Nanuq', but not quite as white.

Lime Frost (Stamile 92) HM Tet, Dor, H65cm (26in), F14.5cm (5¾in), L Rounded to triangular, lightly ruffled, diamond-dusted, somewhat translucent, white with a greenish cast, wide lime-green throat seeping up from the heart. Bloom substance and texture are excellent. Well-branched and budded, it increases well and can proliferate. It is a balanced plant in that the flowers are 7–10cm (3–4in) above the foliage mound. Does not seem to suffer the foliage defects inherent in many white daylilies. Bred from 'Tet Gentle Shepherd' from which it inherits its very near whiteness. Highly recommended for English and European gardens.

Monica Marie (Gates 82) AM Dip (although registered as Tet), Ev (Dor in many areas), H60cm+ (24in), F12cm (5in), EM, Re, Ext, Noc Beautiful, perfectly round, near-white with superb ruffling, green throat. A very 'finished' flower of pansy-form, much used for breeding white daylilies. It does not increase rapidly everywhere and has a lowish bud count although it can produce three sets of scapes; rather top-branched and in cooler climates has scapes much taller than the registered height. A chance seedling out of 'Janet Gayle' (p.57) breeding. A favourite with many growers although it is not successful everywhere; responds to being well watered and well fed; a light winter mulch is beneficial. The tetraploid conversion is also not a good performer everywhere.

Quietly Awesome (Peck 87) Tet, Dor, H60cm (24in), F16.5cm (6½in), M Round, richly ruffled, near-white self, contrasting dark anthers. Heavy substance and high bud count. One of the very best large-flowered near-whites, especially for cold-winter climates.

Radiant Moonbeam (Larch 78) Dip, SEv, H90cm (36in), F16.5cm (6½in), ML Very distinctive, narrow,

Unusual-formed, pink-influenced, near-white, green throat. Well-branched, high bud count, blooms for almost 2 months, an early-morning-opener, very vigorous and fertile both ways. Hardy in regions of winter freeze/thaw cycles. An unusual shape for a near-white daylily and deserves to be better known.

Roman Toga (Millikan 81) Dip, SEv/Ev, H55cm (22in), F11.5cm (4¾in), ML, Re, Ext, SNoc Beautifully formed, ruffled, wide, overlapping, creamy near-white, lemon-green throat. Lush foliage, superbly branched, robust scapes, high bud count and reblooms in many regions. Usually increases well but can be less vigorous than other Millikan whites and needs heat to open satisfactorily.

Schnickel Fritz (Kirchhoff 97) Tet, Dor, H40cm (16in), F12cm (5in), Dd, EM, Re, Ext Rounded, ruffled, petaloid double, near-white to palest pink, tiny green heart. Thoroughly tested in different regions for its cold-winter hardiness although a dormant daylily out of evergreen breeding. Moderately branched with a bud count of approximately 20. Lowish scapes but the blooms are held above the foliage. Sunfast, good substance and consistently double.

Sunday Gloves (Lebegue-Rogers 85) Dip, Dor, H65cm (26in), F14cm (5½in), EM, Fra Ruffled, rather narrowly-segmented, clear, near-white, wide pale yellow throat. Remains a good near-white even after cool nights and adverse conditions. The well-branched scapes are held well above the foliage. Good bud count; some growers report having rebloom but others just have one massive show. Excellent in a clump. Fertile.

Welfo White Diamond (Kraut 97) Dip, Dor, H85cm (34in), F10cm (4in), Sm, ML, Ext, Fra Sunfast, round, recurved, ruffled, diamond-dusted, near-white self, lemon-green throat, heavy substance. Moderate bud count, on top-clustered, graceful scapes. Raised in Germany and should have a great future in European gardens as it is a good performer, opening well in cooler climates.

White Lemonade (Loughry 92) FSC Dip, Dor, H63cm (25in), F9cm (3½in), Sm, M, Fra Round, ruffled, near-white, green throat, pale yellow filaments. Good foliage. Well-branched, floriferous, always opens well; hardy. Excellent and highly recommended.

White Tie Affair (Peck 84) Tet, Dor, H60cm (24in) sometimes less, F15cm (6in), M Shapely, broad, full, lightly ruffled, near-white self, green throat (pale lemon in cooler

'Window Dressing' is a southern-raised, near-white daylily of exceptional form.

weather). Well-branched scapes, multiple top-branching. Dark green foliage. 'Inspired Word' is similar. Much used by Patrick Stamile in breeding for white tetraploids.

ALSO RECOMMENDED: 'Angel Cups', 'Dad's Best White', 'Deloria Irby', 'Green Gage', 'Inspired Word', 'Little Fat Cat', 'Moon Snow', 'Mosel', 'Nanuq', 'Pursuit of Excellence', 'Ruffled Ivory', 'Siloam Ruffled Infant', 'Silver Run', 'Snow Ballerina', 'Sounds of Silence', 'Vivaldi', 'White Temptation' (AM), 'Window Dressing', 'Winsome Cherub'.

CREAM TO LIGHT BEIGE

Cream and ivory can bleach to very near white in hot sun, so this category may overlap with the previous one. The cooler the climate, the richer the pigmentation. There are very few cream self-coloured daylilies, but many have a cream ground with eye patterns (see Bold, contrasting eyes pp.83–87, and Deeper-toned eyes pp.87–93).

Apple Court Champagne (Grenfell 98) Dip, SEv, H65cm (26in), F14cm (5½in), ML, Fra Elegantly ruffled, recurved, diamond-dusted, warm ivory-cream to palest peach polychrome, flaring chartreuse throat, pearly-white depressed midribs, pale yellow filaments. Good substance and velvety to ribbed texture. Long blooming (approx 6 weeks). Scapes are rather top-branched but they produce a well-presented bouquet of blooms well above the foliage, which masks this slight defect. Rebloom has been observed in some European gardens. Hardy in cold-winter regions. This daylily was raised from seed of 'Joan Senior' (above) parentage sent to us by Ron Jinkerson and trialled for suitability for British and European gardens. 'Apple Court Chablis' (Grenfell 97) is similar but with a warmer, melon-blush.

Brookwood Paloma Blanca (Sharp 96) Dip, Dor, H60cm (24in), F7cm (3in), Sm, M Distinctive, ruffled, slightly recurved, smooth, ivory-cream to near-white with a small, lemon-green throat, yellow filaments and contrasting black anthers. Nice plant habit; reasonable bud count. Requires dormant period so suitable only for colder regions. Leo Sharp has introduced many creamy pastel shades suitable for growing in colder climates.

Gleber's Top Cream (Spalding 86) Dip, SEv, H60cm (24in), F15cm (6in), EM, Re, Noc Perfectly round, ruffled, widely segmented, overlapped, diamond-dusted warm cream, flaring lime-green throat, ivory-yellow filaments, prominent wide pearly-pink midribs. Heavy substance, slightly crêped texture. Flowers take 2 days to open and are fully developed and slightly recurved by early morning of the second day. Exquisite presentation on top-branched scapes, one scape per fan; each of the 12 or so buds open at approximately 3 day intervals, thus extending the blooming season over 3 or 4 weeks. Does not perform well in all areas, especially those having winter freeze/thaw cycles where it will have little branching and a lower bud count. Probably prefers a sandy soil.

Guiniver's Gift (E. Salter 90) Tet, Ev, H45cm (18in), F8.5cm (3¼in), Sm, M Round, lightly ruffled, full, overlapped, yellow-influenced cream self, lime-green heart. Heavy substance and smooth texture. Well-branched, floriferous. Fertile.

Helle Berlinerin (Tamberg 81) Tet, Dor, H70cm (28in), F12cm (5in), M Lightly ruffled, wide-open to recurved, melon-influenced cream, yellow throat, matching filaments. Heavy substance and ribbed texture. Well-budded on adequately branched scapes. Perfectly hardy. Very popular in English and European gardens.

Kimmswick (Whatley 82) Tet, SEv, H63cm (25in), F16.5cm (6½in), M, Ext Superlative, ruffled cream to palest melon, lavender midribs, outstanding glowing lime-green throat which lasts all day. The top-branched flowers are set just above the lush foliage. Slow to establish and increase but well worth the wait. Completely hardy to sub-zero temperatures and opens well.

'Little Fruit Cup', a confection in cream, can produce double flowers in hot weather.

Lauren Leah (Pierce 83) Dip, SEv, H50cm (20in), F15cm (6in), EM, Re, Noc Outstanding, beautifully formed, ruffled, pink-influenced cream blend, green throat, ivory-lemon filaments. Healthy, good foliage and moderate increase. Needs time to become established but is then an excellent performer blooming over a long period. An early-morning-opener. Popular in Australasia and Europe.

Lenox (Munson 85) HM Tet, Ev, H75cm (30in), F15cm (6in), M-L Impeccable, full, triangular, diamond-dusted, pink-influenced ivory-cream, with cream-green throat radiating out onto the petals, narrower sepals, white veining, gold-wire edging apparent in hot climates. A heavy bloomer, opening well, healthy and well-branched with handsome, arching foliage. Fertile.

Little Fruit Cup (Guidry 88) Dip, Dor, H50cm (20in), 12cm (5in), Ext, Noc Round, widely ruffled, melon-cream, faint strawberry-pink eye, green throat, pink-tipped filaments. Good substance and smooth texture. Resents transplanting but when established it produces a succession of exotic, sometimes double, flowers on moderately branched scapes.

Magic Lace (Wilson 88) AM Dip, Dor, H58cm (23in), F15cm (6in), EM, Ext, Noc Lacy-edged, exquisite diamond-dusted, cream-influenced pastel pink, lemon-green throat, ivory filaments, darker anthers than its sibling 'Lauren Leah' (above). In many climates 'Magic Lace' is the cream-pink that it is registered rather than cream. Very slow to make a clump but each flower is worth the wait; lovely with creamy shrub roses.

Moon Witch (E. Salter 91) HM Tet, SEv, H65cm (26in), F9cm (3½in), Sm, EM, Re Perfectly round, delicately ruffled, pale ivory-cream with a tiny, lime-green heart; a light red halo is sometimes apparent. Recurved sepals, good substance and smooth texture. Well branched, floriferous, vigorous and opens well in cooler climates. Very fertile and an easy parent. A superb garden plant. A 'Tet Sugar Cookie' offspring (below).

Pear Ornament (Spalding 86) Dip, Ev, H40-50cm (16-20in), F12-15cm (5-6in), M, Noc Very wide, recurved, tailored, cream self, green throat, sometimes with a frill into the heart. Opens well in all climates despite its heavy substance, but its floral segments are more recurved in hotter regions almost forming a ball. Hardy, although slow to increase in cooler areas.

Sugar Cookie (Apps 84) AM, AG Dip, Ev, H50cm (20in), F6cm (2⅜in), Mini, M Perfectly round, ruffled, cream, sometimes with a faint brown halo, lemon-green throat. A bud builder. Not always hardy or opening well in all regions in Europe. Also a tetraploid conversion.

Tylwyth Teg (Whitacre 88) AM, IM, LP Dip, SEv, H1.1m (40in), F20cm (8in), M, Re Fascinating star-shaped, spider-like, pale cream rainbow polychrome, lavender midribs, pale gold throat. Vigorous, multi-branched and floriferous. Rapid in growth and increase. A superb parent.

Vanilla Fluff (Joiner 88) AM, IM, LP Dip, Dor, H85cm (34in), F15cm (6in), Dd, M, Fra Full-formed, fluffy, palest cream-beige self. Rather tall scapes but these are unobtrusive because of the large flowers and excellent foliage. Hardy.

Wendy Glawson (Brown 86) Dip, SEv, H48cm (19in), F12cm (5in), EM Nicely ruffled, yellow-influenced cream self, lemon-green throat. Registered as a near-white but even in areas of high heat does not fit into that category. However, it has one of the most modern shapes of the so-called near-whites.

You Angel You (G. Stamile 93) Dip, SEv, H38cm (15in), F5cm (2in), Mini, Dd, M, Re In very hot regions a tiny full popcorn double. Buff-cream to cream-peach with prominent red eye, repeating on the petaloids, green throat. Floriferous, opens well after cool nights (although possibly as a single), well-branched scapes, low arching foliage. Probably the smallest daylily in its class. Reblooms well in hot climates but takes time to settle down.

ALSO RECOMMENDED: 'May, May', 'Princess Ellen'.

LEMON-CREAM

Alec Allen (K. Carpenter 83) AM Dor, SEv, H65cm (26in), Fl4cm (5½in), EM, Re, Ext, Fra Extremely ruffled, full, flat, wide-open segments, recurved sepals, creamy-yellow blend, lime-green throat. Good branching. Hardy in cold gardens, increases well and opens well everywhere. An all time popular yellow.

Betty Warren Woods (Munson 91) HM Tet, Ev, H60cm (24in), Fl1cm (4½in), Sm, EM, Re Impeccably ruffled, recurved, cream-yellow blushed and shaded lemon-yellow, lightly edged gold, small yellow throat, green heart, wide white midribs, ivory-lime filaments, light orange anthers. Good substance and waxy surface texture. Good foliage, well-branched and a good performer, sending up scape after scape over a long period, opening well and never failing to attract attention. Does not rebloom in

'Video' produces perfectly round, richly ruffled, creamy-yellow flowers.

colder regions, where it may need frost protection. From 'Ruffled Dude', which is outstanding for passing on its ruffling; 'Betty Warren Woods' is a wonderful parent.

Brocaded Gown (Millikan 81) AM, SSM Dip, SEv, H65cm (26in), Fl5cm (6in), EM, Noc, Fra Rain-resistant, perfectly round, ruffled, completely recurved, crêpe-textured, delicate lemon-cream, lemon-green throat. Blooms last in spite of their thin substance. Healthy, dark green foliage and a moderate bud count on somewhat wiry scapes. An early-morning-opener and can rebloom twice in regions where there is a long growing season. Dependable vigour in most regions, needs dividing every 3 years but best divided only into pieces with 3 or more fans to prevent transplant shock in colder areas. Winner of many popularity polls. Parent of 'Marble Faun' and 'Video'. Also a tetraploid conversion.

Kathleen Salter (Salter 90) Tet, SEv, H70cm (28in), Fl5cm (6in), EM Beautifully shaped, full-formed, very ruffled, diamond-dusted, smooth, pale lemon-cream, small green throat. Develops pink highlights on cool evenings. Well-branched scapes and good bud count; may not be hardy in colder climates, where it is often slow to increase.

My Darling Clementine (Salter 88) Tet, Ev, H53cm (21in), Fl1cm (4½in), Sm, E, Re Wide, full, flat, finely ruffled, cream-yellow self, lime-green heart. Rather low, dark green foliage; scapes are beautifully branched. Flowers over a long period and a good rebloomer; slow to increase in cooler climates. Extremely fertile and a super parent.

Tell About It (Kirchhoff 90) Dip, Ev, H60cm (24in), Fl2cm (5in), Dd, EM Consistently double, delicately layered, cool green-influenced creamy-yellow, green throat. Well-branched, outstanding performer. The flower has 'depth' due to the contrast between the light outer colour and the shaded inner layers. Hardy and thoroughly recommended for European gardens.

Video (Millikan 85) Dip, SEv, H50cm (20in), Fl2cm (5in), E-EM, Re, Noc Perfectly round, recurved, flat lemon-yellow, green throat, pearly-white midribs, ivory-yellow filaments. Thinnish substance, like its parent 'Brocaded Gown', with crêped texture. Exceptionally well-branched, very floriferous and very popular in the British Isles and Europe. A faithful, very early bloomer and in hot climates reblooms ML-L.

ALSO RECOMMENDED: 'Fred Ham', 'Marble Faun', 'Pudgie', 'Queen of May', 'Siloam Spizz'.

ACID-LEMON TO GREEN-INFLUENCED YELLOW

Anastasia (Salter 89) Tet, Ev, H63cm (25in), F14cm (5½in), M Unique, heavily ruffled, full, overlapped, bright greenish-yellow, large lime-green throat flows out. The lime-green heart is more obvious in the mornings. Pronounced ruffling can form a pleat in the throat in hot climates. Heavy substance; texture a chenille-like pile. Well-branched scapes. May have difficulty opening after cool nights. Slow to increase; tender in colder regions.

Andrew Christian (Harris-Benz 90) Tet, Dor, H75cm (30in), F12cm (5in), M, Re Flat-open, intense lemon-yellow self, green throat, yellow filaments, black anthers. Heavy substance, lush foliage. Vigorous, widely spaced, 4-way branching with regular, looped ruffling.

Beauty to Behold (Sellers 78) AM, LAA Dip, SEv, H60cm (24in), F14cm (5½in), M, Noc Beautifully recurved, tailored, smooth, lemon-yellow, chartreuse throat. Shiny, deep green foliage. Opens well after cool nights. A bud builder, it can be in flower for up to 3 months. Highly recommended for most climates. A favourite in Germany.

Erin Prairie (Fay 71) Tet, Dor, H68cm (27in), F16.5cm (6½in), M, Noc Widely trumpet-shaped, unusual, smooth deep citrus-yellow, wide grass-green throat. Very floriferous. A dependable performer in Europe. 'Dorethe Louise' is similar in shape but a paler colour.

Green Flash (Hite 82) Tet, Dor, H80cm (32in), F14cm (5½in), EM Triangular to full, ruffled, crêpe-textured, yellow-green self, green throat, recurved narrow sepals. The prominent pearly-white midribs cause the petals to pinch slightly. 3-way branching, good bud count, husky scapes. Many flowers open simultaneously providing an incredible show, but reducing the length of the bloom season. Hardy and an excellent performer.

Green Flutter (Williamson 64) AM, AG, SSM, LAA, RHS/AGM Dip, SEv, H55cm (22in), F7cm (3in), Sm, Her, ML, Ext, Noc Widely star-shaped, ruffled, ribbed canary-green self, matching filaments, vivid green throat radiating outwards giving the impression of greenness. Well-branched and a bud builder, so very floriferous. Quite slow to establish but then multiplies well. One of the greenest in the garden and superb planted near box hedges.

Icy Lemon (Brooks 90) HM Tet, SEv, H85cm (34in), F14cm (5½in), EM, Re Perfectly round, ruffled, slightly recurved, palest lemon-yellow, bright lime-green throat, lighter midribs, chartreuse filaments, large brownish anthers, deeper yellow edge apparent in hot weather. Heavy substance and seersuckered texture. Opens well and a thoroughly good performer. Its superb colour enhances all plants grown with it.

Little Greenie (Winniford 72) AG, AM Dip, Ev, H45cm (18in), F10cm (4in), Sm, M Ruffled, bright yellow to lemon-yellow, the green throat flaring out onto the petals giving an overall green effect. Good foliage. Floriferous and vigorous.

Merinda Honeybunch (Coombes) Tet, Ev, H60cm (24in), F10cm (4in), Sm, EE, Re Rounded, ruffled, citrus-lemon, green throat, yellow filaments, brown anthers. Multiple branching, high bud count. It blooms for 7–8 months of the year in Australia, where it was raised and where it is one of the most popular daylilies.

Omomuki (Stamile 91) Tet, Dor, H65cm (26in), F12cm (5in), EM, Noc Exquisitely ruffled, chartreuse-yellow self, electric-green throat. Excellent branching and high bud count, but the heavy substance of the flowers produces a rather stiff effect in the clump, particularly in cooler gardens. It takes at least 3 years to reveal its fine qualities. A useful yellow hard-dormant tetraploid for European gardens from converted MacMillan breeding. Similar parentage to 'Olympic Showcase' (p.52).

Shaman (Gates 87) HM Dip, Ev, H50cm (20in), F12cm (5in), E, Re, Noc, Fra Very full, slightly recurved, beautifully ruffled, smooth canary-yellow, infused with green at the throat, pearly-cream midribs, darker anthers. Thick substance. Well-branched scapes, high bud count, reblooms well even in cooler regions. Fully hardy once established; in cooler climates looks best after 3–4 years. Resents being disturbed.

ALSO RECOMMENDED: 'Creative Art', 'Emerald Enchantment', 'Evening Bell' (for Fra), 'Green Glitter', 'Green Puff' (AM), 'Isosceles', 'Lustrous Jade'.

LEMON OR PALE YELLOW

Atlanta Full House (Petree 84) AM Tet, Dor, H68cm (27in), F15cm (6in), M Very ruffled, round, recurved, lemon-yellow. Robust and does well everywhere. Slow to increase after transplanting but vigorous when established. Multiple top-branching. Can rebloom immediately.

Bitsy (Warner 62) AM, DFM Dip, SEv, H45cm (18in), F3.5cm (1½in), Mini, Her, EE, Re, Ext, Noc Trumpet-shaped, lightly ruffled, lemon-yellow, small green throat, on wiry black scapes. This daylily has rather poor yellowish grassy foliage, but it is well worth growing for the frequent flushes of flower it produces throughout the summer, even in cooler regions, and because it is one of the earliest to flower. Not an early-morning-opener. Also a tetraploid conversion.

Corky (Fischer 59) DFM Dip, Dor, H80cm (32in), F7cm (3in), Her, M Bell-like, yellow flowers with brown backs and brown buds on brown, wiry scapes. A classic. Similar to, but paler in colour, than 'Golden Chimes' (p.51). Lovely naturalized in less formal plantings.

Crystal Cupid (E. Salter 85) HM Dip, Ev, H40cm (16in), F5cm (2in), Mini, EM, Re Full, overlapped, bright lemon-yellow self, deeply etched and ruffled edge. Well-branched, floriferous. Excellent rebloomer; lovely *en masse*. Fertile.

Devonshire (Munson 87) Tet, Ev, H75cm (30in), F17cm (7in), EM Broad, full overlapped petals of ivory-yellow, lemon-green throat, gold-wire edging apparent in hot climates, bright yellow sepals also gold-edged. Heavy, waxy substance, slightly crêped surface. Superbly branched,

'Corky', a delightful miniature raised by Hubert Fischer, is a lighter yellow than his better-known 'Golden Chimes'.

heavy scapes, well-budded. Establishes well, vigorous. Reblooms in hot climates. Very fertile.

Forsyth Bonanza (Lefever 88) Dip, Dor, H58cm (23in), 9cm (3½in), Sm, M Tailored, light yellow, prominent midribs. A very early-morning-opener in cool climates, always perfect regardless of weather and indispensible for European gardens.

Happy Returns (Apps 86) HM Dip, Dor, H40cm (16in), F7cm (3in), Sm, E, ERe, Ext Slightly ruffled, light yellow self, lemon-green throat. Reliable rebloomer in most areas provided it is kept well-watered but not an early-morning-opener. Suitable for growing in containers. Out of 'Stella de Oro' (p.52) and a more pleasing shade of yellow. According to research 'Happy Returns' is probably the third most popular daylily on sale in the United States, after 'Stella de Oro' and 'Hyperion' (below). Very fertile.

Hyperion (Mead 24) AM/RHS 1931 Dip, Dor, H90cm (36in), F14cm (5½in), Her, M, Ext, Very Fra Trumpet-shaped, lemon-yellow, grown for its famous exquisite fragrance. Sometimes produces polytepals and fused buds. Very thin substance and its pigment can melt in hot weather. A classic of real historical interest which was used in the early breeding of spider daylilies. 'Tetrina's Daughter', also fragrant, is worthwhile.

Lemon Lollypop (Simpson 85) LP Dip, Dor, H60cm (24in), F6.5cm (2¾in), Sm, E, Re, Ext, Noc, Very Fra Superb, ruffled, lemon-yellow self, green throat. In bloom for a long time and reblooms well in many areas. Very nocturnal so the next day's blooms start to open when the present ones are still flowering.

Marion Vaughn (Smith 51) Dip, Ev, H90cm (36in), F12cm (5in), Her, M, Very Fra Tapered, lily-like, pale lemon-yellow self, paler midribs, tiny green heart. Graceful, narrow foliage. The trumpet-shaped flower never opens wide but that is part of its charm; it is also treasured for its delicious fragrance.

Penny's Worth (Hager 87) Dip, Dor, H25cm (10in), F3cm (1¼in), Mini, E, Re Dainty, bell-shaped, lemon-yellow self, tiny green heart, yellow filaments, brown anthers. Thin substance and smooth texture. Mounding, grass-like foliage. Valuable for its long bloom season, reblooming qualities and dwarf habit. Ideal for sunny rock gardens.

Prairie Moonlight (Marsh 66) Dip, SEv, H85cm (34in), F20cm (8in), Her, E, Noc, Very Fra Huge, star-

PLATE V
PINK DAYLILIES

H. 'Stoke Poges'

H. 'Jolyene Nichole'

H. 'Pink Cotton Candy'

H. 'My Belle'

All flowers are shown at approximately ¼ size

H. 'Ann Kelley'

H. 'Strawberry Candy'

H. 'Edna Spalding'

H. 'Smoky Mountain
Autumn'

H. 'Pastel Classic'

H. 'Barbara Mitchell'

shaped, sunfast, ruffled, creamy to pale yellow. Although an older cultivar it is still treasured for its strong fragrance. Vigorous.

Quick Results (Brooks 87) Tet, SEv, H83cm (33in), F14cm (5½in), EM, Re, SlFra Full, nicely ruffled, diamond-dusted, intense lemon-yellow self, matching yellow filaments, light brown anthers, olive-green heart, pearly-cream midribs. Heavy substance and ribbed texture. Excellent scapes with good branching, increases rapidly. Opens well in cooler climates.

Siloam Mama (Henry 82) LP Dip, Dor, H60cm (24in), F14.5cm (5¾in), Ext, Noc, Very Fra Wide-open, ruffled, recurved, light yellow, matching filaments and midribs, green throat. Blooms fully open early in the morning, holding well beyond midnight. Multiple top-branching but displays its flowers well above the narrow foliage. A rapid increaser and a bud builder so has a long bloom period.

ALSO RECOMMENDED: 'Hudson Valley' (for Fra), 'Ruffled Ballet', 'Ruffled Perfection', 'Siloam Amazing Grace', 'Siloam Harold Flickinger', 'Whichford', 'Yellow Mammoth'.

MID-YELLOW

Atlanta Fringe Benefit (Petree 85) Tet, Dor, H53cm (21in), F11.5cm (4¾in), EM, Ext, Noc, Fra An unusual yellow self of wide, rounded form with bubbly, fringed edges, which can turn gold by the end of the day. Good increase, one of the better openers among daylilies with heavy edges, and now inexpensive.

Blond is Beautiful (Harris-Benz 85) HM Tet, SEv, H70cm (28in), F15cm (6in), M, Very Fra Ruffled, pinched, pleated, diamond-dusted, bright yellow self, green heart, contrasting brownish anthers. Near-white midribs which widen towards the outer edges of the petals. Petal edges are deeper yellow. Recurved sepals are lighter at the edges. Heavy substance and seersucker texture. Opens well after cool nights. Fertile.

Eenie Weenie (Aden 76) Dip, Dor, Ext, H25cm (10in), F5cm (2in), Mini, E-EM, Re Recurved, lightly ruffled, chrome-yellow, tiny green heart, depressed midribs. Rather pointed, flat sepals, light brown anthers. Top-branched with multiple blooms giving a rather crowded appearance but the extra early blooms are so welcome that

they make this defect insignificant. Suitable for rock gardens. Not a good performer everywhere in Europe as it often suffers from green sepal disfigurement.

I'm Different (Beckham 81) Dip, SEv/Ev, H50cm (20in), F19cm (7½in), M, Re, Ext, Fra Ruffled, round-tipped, oval segments of soft, warm yellow. Nearly 100 per cent of the blooms are polytepal. Completely hardy.

Jen Melon (Oakes 87) Dip, Dor, H65cm (26in), F17cm (7in), L, Re, Fra Huge, wide-segmented, ruffled, recurved, apricot-influenced warm yellow, light green throat, yellow filaments, black anthers, ribbed texture. Well-branched, floriferous, vigorous and valuable for its late flowers.

Lights of Detroit (Weston 82) Tet, SEv, H63cm (25in), F14cm (5½in), M, Noc Distinctive, flat, cinnamon-dusted tips, mid-yellow. Good substance, smooth surface. Takes 2 days to open but opens early on the second day. Bud count about 24. 'Lights of Detroit' is a cross between a Diploid and a Tetraploid resulting in an anomaly; it will cross with both Dips and Tets, though using it with Dips is much easier.

Lion Dance (Harris-Benz 86) Tet, Dor, H53cm (21in), 15cm (6in), M Perfectly round, pansy-like, diamond-dusted, brilliant sunshine yellow, wide, recurved sepals, jagged fringed border, yellow filaments, dark brown anthers. Heavy substance and crêpe-velvet texture. Popular in Germany and hardy in cold-winter regions although it can be slow to settle down and the blooms can be too close to the foliage.

Molokai (Whatley 76) AM Tet, Dor, H68cm (27in), F16.5m (6½in), M, Ext Attractively ruffled, flat, diamond-dusted, bright yellow self, olive-green throat, dark yellow filaments. The ruffling goes deep into the throat. Heavy substance and seersucker texture. A superb older variety, popular in Europe.

Rachel My Love (Talbott 83) AM, IM Dip, SEv, H45cm (18in), F12cm (5in), Dd, EM, Re Full, pompom-type, medium yellow, green throat. Well-branched. Cold-hardy but also performs well in Australia and New Zealand.

Sandra Elizabeth (Stevens 83) EFA Tet, Dor, H70cm (28in), F15cm (6in), Very L (marker) Older-style, open, clear bright yellow. Excellent dark green foliage and well-branched scapes. A marker for Very Late Flowerers and one of the last to begin flowering therefore very valuable but slow to increase and difficult to breed with.

Yellow Lollipop (Crochet 80) DF, HM Dip, Dor, H27-35cm (11-14in), F5.5cm (2¼in), Mini, ML, Re, Ext Floriferous, medium yellow self. Increases well, and long and repeat blooming. Blooms immediately after the main flush of 'Stella de Oro' (p.52) and can be used to extend the blooming season of that particular shade of yellow. An excellent small, landscaping daylily, reblooming in many areas.

ALSO RECOMMENDED: 'Ava Michelle', 'Butterpat', 'Demetrius', 'Limited Edition', 'Little Dart', 'Susie Wong', 'Yellow Explosion'.

GOLDEN-YELLOW AND GOLD

Betty Woods (Kirchhoff 81) AM, SSM, IM Dip, Ev, H55cm (22in), F14cm (5½in), Dd, EM, Re, Fra (hot climates) Perfectly-formed, peony-type, deep golden-yellow self, green throat. Excellent branching. It maintains a high bud count if it is moved to different soil every 2–3 years. Flowers all summer until the first frosts, but requires high even temperatures to open fully and needs protecting during its first winter. 'Betty Woods' is still on many popularity polls and performs well in Australasia.

Bill Norris (Kirchhoff 93) PC Tet, SEv, H74cm (29in), F12cm (5in), M, Re Perfectly formed, extravagantly ruffled, flat, superb, glowing golden-yellow, green throat. Well-branched scapes, leathery texture, floriferous and vigorous. Very hardy and usually opens well after cool nights; long bloom season. Although much in demand as a breeding plant, 'Bill Norris' has superb garden value.

Brookwood Winner's Circle (Sharp 87) Dip, Dor, H50cm (20in), F11cm (4½in), Sm, EM Round, ruffled, recurved, brilliant golden-yellow, intense lime-green throat. When established will produce up to 47 buds and was bred to open at cooler night temperatures.

Camden Gold Dollar (Yancey 82) AM Dip, SEv, H48cm (19in), F7cm (3in), Sm, EM, Re Ruffled, very full, deep yellow self, green throat, deep yellow filaments, contrasting black anthers. Good bud count, an extra long bloomer and an excellent rebloomer in many locations, 3-way branching. Very hardy. Ideal for landscaping.

Condilla (Grooms 77) AM, IM, LAA Dip, Dor, H50cm+ (20in), F11cm (4½in), Sm, Dd, ML Round, carnation-like, deep golden-yellow, contrasting black anthers, subtly serrated gold edges. A distinctive, very well-branched clump (50+ buds) with smooth, dark green

foliage. Although at its best in colder regions it opens well in all weathers.

Ever So Ruffled (Stamile 83) AM Tet, SEv, H55cm (22in), F12cm (5in) or less, M, Noc, Fra Beautifully formed, extravagantly ruffled, perfectly round, golden-yellow, lemon-green throat. Well-branched; a long bloom season but needs time to become established. Responsible for introducing ruffled edges into many breeding lines.

Golden Chimes (Fischer 54) DFM, AM, RHS/AGM Dip, Dor, H65cm (26in), F6cm (2½in), Mini, Her, E Masses of golden, bell-shaped flowers, from mahogany-brown buds, atop multi-branched, mahogany-brown stems. This graceful and charming daylily is at home at the edge of woodland and in a wilder garden setting; used in mass plantings.

In Maxine's Honour (Alexander 93) Tet, Ev, H90cm (36in), F14cm (5½in), E, Re Vibrant, golden daffodil-yellow. Tall and well-branched. Hardy in most areas and reblooms well in Australia and New Zealand and excellent *en masse*.

Jerusalem (Stevens-Seawright 85) Tet, Dor, H70cm (28in), F12cm (5cm), M, Ext Heavily ruffled, intense rich gold to pumpkin-orange self. Well-branched with a high bud count. Very good reports of this one, although not always a good performer in European gardens. Has 'Dance Ballerina Dance' (p.54) in its background. Usually sterile.

Layers of Gold (Kirchhoff 90) HM Tet, Ev/SEv, H60cm (24in), F12cm (5in), Dd, EM, Re, Ext, Fra Ruffled, hose-in-

An exquisitely ruffled, saturated brilliant gold self, 'Olympic Showcase' blooms and increases well.

hose, recurved golden-yellow self, green heart. Consistently double, well-branched and a good parent but can be slightly tender.

Mary's Gold (McDonald 84) AM Tet, SEv, H85cm (34in), F16.5cm (6½in), M Ruffled, recurved, diamond-dusted, brilliant golden-yellow self, deep yellow filaments, large contrasting dark brown anthers. The olive-green throat flares out from the heart on each side of the pale yellow midrib. Heavy substance and seersuckered texture. Opens well in cooler regions and described as a golden beacon in the garden. Well-branched, floriferous, vigorous, producing side shoots very quickly and can produce polytepal blooms. Very popular in Europe.

Olympic Showcase (Stamile 90) Tet, SEv, H60cm (24in), F12cm (5in), EM, Ext, Noc, Fra Wide open beautifully ruffled, gently recurved, deeply saturated brilliant golden-yellow, green throat. Vigorous, well-branched and with heavy substance. A long-season bloomer. Does well in many European regions and highly recommended by Matthias Thomsen-Stork.

Pearl Lewis (Peck 86) AM Tet, Dor, H60cm (24in), F15cm (6in), ML Rainproof, wide, heavily ruffled, superb pink-influenced soft golden-yellow to golden-apricot, with a narrow gold edge sometimes apparent. Opens flat, the colour holding all day and a consistently high performance daylily of great refinement, which opens well everywhere. The number of scapes producing beautifully opening flowers makes up for the moderate bud count. 'Has 'Dance Ballerina Dance' (p.54) in its background. Usually sterile.

Sir Blackstem (Hager 89) Dor, Ev, H45cm (18in), F5.5cm (2¼in), Mini, ML Bell-shaped, deep yellow self, matching filaments, black anthers, mahogany-brown reverse to floral segments. The sturdy scapes are also dark mahogany-brown, contrasting well with the flowers and the foliage. Floriferous. Reblooms in the British Isles and in New Zealand where it is very popular. An unusual daylily which would associate well with *Anthriscus sylvestris* 'Ravenswing' and other dark reddish-brown foliage plants.

Stella de Oro (Jablonski 75) DFM, AM, SSM Dip, Dor, H30cm (12in), F6cm (2½in), Mini, EE, MRe Well-known, circular, recurved bell-shaped, harsh shade of golden-yellow, tiny green heart. One of the first to bloom in many regions but may not open fully under cool night conditions. Needs regular deadheading to keep up flowering impetus: removing the seed pods also helps. Also requires moving every 2–3 years to new soil to retain its re-blooming qualities. Tends to go dormant quite early. Also a tetraploid conversion.

Texas Sunlight (Lewis 81) DFM, AM Dip, Dor, H70cm (28in), F6.5cm (2¾in), Mini, M Showy, perfectly round, ruffled, very recurved bright gold self, tiny green heart. Well-branched, floriferous and always a good performer.

Victorian Collar (Stamile 88) AM Tet, SEv, H60cm (24in), F15cm (6in), EM, Ext, Fra Large, wide, overlapped, heavily ruffled, very lovely light gold to golden-yellow self, yellow filaments, brown anthers, green throat. Good substance and ribbed texture. Strong, well-branched scapes, high bud count.

ALSO RECOMMENDED: 'All American Gold', 'Burning Day Light' (AM), 'Cartwheels' (AM, SSM), 'Chicago Sunrise', 'Daily Bread', 'Daily Dollar', 'Delores Gould', 'Eighteen Carat', 'Golden Prize' (LAA), 'Sun King', 'Sunny Bit'.

ORANGE TO TANGERINE

Berlin Tallboy (Tamburg 89) Tet, Dor, H1.5m (5ft), F19cm (7½in), ML Widely strap-shaped, recurved, vivid fulvous-dusted orange, faint maroon halo, orange throat flares into the orange midribs, contrasting large black anthers. Good substance and ribbed texture. Rather top-branched but the huge flowers glow like a beacon especially against a dark background. Useful for its height and late-flowering blooms. Dr Tamburg writes to Gerald Sinclair (collector of European hybrids) "I had access to pollen of 'Norton Tallboy' (Coe) and I made a cross with the American tetraploid 'Lucretius'. This produced 'Berlin Tallboy'...and so, surprisingly, 'Berlin Tallboy' has no *H. altissima* blood."

Brookwood Orange Drop (Sharp 87) Dip, Dor, H50cm (20in) F7cm (3in), Sm, E Perfectly round, orange self, matching filaments, tiny green throat, prominent midrib. Ribbed texture; well-branched, rigid scapes with up to 25 buds. 'Brookwood Orange Drop' is a good performer everywhere.

Country Pride (Joiner 89) Dip, Ev, H70cm (28in) F12cm (5in), Dd, E, Re, Ext, Noc Round (with the inner segments bunched together), tangerine-peach, tangerine filaments, contrasting black anthers, green throat, on an arching scape with up to 24 buds. Flowers early and repeats

Exquisitely scallop-ruffled, soft tangerine-orange 'Golden Scroll' is valued for its late-flowering qualities. Lovely with *Agapanthus* 'Dark Navy Blue'.

well even in cooler climates. Light to medium green foliage. From 'Golden Scroll' (below).

Golden Scroll (Guidry 83) AM, LP Dip, Dor (in most areas), H48cm (19in), F14cm (5½in), L, Re, SlFra Immaculately ruffled, well-formed, muted tangerine-orange to deep peach, green throat. Heavy substance, ribbed texture, rain-resistant and an early-morning-opener. Can bleach in very hot sun to palest creamy-peach, the darker midribs making a wonderful contrast. When well tended may produce side branching. Beautiful, lush foliage. A very good breeding plant. Lovely end of season daylily; a useful companion to agapanthus, crocosmia, kniphofia and miscanthus varieties.

Mauna Loa (Roberts 79) Tet, Dor, H60cm (24in), F12cm (5in), M, Re Rounded, lightly ruffled, subdued tangerine-orange blend, matching filaments, black anthers, green throat. Reasonably well-branched, floriferous. Performs well in British gardens; bloom period is only 2–3 weeks.

Orange Velvet (Joiner 89) Dip, SEv, H75cm (30in), F16.5cm (6½in), M, Re Sunfast, rain-resistant, opulent, rounded, ruffled, intense glowing creamy-orange petals, lighter sepals, green throat. Soft, velvety texture, good substance. Very free flowering, a rapid increaser. The only

slight fault is that the tall blooms are slightly out of proportion to the excellent, healthy foliage. Hardy in most areas.

Show Amber (Blyth 88) Tet, Dor, H75cm (30in), F14cm (5½in), ML, Very Fra Ruffled, tawny-orange, deeper tawny-brown halo, surrounding prominent yellow midrib, tangerine throat, green heart, orange filaments. Good substance and ribbed texture. Well-branched, floriferous. A popular Australian variety.

Tuscawilla Tigress (Hansen 88) Tet, SEv, H50cm+ (20in), F18.5cm (7¼in), EM, Re, Ext, Noc Sunfast, recurved, tawny-orange to russet-red, deeper veining, slightly darker eye around orange throat which flares into the pale orange midribs, tiny green heart, tangerine-orange filaments, dark brown anthers. Thick substance and ribbed surface texture. Multiple wide-branched scapes. Height depends on soil. Dormant in cold-winter climates.

Viracocha (Roberts 76) Tet, Dor, H63cm (25in) F12cm (5in), EM Ruffled, crêpe-textured, brilliant tangerine to deep orange self, heavy substance, lemon-green throat, tangerine filaments. Well-branched, high bud count and increases well. Recommended for English gardens.

ALSO RECOMMENDED: 'Autumn Minaret', 'Burning Daylight', 'Earlianna', 'Jersey Spider', 'Knick Knack', 'Krakatowa Lava', 'Orange Vols', 'Pure and Simple', 'Sampson'.

PALE MELON TO LIGHT APRICOT

Brookwood Simpatico (Sharp 97) Dip, Dor, H55cm (22in) F7cm (3in), Sm, Very L Evenly ruffled, gently recurved, bright melon, matching filaments, very large contrasting black anthers, tangerine throat, tiny green heart. Multiple-branched scapes carrying up to 25 buds on an established plant. Will not thrive without some dormancy. 'Naomi Ruth' is similar but with less distinctive black anthers.

Bubbly (J. Joiner 89) Dip, SEv, H50cm (20in), F6.5cm (2¾in), Mini, Dd, M Full, lightly ruffled, apricot self, green throat. Graceful, well-branched scapes can carry well over 20 buds of perfect tiny rosettes. An important introduction from one of the best-known breeders of small popcorn doubles. Lighter in colour, and with smaller flowers, than 'Country Pride' (p.52).

Curly Ripples (Guidry 79) Dip, Ev, H65cm (26in), F16.5cm (6½in), E, Re, Ext, Noc, Fra Round, wide, rippled-edged, light apricot and cream blend, deep olive-green throat which lasts all day. Rather top-branched, but a bud builder, adding 10 to 12 buds to an original count of about 25; of moderate increase but an unusual and attractive daylily, hardy in many parts of Europe.

Dance Ballerina Dance (Peck 78) AM Tet, Dor, H60cm (24in), F15cm (6in), M Legendary parent of the modern ruffled daylilies but not always satisfactory as a garden plant since it only opens well in hot climates. The heavily ruffled flowers are melon-apricot, frosting to an ethereal pink in hot sunshine. Can produce polytepal blooms.

Fabulous Prize (E. Brown 74) Tet, Ev, H68cm (27in), F12cm (5in), E, Re Recurved, lightly ruffled, smooth-textured, pink-influenced palest apricot, yellow-gold throat flaring onto the petals and sepals, tiny green heart, depressed pearly-apricot midribs, tangerine filaments. Good substance. An older variety but still good.

Femme Osage (Whatley 85) Tet, SEv, H63cm (25in), F16.5cm (6½in), M, Ext, SlFra Opulent, scallop-ruffled, rounded, flat, diamond-dusted melon-peach to tangerine self, deeper orange veining, prominent, wide pearly-lavender midribs, orange filaments and anthers, tiny green heart. 3-way branching. A superb daylily: rain-resistant and an early-morning-opener.

Lady of Fortune (Salter 92) Tet, SEv, H65cm (26in), F9cm (3½in), Sm, M, Re Round, full, overlapped, lightly ruffled, cream-ivory to palest melon-peach, lemon-green throat, ivory-peach filaments, dark anthers. Heavy substance and smooth, leathery texture. Rather stiff habit, but beautiful branching and a wonderful soft pastel colour. Increases exceptionally well. Out of 'Tet Sugar Cookie'. Fertile.

Michele Coe (Coe 69) RHS/AM, RHS/FCC Dip, SEv, H75cm (30in), F12cm (5in), Her, EM, Re Ruffled, widely segmented, diamond-dusted, melon-cream with pearly-lavender midribs, light tangerine throat, deep melon filaments. Good substance and smooth texture. Bred for the British climate and performs equally well in Europe. A superb garden plant. Very fertile. One of the best from one of England's few hybridizers.

Molino Cascade (McCord 91) Dip, SEv, H60cm (24in), F11.5cm (4¾in), EM, Re, Ext Perfectly round, ruffled, pale apricot with rose-pink halo, yellow throat, green heart, tangerine-cream filaments, brown anthers. Heavy substance and smooth texture. Hardy.

Monica Mead (Kirchhoff 91) Dip, Ev, H50cm (20in), F11cm (4½in), Sm, Dd, E, Re, Ext Full, ruffled, flat, over-lapped, palest melon-apricot, green throat. Good scapes with 3–5-way branching. A superb double daylily but may not be hardy everywhere.

Scatterbrain (Joiner 88) Dip, SEv, H80cm (32in), F15cm (6in), Dd, M, Re, Fra Loose, frilly, full, pale peach-pink self, pale green throat, good substance. The scapes can carry up to 6 open blooms at the same time, in a bouquet-like effect. Long blooming season.

Second Glance (Sellers 84) Tet, SEv, H70cm (28in), F15cm (6in), M Recurved, lightly ruffled, melon-persimmon blend, matching filaments, brown anthers, green throat, wide pearly-lavender midribs. Well-branched, floriferous, hardy.

Spanish Serenade (Guidry 87) Dip, Ev, H55cm (22in), F14cm (5½in), M, Re Perfectly symmetrical, ruffled, mid-apricot blend, tangerine-yellow throat. Good substance and ribbed texture. Very well-branched. Superb in European gardens although tender and needing frost protection in cold-winter regions where it is slow to increase.

ALSO RECOMMENDED: 'Baby Fresh', 'Frances Fay', 'George Cunningham', 'Lynn's Delight', 'Netsuke'.

APRICOT-PEACH

Bertie Ferris (Winniford 69) AM, SSM, DFM Dip, Dor, H45cm (18in), F6cm (2½in), Mini, Her, E-EM, Re, Ext, Noc Eye-catching, ruffled, bright persimmon-orange self, fitting into no exact colour category. Can be slightly tender as a young plant and needs some heat to open fully. Long-flowering, sometimes into early autumn. Excellent foliage, superb branching, high bud count.

Canton Harbor (Munson 87) HM Tet, Ev, H80cm (32in), F12cm (5in), EM Sun-resistant, broad, flat, faintly coral- to lavender-influenced warm apricot, gold throat, small dark olive-green heart. There is a hint of tangerine in the veining and ruffles and a slight watermark can appear in very hot weather. An abundance of well-branched scapes. Fertile and a good parent. Outstanding in some European gardens and in Australia.

Decatur Piecrust (Davidson 82) Tet, Dor, H55cm (22in), F12cm (5in), M, Ext Very heavily piecrust-ruffled, round, deep apricot to salmon pink, tangerine throat, apricot filaments, contrasting black anthers, pearly-lavender midribs. Heavy substance and crêped to velvety texture. Although hardy it needs hot sunshine to open and recurve well. Out of 'Round Table' (Peck) a very round, pink blend.

Elizabeth Salter (Salter 92) Tet, SEv, H65cm (26in), F12cm (5in), M, Noc Lavishly ruffled, full, overlapped, peach to peach-pink (in cooler climates), pale apricot to salmon shading nearer the throat, pearly-apricot midribs, light apricot throat. In the folds of the ruffling, there can be a salmon influence. Can take up to mid-day to open fully. Heavy substance and velvety texture. Beautifully branched scapes carry multiple blooms. Increases well, stoloniferous. A superb daylily and a popularity poll winner. A favourite in European gardens and first winner of Hemerocallis Europa's Roswitha Waterman Award.

Evelyn Lela Stout (Munson 87) Tet, Ev, H60cm (24in), F14cm (5½in), EM, Ext Superb, generously ruffled, pastel apricot-peach with pink tints in cool climates, sometimes narrowly gold-edged, lemon-green to green throat, peach filaments, dark anthers, pearly-lavender midribs. Heavy substance and smooth texture. High bud count, very vigorous but the scapes can be rather low if the temperature is not high enough and it needs even night and day temperatures to open well.

In Excess (Alexander 93) Dip, Ev, H70cm (28in), F12cm (5in), Dd, EM, Re, Very Fra Very full, ruffled apricot-peach. Very popular in Australia where it was raised.

Jedi Irish Spring (Wedgeworth 87) Dip, SEv/hard-dormant, H65cm (26in), F12cm (5in), M, Fra, Nicely ruffled, recurved, apricot, tiny green heart, depressed midribs, prominent veining, orange filaments, brown anthers. A warm pink flush appears on the segment tips in hot weather but several blooming seasons are needed to produce this subtle colouration. Heavy substance and velvety texture. Good branching, many blooms and often reblooms in favourable areas once established.

Maggie Fynboe (Reinermann 95) Dip, Dor, H70cm (28in), F11cm (4½in), ML Ruffled, flat, gently recurved, salmon-apricot blend, green throat. Branching is 2–3-way, bud count around 15–20, an early-morning-opener. Very popular in Europe and an outstanding daylily raised from 'Rose Emily' (p.62).

Maison Carree (Munson 88) HM Tet, Ev, H70cm (28in), F12cm (5in), M Broad, ruffled, peach-yellow gold, blushed pink, pink midribs. Small, green-gold throat.

'Maggie Fynboe' is a lovely green-eyed apricot-orange from Werner Reinerman, one of Europe's leading daylily breeders.

Heavy, smooth and waxy substance. Well-branched with a high bud count. Strong, healthy and fertile. A sibling to 'Evelyn Lela Stout' (above) with a more refined form.

Selma Timmons (Munson 88) HM Tet, SEv, H45cm (18in), F11cm (4½in), Sm, EM, Re Ruffled, recurved, rich apricot-pink, small round, greenish-gold throat. Full-formed with tightly pleated ruffles on the narrowly yellow-edged petals and sepals. Well-branched, fertile. A subtle colour, very difficult to describe accurately.

Spanish Glow (Salter 88) Tet, SEv, H65cm (26in), F12cm (5in), ML, Re Well-formed, overlapped, slightly recurved, pink-influenced, soft apricot-peach, green throat. Good substance, smooth texture with slightly ruffled petals. Vigorous, producing many well-branched scapes with a high bud count. Reliable, opens early and performs well everywhere. Fertile.

ALSO RECOMMENDED: 'Chemistry', 'Doll House', 'Fall Guy', 'Leprechaun's Lace', 'Madge Cayse', 'Melon Balls', 'Pixie Parasol', 'Simply Pretty', 'Sarsaparilla', 'Song of Spring', 'Totally Tropical', 'Upper Class Peach'.

BRONZE AND COPPER
Most of the daylilies that appear bronze are, in fact, over-lays or deeper veining.

Cajun Gambler (Guidry 86) AM Dip, Ev, H60cm (24in), F17cm (7in), E, Re, Ext, Noc, SlFra Round, ruffled, amber-influenced, copper-orange, bronze veining, subtle

darker eye, olive-green throat. A hardy evergreen but it is worth protecting it for the first two winters. Very large flowers on a small, compact plant.

Judah (Harris 79) Tet, Dor, H75cm (30in), F16.5cm (6½in), M, Re, Ext, Fra Large, ruffled, recurved, orange-bronze, wide sunburst orange throat flaring out into the orange midribs, tiny green heart, orange filaments, brown anthers. A popular, floriferous daylily.

Little Deeke (Guidry 80) AG, AM Dip, Ev/SEv, H50cm (20in), F11cm (4½in), Sm, E, Re, Fra Ruffled, crêped, true bronze, deep olive-green throat. Fully open and ruffled by dawn in cool weather. Hardy. Increases moderately to well. Gives good branching if well tended.

ALSO RECOMMENDED: 'Bronze Age', 'Wilhelm'.

TAN, GINGER, OXBLOOD AND DARK BROWN

Brunette (breeder not known) Dip, Ev, H50cm (20in), F7cm (3in), EE, Very Fra Graceful, lily-like, tan-brown, yel-low throat. Arching, narrow foliage. Flowers with *H. lil-ioasphodelus*, of which it is presumably an offspring, and is equally fragrant. While this description does not tally with the registration details of 'Brunette' (Stout) I thought the daylily we grow as 'Brunette' well worth including. Delightful in the May garden when planted with blue Siberian irises or as a companion to early-flowering, yellow daylilies. Popular in the British Isles and Europe.

'Judah' is a reliable, free-flowering daylily and is very effective with agapanthus and kniphofia.

Chocolate Dreams (Shooter 97) Dip, Dor, H60cm (24in), F12cm (5in), M, Re Triangular, flared, overlapped, very ruffled, chocolate-brown, prominent purple veins, matching triangular, lemon-green throat, chocolate-brown tipped filaments; the gathered ruffles are shot through with a thread of gold. Good substance and velvety texture. 4-way branching with a bud count of approximately 15–18.

Chocolate Ripples (Shooter 92) Dip, Dor, H75cm (30in), F12cm (5in), M Ruffled and serrated-edged, flat-formed, rich chestnut-brown, prominent burgundy veins, lemon-green throat. Heavy substance and crêped texture. 4-way branching and high bud count but slow to increase in some areas.

Fudge Sundae (Mercer 89) Tet, SEv, H75cm (30in), F16.5cm (6½in), M Big, wide-petalled, oxblood red-brown, darker, darker eye, yellow throat. Well-branched, floriferous, vigorous and hardy.

Mahogany Magic (Stamile 95) Tet, SEv, H53cm (21in), F10cm (4in), Sm, M Round, full, nicely ruffled, sunfast, rich mahogany-red, deep mahogany eye, gold-green throat. A lighter orange edge is sometimes apparent. Strong scapes with 3-way branching. Fertile both ways but a difficult pod parent. Patrick Stamile bred this when he was developing a line of dark reds and purples. A welcome addition to the daylily colour palette. Good with *Carex* 'Small Red'.

Mary Brown (Verhaert 97) Dip, SEv, H65cm (26in), F15cm (6in), Dd, M Full, beautifully opening, ginger-brown, narrow mahogany-brown eye, deep yellow throat, tiny green heart. Ribbed texture. Named by François Verhaert for a friend who is a keen daylily collector.

Matthew Martian (Dougherty 92) Tet, Dor, H70-75cm (28-30in), F14cm (5½in), M, Ext Brown self, healthy foliage all season. 6-way branching, very floriferous and opens well in cool weather.

Silkwood (Chesnik 85) Tet, Dor, H90cm (36in), F12cm (5in), EM Unusual full-formed, nicely ruffled, pale ginger-brown with yellow undertones, mahogany-brown halo, yellow throat and filaments, contrasting black anthers, wide pearly-yellow midribs. The edges have even, lacy pleated ruffling on all floral segments. Heavy substance and crêped texture; opens well. Candelabra branching. A daylily of quiet, subtle colouring which associates well with ornamental grasses. Out of 'Dance Ballerina Dance' (p.54).

ALSO RECOMMENDED: 'Little Bronzene', 'Cherry Smoke', 'Chestnut Lane', 'Chocolate Splash', 'Double Bourbon', 'Double Coffee', 'Gingerbread Man', 'Jenny Wren', 'Mama's Hot Chocolate', 'Milk Chocolate', 'Mojave Sunset', 'Tawny Gold'.

PALE MELON-PINK AND FLESH TONES

All the daylilies listed below will be melon or melon-pink in cool climates. However, in hot weather and strong light most will frost to a purer pink.

Beijing (Munson 87) HM Tet, SEv, H60cm (24in), F12cm (5in), M, Re Opulently ruffled, broadly-segmented, sunfast, pale flesh-pink, small cream-green throat, pearly-lavender midribs, melon-cream filaments, dark anthers. Good substance and smooth texture. Opens well and stays open late. Strong, well-branched, wiry scapes; narrow foliage.

Fairy Tale Pink (Pierce 80) AM, SSM, PC Dip, Dor, H60cm (24in), F14cm (5½in), M, Re Very ruffled, diamond-dusted, creamy-beige to melon-pink self of superb substance, needing warm evenings to open properly. Sometimes produces double flowers in hot weather. A healthy, fertile plant improving all its offspring with its positive attributes (see 'Barbara Mitchell', p.59, 'Betty Benz', p.58, and 'Xia Xiang', p.61) but it increases slowly. Does not perform well in some climates being too dormant for regions with very long growing seasons, but despite its faults is probably one of the quintessential so-called pink daylilies of our time.

Janet Gayle (Guidry 76) AM, SSM Dip, Ev, H65cm (26in), F16.5cm (6½in), M Heavily ruffled, diamond-dusted, pale melon-pink to cream-pink, lemon-green throat. Heavy substance and ribbed texture. The foliage is thin and wispy, going brown in dry weather and disappearing very early in autumn. Some flowers will be semi-double in hot weather. Not a good performer in Florida and similar climates or in areas of severe winter weather, including parts

The voluptuously formed and opulently ruffled Southern beauty 'Beijing' performs equally well in colder climates.

of Europe. However, it is a landmark in daylily breeding and is a beautiful plant where it can be grown successfully.

Mini Pearl (Jablonski 82) Dip, Dor, H40cm (16in), F7cm (3in), Sm, EM, Re, Ext Round, recurved, widely ruffled, diamond-dusted, melon to blush pink, bright yellow throat and filaments, tiny green heart. Excellent glossy foliage; very floriferous, rain-resistant and an early-morning-opener.

Moonlight Mist (E. Salter 82) Dip, Ev, H45cm (18in), F6.5cm (2¾in), Mini, M, Re Superb, full, ruffled blend of pale ivory and cream-pink, lemon-green heart. Well-branched scapes; rain-resistant and an early-morning-opener. Resents division into single fans and takes time to recover but should be in every collection.

Peach Whisper (Stamile 91) Tet, Dor, H63cm (25in), F14cm (5½in), EM, Re, Ext Soft peach-pink (colour often varies from registration), lemon-green throat. Well-branched, increases rapidly and a prolific bloomer.

ALSO RECOMMENDED: 'Peach Jubilee', 'Southern Love', 'Yazoo Mildred Primos'.

LIGHT PINK-CREAM

Betty Benz (Harris-Benz 87) Dip, Dor, H80cm (32in), F16.5cm (6½in), ML, Ext, Fra Heavily ruffled, diamond-

'Bogie and Bacall' is a delicate cream pink becoming more opulent in hot climates.

dusted, ethereal cream-pink to cream-beige, large deep green throat which flares out onto the segments. Vigorous, husky foliage and sturdy scapes, 4–5-way branching, high bud count. Recommended for cooler gardens where it reblooms.

Bogie and Bacall (Hansen 92) Dip, SEv, H53cm (21in), F12cm (5in), Dd, EM, Re, Ext, Noc Round, ruffled, cream-pink, cherry-red eyeband, green throat. Blooms become fuller and more ruffled in hot weather but reputed to be hardy in cold-winter regions.

Mount Herman Starlight (J. Carpenter 94) Dip, Dor, H70cm+ (28in), F15cm (6in), E, Re, Fra Round, ruffled, flat, cream, blushed pink, large green throat radiating out onto the petals. Opens flat at dawn after cool nights so highly recommended for cooler climates. Deserves to be better known.

Nagasaki (Kirchhoff 79) Dip, Ev, H48cm (19in), F11cm (4½in), Dd, Sm, EM, Re, Ext, Fra Symmetrical, pastel blend of cream, pink and lavender, yellow halo. An exceptionally good parent; a milestone in double daylilies.

Pastel Classic (Millikan-Soules 87) AM Dip, SEv, H58cm (23in), F15cm (6in), M, Re, Fra Heavily ruffled, diamond-dusted, cream-influenced, soft pink, subtle darker veining, flaring green throat. Heavy substance and ribbed texture. The husky scapes can produce some branching if well cultivated. Hardy although the somewhat low foliage can be badly affected in severe winters. Vigorous, floriferous; proliferates and reblooms in cooler climates. The pigment deepens after cool evenings becoming a rich pastel-pink; in heat the colour lightens to a salmonish-buff.

Peace & Plenty (Simpson 94) Dip, SEv, H80cm (32in), F14cm (5½in), E-M Superb creamy-pink, lemon-yellow throat blending to chartreuse-green deeper into the heart. 5-way branching, a bud count of 30+, a bud builder and a good rebloomer. Opens early and is hardy in cold-winter regions.

ALSO RECOMMENDED: 'Ars Vivendi', 'Luverne', 'Siloam Betty Woods'.

PINK BLENDS AND POLYCHROMES

Ellen Christine (Crochet 87) AM, IM Dip, SEv, H58cm (23in), F16.5cm (6½in), Dd, M, Re Ruffled, sunfast melon with a subtle pink influence that can frost in sunshine to two tones of melon. The segments and petaloids have saw-toothed edges. An outstanding double.

Kate Carpenter (Munson 80) AM, LAA Tet, Ev, H70cm (28in), F15cm (6in), EM, Re, Fra Round, recurved, widely ruffled, diamond-dusted, shimmering palest pink blend, yellow throat flaring onto the petals, small glowing-green heart (in Florida, just green elsewhere), pearly-lavender midribs, ivory-lime filaments, light brown anthers. Heavy substance and smooth texture. It is healthy but slow to establish and to increase, is not rainproof and the buds are so close together that new blooms, on top multiple-clustered scapes can be spoiled. It may not always perform well everywhere.

Ming Porcelain (Kirchhoff 81) AM Tet, Ev, H70cm (28in), F13cm (5¼in), EM, Re, Ext Opulent, ruffled, smooth-textured, gold-dusted, pastel ivory-yellow to peach-pink blend, lemon-green throat. Excellent, wide, lush and upright foliage but rather stiff scapes. Needs high even temperatures to open well and in chilly weather the early blooms are not as good as those that follow later. Fertile.

Senegal (Kaskel 97) Tet, Ev, H60cm (24in), F14cm+ (5½in), M, Re Full, sculpted and ruffled, polychrome in shades of pink and coral, blended with pastel orange-yellow, lavender midribs, apricot filaments, orange anthers. Heavy substance and velvety texture; an early-morning-opener. The blooms appear just above the healthy husky foliage. Hardy in cold-winter regions with no protection even though raised in Florida. Fertile.

Serena Sunburst (Marshall 86) Tet, Dor, H58cm (23in), F12cm (5in), M, Re Showy, recurved, heavily ruffled, yellow overlaid with frosty salmon-pink with lemon-gold highlights, gold-green throat, peach-gold filaments. In hot weather a narrow, lacy gold edging is apparent. Compact and dense with great visual impact. A superb plant, flowering for a long time.

Vision of Beauty (K. Carpenter 85) Dip, Dor, H53cm (21in), F15cm (6in), M, Re, Ext, Fra Widely segmented, round, ruffled, flat, diamond-dusted, yellow-influenced pink, faint deeper pink halo, yellow throat blending into a lime-green heart, warm yellow filaments, prominent cream-yellow midribs. Heavy substance and smooth texture. Well-branched, floriferous. Opens superbly in English and European gardens.

ALSO RECOMMENDED: 'Fragrant Bouquet', 'Nob Hill', 'Surprisingly Pink' (HM).

PALE PINK

Ah Youth (Simpson 87) Dip, Dor, H70cm (28in), F11cm (4½in), Sm, M, Ext, Noc, Fra Ruffled, true clear pale pink, deeper pink eye, lemon-green throat. The rebloom flowers are a deeper colour than the hot summer blooms. Opens well in all weathers; a rapid increaser and fertile.

Barbara Mitchell (Pierce 85) SSM Dip, Dor (in most areas), H55cm (22in), F15cm (6in), M, Re Voluptuous, wide, recurved, ruffled, soft light pink with overlapping petals, faintest rose band in hot climates, green throat. The pink pigment may have beige undertones in cooler climates; deeper pink veins create the impression of corduroy texture. Well-branched scapes. Slightly tender without snow cover or mulch in cold-winter regions but consistently good in most areas. Also a tetraploid conversion which is used by many breeders to produce better substance in the flowers, eg 'Pink Ambrosia' (p.81). 'Tet Barbara Mitchell' (John Benz) is also known to double the fragrance in its offspring.

Lullaby Baby (Spalding 75) AM, AG, LAA Dip, Dor, H45cm (18in), F9cm (3½in), Sm, M, Noc Exquisite, rounded, ruffled, diamond-dusted, crystalline ice-pink. Healthy dark green foliage. Well-branched, floriferous, long-blooming and can be a bud builder. Hardy. Also a tetraploid conversion, one of its more important offspring being 'Ming Porcelain' (above) which now figures in most modern tetraploid pinks.

Millie Schlumpf (Guidry 81) HM Dip, Ev, H50cm (20in), F15cm (6in), E, Re, Noc, Fra Round and ruffled, true pale pink, vivid green throat, pink filaments. The orange anthers are the only discordant note in this otherwise superb pink. Consistent 3-way branching, delicate arching foliage and moderate growth. A faithful rebloomer in cooler climates and very popular in British and European gardens.

My Belle (Durio 75) AM, SSM Dip, Ev, H65cm (26in), F16.5cm (6½in), E, Re, Ext Broad, ruffled, palest light pink shaded lavender at the edges, pale pink midribs, lemon-green throat. More colourful in cooler regions. Husky foliage and a stoloniferous habit. Vigorous and a fast increaser. Ideal for beginner daylily growers.

Speak of Angels (Simpson 91) HM Dip, SEV/Dor, H65cm (26in), F15 (6in), M, Ext, Noc Ruffled, wide-petalled, pale pink, soft lavender-pink halo, very large chartreuse-green throat. Vigorous, increases rapidly, opens serenely every time. "Totally undaunted by wet, chilly weather" says Al Rogers of Caprice Farms, who regards it as an excellent daylily for the Pacific North West, the British Isles and Europe.

Thelma Elaine (Wilson 93) Dip, Dor, H53cm (21in), F15cm (6in), EM, Ext Huge, loosely ruffled, flat, smooth, porcelain-textured, rich light pink. Well-branched; low scapes make it beautiful to look down into.

Tonia Gay (Spalding 84) Dip, Ev, H38cm (15in), F14cm (5½in), E, SlFra Ruffled, pale-pink blend over an ivory-white base, pearly-white midribs, soft yellow throat, green heart. Its relative lack of branching may explain why it has not won any awards, the other reason being that it can exhibit sepal quilling, which some growers find unattractive. An excellent performer in European gardens; earlier to flower, with larger, clearer-coloured blooms than 'Lullaby Baby' (p.59).

Tuscawilla Princess (Hansen 90) Dip, SEv/Dor, H65cm (26in), F12cm+ (5in), ML, Re, Noc Attractively ruffled, gently recurved, pale pink self, yellow throat flaring onto the petals, tiny soft olive-green heart, pale lime-green filaments. Good substance and ribbed texture. Multiple branching, high bud count (30+ in Florida). Vigorous, hardy, a long-season bloomer and an early-morning-opener. From 'Barbara Mitchell' (p.59).

Vi Simmons (Talbott 87) Dip, Ev, H60cm (24in), F15cm (6in), M, Re, Fra Gracefully formed, lushly ruffled, smooth-textured, clear baby-ribbon pink, bisected by a white midrib, lemon-green throat with matching filaments. Heavy substance and rain-resistant, a good early-morning-opener. Healthy foliage, vigorous, moderate increase and 3–4-way branching. Reputedly not always hardy in the coldest areas but has survived in Zone 6.

ALSO RECOMMENDED: 'Balaringa Promise', 'Booger', 'Quiet Pink', 'Silver Ice'.

CLEAR, MID-PINK

Codie Wedgeworth (Pierce-Wilson 87) AM Dip, Ev, H65cm (26in), F15cm (6in), EM, Re Round, ruffled, pastel-pink of exceptional quality and exquisite form. The flowers have heavy substance and waxy texture. Well-branched and a bud builder. Somewhat tender in some cold-winter areas, generally needing a hot climate to perform well. Popular in Australasia.

Delightsome (Sikes 85) Dip, SEv, H40cm (16in), F10cm (4in), Sm, M Extremely ruffled, flat, clear medium pink, chartreuse throat. Good substance and smooth, silky texture. Perfectly branched, vigorous and hardy in cold-winter climates; much taller in cool climates. A delight wherever it is seen.

Fashion Page (Bennett 89) Dip, SEv, H70cm (28in), F16.5cm (6½in), EM Beautiful mid-pink with a rose halo, which deepens in colour in colder climates, lemon-green throat. A good performer with above average bud count, hardy. From a breeder whose work deserves to be better known outside his own locality.

Jedi Brenda Spann (Wedgeworth 90) Dip, SEv, H60cm (24in), F15cm (6in), M, Ext, SlFra Full, ruffled, diamond-dusted, buff-influenced (in cooler climates), light to mid-pink, deeper veining, narrow deeper pink halo, vivid lemon-green throat, pink-influenced buff-ivory filaments. The extravagant ruffling goes deep into the throat. Good substance and slightly ribbed texture. Its hardiness in colder European gardens is still being tested.

Jedi Sue McCord (Wedgeworth 88) Dip, SEv, H55cm (22in), F14cm (5½in), E, Re, Ext, Noc, Fra Superb, wide, ruffled, clear pink, darker rose-pink halo, vivid green throat. The top-clustered scapes bear flowers just above the foliage and open over a 3-week period. Has 'Janet Gayle' (p.57) in its ancestry as do most of the Jedi series.

Little Celina (Williamson 70) DFM, AM Dip, Ev, H35cm (14in), F5cm (2in), Mini, E, Re, Ext Pink self. An important parent in Pauline Henry's breeding lines.

Mary Frances Ragain (J. Carpenter 93) Dip, SEv, H65cm (26in), F15cm (6in), ML, Re, Fra Round, evenly ruffled, very flat, clear mid- to deep pink, raised midribs, pink-tipped filaments, lemon-green throat. Heavy substance and leathery texture.

Pink Flirt (DeKerlegand 87) AM Dip, SEv, H50cm (20in), F15cm (6in), E, Re, Ext, Fra Ruffled, bright peppermint-pink self, green throat. An outstanding and very popular daylily, renowned for its fragrance but a better performer in hotter climates.

Sabra Salina (Wilson 91) Dip, Dor, H55cm (22in), F15cm (6in), EM, Re, Ext, Fra Heavily ruffled, light to mid-pink, gold halo, tiny green heart, pink-tipped, yellow filaments. Low-growing for the flower size and one of the most beautiful, ruffled pinks. Hardy in cold-winter regions.

'Speak of Angels', a charming pale pink, thoroughly recommended for cooler climates where it opens well in all weathers.

Sharon Voye (Hansen 94) Dip, Ev H70cm (28in), F12cm (5in), ML, Re, Ext Sunfast, voluptuously ruffled, perfectly formed, bright medium pink, glowing green throat. Heavy substance and waxy, ribbed texture. Hardy in cold-winter regions.

Siloam Double Classic (Henry 86) AM, SSM, IM, LP Dip, SEv, H50cm (20in), F14cm (5½in), Dd, EM, Re, Ext, Fra Full-formed, bright pink, green throat of exquisite colour and shape. Rain-resistant and an early-morning-opener. An outstanding double although the earliest flowers are usually single and can be distorted if the nights are still cool. Performs better in cold-winter regions.

Virginia Franklin Miller (Kirchhoff 93) Dip, Ev, H70cm (28in), F16.5cm (6½in), M, Re, Fra Ravishing double with fused stamens and flat to recurved sepals, light to mid-pink, deep green throat. Very vigorous, well-branched with a good bud count. Now also a tetraploid.

Xia Xiang (Billingslea 88) AM Dip, SEv, H70cm (28in), F15cm (6in), M, Ext, Fra Round, wide-petalled, flat-formed, clear, deep pink self, green throat, cream to pink midribs, yellow-flushed pink filaments and pistil. The sepals have tailored ruffling with a corduroy-like texture from its 'Fairy Tale Pink' ancestry. A superb and unusual shade of pink with heavily looping ruffles, on 4-way branched scapes, opening flat every morning with perfect form, colour and substance. Vigorous and blooms for weeks. "The queen of pinks, having the look of a southern beauty and the sturdiness of a northern performer": Lynn Purse.

ALSO RECOMMENDED: 'Cantique', 'Corryton Pink', 'Edna Spalding', 'Gentle Rose', 'Lake Norman Sunset', 'Little Monica', 'Olallie Mack', 'Preppy', 'Second Thoughts', 'Tootsie Rose'.

ROSE-PINK

Betty Jenkins (Wilson 89) Dip, SEv, H55cm (22in), F15cm (6in), EM, Re, Ext Heavily ruffled, rose-pink, green throat. Good branching, bud count, and an early-morning-opener, but can be slow to increase. A very lovely daylily of good substance.

Coming up Roses (Hager 90) HM Dip, Ev, H75cm (30in)(usually less), F9cm (3½in), Sm, E, Re Superb, perfectly round, wide-petalled, recurved, exquisitely ruffled, lavender-influenced, deep rose-pink, palest pearly-lavender-pink midribs, lemon-green heart. Opens well with a profusion of flower lasting for weeks and reblooms in cooler gardens. 'Coming up Roses' is worthy of inclusion in any collection.

Farmer's Daughter (Kirchhoff 91) Tet, Ev, H70cm (28in), F14cm (5½in), E Sunfast, tightly pleated, full, overlapped, coral-influenced deeply saturated rose-pink of satiny texture, deeper rose-gold edge apparent only in hot climates, green throat fades to yellow but the heart remains green, pearly-pink midribs only just visible, pink-tipped yellow filaments, brown anthers. Hardy, vigorous, rainproof, very well branched. Very popular and a superb performer even in colder European gardens.

Frances Joiner (Joiner 89) AM, IM Dip, Dor, H60cm (24in), F14cm (5½in), Dd, M, Re, Fra Unusual, hose-in-hose double with distinctive rose colouration on the outer edges blending into rose-apricot towards the green throat. The scapes have good branching, and this is a vigorous, floriferous, consistent high-performance daylily. Easy to grow and one of the most popular double daylilies available. Also a tetraploid conversion.

Jedi Dot Pierce (Wedgeworth 89) Dip, SEv, H50cm (20in), F15cm (6in), EM, Re Very ruffled, slightly recurved, muted rose-pink with slightly deeper veining, a faint darker pink halo and green throat. Top-branched scapes with blooms just above the foliage so that it is lovely to look down on. Opens well after cool nights. A rapid increaser. A superb daylily.

Jolyene Nichole (Spalding-Guillory 84) AM Dip, Dor, H35cm (14in), F15cm (6in), M, Noc Richly ruffled, recurved, glowing rose-pink, deeper pink veining, green throat soon turns yellow. A much paler colour in very hot regions. Lowish scapes, just above the lush dark green foliage, means the clump resembles a bouquet when in full flower but that proportions are rather unbalanced. A vig-

'Langley Rose Explosion' is a hardy, double daylily raised by one of Canada's leading breeders.

orous increaser responding well to frequent feeding. Rain-resistant, an early-morning-opener, needs protection in very cold-winter regions. Dormant although registered as an evergreen or semi-evergreen.

Langley Rose Explosion (Erikson 96) Dip, Dor, H80cm (32in), F12cm (5in), Dd, M, Fra Ruffled, rose with slightly deeper rose eye, yellow-green throat.

Mabel Nolen (Nolen 84) Dip, Dor, H70cm (28in), F15cm (6in), M, Fra Beautiful, ruffled, clear light rose-pink, green throat bisected by contrasting wide white midribs, pearly-pink anthers. Exquisite branching, the blooms set at a nice height above the foliage. Best in cold-winter climates.

Rose Emily (Pierce 82) AM Dip, SEv, H50cm (20in), F12cm (5in), M, Re, SNoc Celebrated, round, elaborately ruffled, fully recurved, light rose-pink self (with a salmon influence in cooler climates), deeper rose-pink veining, pale pink depressed midribs, yellow filaments, bright lime-green throat, which forms a circular spot in the heart of the flower. Heavy substance and smooth texture. Appreciates a mulch in regions with very cold winters; when the nights are consistently warm it is a superb performer in Europe, although slow to increase.

Seminole Wind (Stamile 95) Tet, Ev/SEv, H58cm (23in), F16.5cm (6½in), EM, Re, Ext, Fra Perfectly round, scallop-ruffled, flat to slightly recurved, waxy, deep rich clear pink to rose-pink in cooler regions, narrow yellow throat, olive-green heart. 3–4-way branching in hot regions. Dark olive-green foliage. The influence of its parent, the tetraploid form of 'Barbara Mitchell' (p.59) is apparent. A breakthrough in pink tetraploids. Fertile.

Silken Touch (Stamile 90) Tet, Dor, H58cm (23in), F15cm (6in), EM, Re, Ext, Noc, Fra Widely ruffled, smooth, soft bluish-rose-pink (becoming paler in high temperatures), green throat. Rather top-branched and slow to increase in cooler climates, it opens well, however, and these defects become insignificant when looking down at its superb blooms. From 'Tet Martha Adams', a southern-raised pink, it needs a few seasons to settle down, then increases rapidly. An excellent parent for breeding tetraploid pinks.

Siloam Double Rose (Henry 79) AM, IM, LP Dip, Ev, H50cm (20in), F15cm (6in), Dd, M, Ext, Fra Bright pink, with deeper veining, giving the overall impression of rose, ruby-red eye, green throat. Good substance and ribbed texture. Doubling more apparent in cold-winter climates. The first flowers are usually single.

Siloam Olin Frazier (Henry 90) Dip, Dor, H55cm (22in), F13.5cm (5¼in), Dd, E, Ext Hot bright pink (between rose-pink and rose-red) with a touch of creamy-white in the ruffling. Always perfectly formed with great bloom habits but not always a rapid increaser.

Siloam Ribbon Candy (Henry 81) Dip, Dor, H55cm (22in), F6cm (2½in), Mini, ML, Re Round, ruffled, deep rose-pink, rose-red veining and eye, vivid green heart, narrow buff midribs, pale pink filaments. Flowers are smaller than the registration indicates. Although floriferous it does not open perfectly until almost the end of the flowering season but is nonetheless very popular.

Sitting Cool (Bennett 96) Dip, SEv, H60cm (24in), F16.5-17cm (6½-7in), M Ruffled, creamy-peach to cherry-rose blend, lemon-green throat. Very heavy substance and corduroy texture. Good branching and bud count. Very vigorous and hardy. Beckons across the garden.

Sue Rothbauer (K. Carpenter 83) Dip, SEv, H50cm (20in), F16.5cm (6½in), EM, Re, Fra Ruffled, recurved, silky-textured, intense saturated rose-pink, lemon-green throat, the colour being noticeably darker in cloudy weather. Blooms and reblooms consistently and is never damaged by varying weather conditions although it needs warm nights to open flat.

Vera Biaglow (Moldovan 86) AM Tet, Dor, H70cm (28in), F15cm (6in), ML, Ext Broad, circular, ruffled, rather vivid rose-pink, yellow throat. A silvery-grey edge is sometimes apparent. Well branched, but rather thick scapes; can be a reluctant opener. Highest quality and a superb colour for those who like this rather harsh shade of rose-pink.

ALSO RECOMMENDED: 'Addie Branch Smith', 'Ann Kelley', 'Bug's Hug', 'Classic Rose', 'Jedi Rose Frost', 'Lake Norman Spider', 'Little Rosy Cloud', 'Mumbo Jumbo', 'Neal Berry', 'Rose Talisman', 'Thy True Love'.

SALMON-PINK AND CORAL-PINK
Salmon- and coral-pinks are often lavender-influenced and this is clearly apparent in the daylilies listed here.

Bermuda Coral (Marvin 85) Tet, Dor, H1.1-1.2m (42-48in), F16.5cm (6½in), L-Very L Triangular, tailored, slightly recurved, creamy-pink to pink-coral with subtle shadings of peach and pink and sometimes flushes of blue, especially in cool weather; tiny green heart early in the morning, creamy-orange throat, matching filaments and pistil. Tall, 3-4-way branching, with a bud count of 18+. Opens well on cool mornings and can establish quickly, although a modest increaser; completely hardy. A difficult parent which is a pity since it could pass on very late blooming characteristics in a colour other than yellow.

Classy Cast (Brooks 93) Tet, SEv, H1m (3ft), F12cm (5in), EM, Re Gently ruffled, flat, slightly recurved, pale coral-rose, yellow throat, green heart, pink-tipped lime-green filaments, prominent pearly-pink midrib. A robust daylily of waxy texture, well-branched, floriferous and performs well in cooler climates. 'Classy Cast' takes a year to establish and is more vigorous than its parent 'Kate Carpenter' (p.59).

Cool Jazz (Kirchhoff 87) Tet, Ev, H70cm (28in), F14cm (5½in), E, Re, Ext Wide, ruffled, overlapped, gold-dusted, shell to pale coral-pink, wide lemon-green throat; narrow gold-wire edges become apparent in hotter climates. Robust, wide, dark green foliage. A vigorous and showy daylily.

Diva Assoluta (Morss 85) HM Tet, SEv, H63cm (25in), F15cm (6in), M Ruffled, creamy salmon-pink to near-ivory, pale salmon to gold edges (only apparent in very hot climates), green throat. Good substance, very hardy, fertile. Not always a clear colour in cooler climates and can be a reluctant opener.

Near-ivory with pale salmon to gold edges in hot climates, 'Diva Assoluta' reveals tints of creamy salmon-pink in cooler regions.

Frank Gladney (Durio 79) AM Tet, Ev/SEv, H65cm (26in), F16.5cm (6½in), EM, Re, Ext Full, widely segmented, fascinating lavender-influenced blend of hot coral to salmon-pink, light tangerine throat. The colour is exquisite after cool evenings, but the thin substance can result in rain damage in heavy downpours. Healthy foliage, flowers for months and multiplies well but needs daily deadheading. 'Frank Gladney' is outstanding in most gardens even though the shape of the flowers is not perfect. An early-morning-opener.

Smoky Mountain Bell (Guidry 92) Dip, Ev, H63cm (25in), F14cm (5½in), E, Re Showy, round, extravagantly ruffled into the throat, diamond-dusted, salmon- to terracotta-pink with a lavender hue visible on some mornings, similar to 'Smoky Mountain Autumn' (below), but with a richer pink influence and more recurved, wide, light orange throat, matching filaments, tiny green heart. 2-way branching. Can be slightly tender in some climates, needing a mulch during its first winter, slow to increase. Impeccable Guidry form.

Tropic Sunset (Harris-Benz 87) Tet, Dor, H60cm (24in), F17cm (7in), EM, Ext Huge, coral-rose blend. With good branching and bud count, this daylily opens and increases well.

ALSO RECOMMENDED: 'Coral Dawn', 'Coral Moon', 'Tang Porcelain'.

TERRACOTTA-PINK BLENDS

Cajun Lady (Guidry 85) Dip, Ev, H75cm (30in), F15cm (6in), E, Re, Noc, Fra Perfectly formed, exquisitely ruffled, saturated salmon-rose to terracotta-blend blushed lavender on the segment tips, golden-green throat, pale pink filaments, contrasting large black anthers, wide pearly-lavender midribs. Opens well and blooms perfectly in southern England and is completely hardy, but in colder climates it can be slow to increase and a poor performer.

Pink Damask (Stevens 51) AM, RHS/AGM Dip, Dor, H90cm (36in), F10cm (4in), Sm, Her, M Lily-shaped, buff-pink to terracotta-pink with an underlying yellow base, distinctive white midribs, black anthers, tangerine-yellow throat. Narrow foliage. Floriferous and vigorous but the colour is poor compared with modern clear, pure pinks.

Smoky Mountain Autumn (Guidry 86) AM, LAA Dip, Dor, H45cm (18in), F14cm (5½in), E, Noc, Fra Deeply ruffled, slightly recurved, subtle lavender-influenced smoky copper-rose blend, slightly darker towards the throat, olive-green heart. Narrow leaves, top-branched, but the flowers are well presented on the scapes. Opens very well in all weathers but does not increase rapidly. Has topped many popularity polls since its introduction and performs well in most regions.

ORANGE-RED TO RUSTY-RED

Aztec Furnace (Stamile 87) Tet, Dor, H68cm (27in), F12cm (5in), EM Elegantly formed, round, wide-petalled, conspicuously veined burnt-orange to rusty-red, faintly darker eye, green throat, recurved sepals. A sun-resistant, thoroughly good performer in most climates and very popular in European gardens.

Captain Joe (Faggard 91) Tet, SEv, H82cm (32¼in), F12cm (5in), M Round, ruffled, recurved, russet-coral to light red, tangerine throat, matching filaments, small green heart. Good substance and corduroy texture.

Clovette Adams (Kirchhoff 93) Tet, Ev, H55cm (22in), F15cm (6in), Dd, E, Re, Ext, Fra Round, ruffled, smooth-textured, deepest orange to russet-red, gold to green throat. A gold edge is apparent in very hot climates. Consistently double with wide, overlapping segments. If there is rebloom it becomes hose-in-hose. Well-branched. Fertile both ways. While still not widely available it is one to look

out for as it is reputed to be hardy in cold-winter climates and has reached the standard of the best diploid doubles.

Hot Ember (Stamile 86) HM Tet, Ev/SEv, H75cm (30in), F14cm (5½in), M, Re Sunfast, lightly ruffled vivid reddish-orange to light russet-red, orange eye, deep yellow throat flaring into the midribs, tiny green heart, tangerine filaments, black anthers. Relishes strong sun, a rapid increaser and a superb colour. Hardy. Fertile.

House of Orange (Weston 91) Dip, Dor, H68cm (27in), F13.5cm (5¼in), M Flawless, slightly recurved, smooth, velvety, intense bittersweet russet-orange, dark green throat. A good performer in most regions, very hardy. Its unusual colour needs to be seen close up.

Old Tangiers (Millikan 85) HM Tet, SEv, H70cm (28in), F12cm (5in), ML Eye-catching, nicely ruffled, wide, darker veined, tawny-orange, faint russet eye, narrow yellow throat bisected by pale yellow midribs, tiny green heart, orange-tipped yellow filaments. Reliably hardy, an early-morning-opener and a good performer everywhere. Very popular.

Pat Mercer (Joiner 84) Dip, SEv, H70cm (28in), F17cm (7in), M, Re Rain-resistant, ruffled blooms begin to open a

'Smoky Mountain Autumn' is a beautifully ruffled, subtle-toned smoky copper-rose blend of exquisite shape.

full day before they fully recurve, which may not be achieved in cooler climates. The first day it appears to be deeply saturated orange-red with a very green throat, and sometimes a halo can be visible. The second day the colour changes to mars-orange with a yellow-green throat. Beautifully branched but on rather low scapes. Broad, blue-green foliage. The roots are large and very long. Incredibly vigorous; can be tender in very cold-winter regions. Needs daily deadheading.

Sound and Fury (Sikes 78) HM Tet, SEv, H65cm (26in), F14cm (5½in), M Spectacular, triangular, ruffled, red-veined, bright russet-orange, darker red halo, small gold throat that seeps into a short yellow midrib. Rather thin substance but nevertheless sunproof and performs best in humid climates. Reblooms and grows well everywhere making a great show over a long period.

Southern Summer (Sikes 93) Tet, SEv, H70cm (28in), F11cm (4½in), Sm, M, Re Very ruffled, slightly recurved, vibrant hot orange-red with small deeper orange-red eye, yellow throat, green heart. Heavy substance. Good branching and bud count. Fertile.

Timeless Fire (Guidry 86) Dip, SEv, H45cm (18in), F12cm (5in), E-M, Noc Sumptuous, full, recurved, lightly ruffled, smooth, rusty-red to blood-red (in cool weather), yellow throat, green heart, contrasting wide cream midribs, red-tipped yellow filaments. Lush, wide, blue-green foliage. Moderately vigorous, excellent form and substance. Opens perfectly, fully hardy and performs well in many parts of Europe.

ALSO RECOMMENDED: 'Bologongo', 'Pixie Pipestone', 'Red Rum' (AM, AG, LAA), 'Summer Jubilee', 'Tropical Heatwave'.

SCARLET

Aramis (Benz 91) Tet, Dor, H75cm (30in), F12cm (5in), ML, Re Round, elaborately ruffled and frilled, sunfast brilliant red, glowing green throat. Fully hardy.

Broadway Valentine (G. Stamile 94) Tet, Dor, H60cm (24in), F6.5cm (2¾in), Mini, EM, Re Ruffled, recurved, rusty-scarlet, yellow throat. The first of many in a new direction for this talented hybridizer who is turning her attention to small and mini tetraploids. 'Broadway Valentine' is particularly recommended for those growing daylilies in cooler climates.

Chicago Apache (Marsh-Klehm 81) Tet, Dor, H70cm (28in), F12cm (5in), M Rich, velvety, scarlet self, with a silky finish, lemon-green throat, red filaments and black anthers. The petals have lightly ruffled edges of a deeper tone and a paler midrib. A thoroughly hardy and dependable daylily with a wide range of adaptability and excellent for its late bloom. One of the best reds for European gardens although the lush foliage can be somewhat coarse and stiff.

Christmas Is (Yancey 80) Dip, Dor, H50cm (20in), F11cm (4½in), Sm, M, Re Full-formed, brilliant scarlet, spectacular deep sunburst lime-green throat, red-tipped, ivory-lime filaments, raised midribs. Scapes only just above foliage on young plants. Vigorous, rapid increaser but sometimes a reluctant bloomer. Lovely when planted in front of 'Green Flutter' (p.46). Also a tetraploid.

Dragon King (Kirchhoff 92) Tet, Ev, H55cm (22in), F12cm (5in), E Sumptuous, widely ruffled, rich orange-influenced scarlet, huge contrasting chartreuse sunburst throat, the throat colour also visible on the sepals when fully recurved, tiny green heart gradually turns yellow, red-tipped lemon-green filaments, contrasting black anthers,

'Timeless Fire' has pale yellow midribs that contrast well with the rusty-red ground colour.

inner petal pleating. The throat colour can be deep green on cool mornings. Beautiful foliage and excellent wide-branching but rather slow to increase.

James Marsh (Marsh-Klehm 78) HM Tet, Dor, H70cm (28in), F16.5cm (6½in), EM Slightly crimped-petalled, scarlet self, contrasted with smooth sepals thinly outlined in creamy-yellow, yellow-green throat. Thoroughly reliable in most locations and recommended for new growers.

Kent's Favourite Two (Kirchhoff 89) HM Tet, Ev, H65cm (26in), F13.5cm (5¼in), EE, Re, Ext Wide-segmented, full, overlapped, recurved, lightly ruffled, velvety, clear bright red to near rusty-red (in cooler climates), narrow deep yellow throat blending into a bright green heart. Exceptionally sunfast, hardy in cold-winter regions, a good performer in European gardens and a rapid increaser. Very fertile.

Leonard Bernstein (Kirchhoff 93) HM Tet, Ev, H63cm (25in), F14cm (5½in), EM, Re, Noc Beautifully presented, round, deeply ruffled, recurved, velvety, clear rich red, green throat, red-tipped, ivory-green filaments. Superb substance, colour and form with exquisite candelabra branching. Hardy but the foliage can suffer in severe winters although it rejuvenates quickly as the temperature warms up. Very fertile.

Red Joy (Sellers 82) Tet, SEv, H80cm (32in), F15cm (6in), M Wide-open, slightly recurved, velvety, brilliant scarlet, wide yellowish-green throat, red-tipped lemon-green filaments. Not widely grown in the US but popular in the British Isles where it is a good performer.

Red Volunteer (Oakes 84) AM Tet, Dor, H75cm (30in), F17cm (7in), M, Fra Sunfast, open, clear candlewax-red self, gold throat, pointed sepals. Good substance, high bud count, a superb performer in all regions; a useful landscape daylily and suitable for novice growers. Hardy, adaptable, fertile.

Scarlet Orbit (Gates 85) AM Tet, SEv, H55cm (22in), F15cm (6in), E, Re Round, lightly ruffled, flat, scarlet with faint, darker red halo, precise lemon-green throat. A superb daylily but can require some shade in hot, humid conditions. After late, hard frosts or drought conditions, it may bloom within the foliage and, even when well tended, the flowers only ever sit on the foliage. Performs well in Australia and New Zealand.

Seductor (Gates 83) AM Tet, Ev, H45cm (18in), F15cm (6in), EE Ruffled, wide, overlapping petals of brilliant scarlet, small vivid green throat, red-tipped yellow filaments. Very early, long-blooming and reblooms many times in favourable areas. Healthy, dark green foliage which looks good all the summer. The individual blooms are hardly ever perfectly formed but it is excellent *en masse* as a landscaping daylily. Can proliferate. Needs some winter protection in colder regions.

Spider Man (Durio 82) Tet, Dor, H60cm (24in), F17cm (7in), EM, Re Wide open, star-shaped, sunfast, saturated velvety, fire-engine-red, yellow throat flaring a little onto the floppy segments, red-tipped yellow filaments, prominent midribs. Floriferous with a long bloom season. The flowers have an unusual spider-like form although the tepal ratio is too wide to classify this daylily as a Spider Variant.

ALSO RECOMMENDED: 'Amadeus', 'Bedarra Island', 'King Haiglar', 'Lusty Lealand', 'Red Precious', 'Scarlet Chalice', 'Stafford'.

BLOOD-RED TO DARK RED

Bama Bound (Webster 86) Tet, SEv/Dor, H60cm (24in), F12cm (5in), M, Re, Fra Round, nicely ruffled, recurved, velvety, deep red, yellow throat, green heart, red-tipped yellow filaments. Sunfast in hot, humid regions. Hardy and a superb performer in cold, mountainous regions in Europe, opening well everywhere. Very fertile. Highly recommended.

Claudine (Millikan 86) Tet, Dor, H60cm (24in), F12cm (5in), M Outstanding, triangular, full-formed, lightly ruffled, blood-red with a faint darker eye, bright yellow throat, red filaments, prominently raised midribs, very recurved sepals. Heavy substance and velvety texture with a glistening metallic finish. One of the best dark reds in our garden and there are many other good reports of its performance, especially from cold-winter regions.

Dark Avenger (E. Salter 90) HM Dip, SEv, H45cm (18in), F6cm (2½in), Mini, M, Re Round, recurved, full-formed, clear velvety, dark-red, lemon-green throat, dark red-tipped yellow filaments. Well-branched, high bud count, the buds attractively coloured black-red. Hardiness is doubtful in some areas.

Hot Ticket (Brooks 93) Tet, SEv, H74cm (29in), F14cm (5½in), EM, Re Wide open, lightly ruffled, superb, fully saturated rich dark red, slightly darker halo, deep yellow throat, green heart, red-tipped yellow filaments, black anthers. Leathery substance, slightly ribbed surface texture. Excellent in cooler climates.

Lowenstine (Millikan 79) Tet, Dor, H70cm (28in), F16.5cm (6½in), M Eye-catching, large, triangular-shaped, lacquer-like deep-red, narrowish segments, wide lemon-green throat. Stoloniferous habit. Performs well in colder climates.

Nebuchadnezzar's Furnace (Talbott 88) Dip, Ev, H55cm (22in), F12cm (5in), Dd, M Darkest red, red-black eye. Hardy in many areas but can be affected by freeze/thaw cycles.

Night Raider (Webster 86) Tet, Dor, H70cm (28in), F14cm (5½in), M, SNoc Weatherproof, full, slightly recurved, dark red, seemingly darker due to the near-black veining and edges, vivid green throat, deep red-tipped filaments, dark anthers. Very healthy with lush, husky foliage. Well-branched, blooms heavily for over a month, moderate to good increase. Although registered as an M, it blooms as an EM or even an E, taking over just as 'Scarlet Orbit' (above) is reaching its peak.

Rue Madelaine (Carr 92) Tet, SEv, H68cm (27in), F14cm (5½in), EM, Re Ruffled, rich black-red-influenced burgundy-purple self, green throat. Well-branched, vigorous, hardy in many colder areas and an early-morning-opener. Fertile. Excellent but not as dark as some.

'Seminole Blood' is a sombre blood-red of beautiful proportion, with a strikingly contrasting throat – a wonderful performer in many climatic regions.

Seminole Blood (Kirchhoff 94) Tet, Ev, H75cm (30in), F15cm (6in), E, Re, Ext Wide, ruffled, overlapped, sombre blood-red, perfectly contrasting triangular orange throat, tiny green heart, red-tipped yellow filaments, near-black anthers. Well-branched and vigorous. Hardy in cold-winter climates. Fertile.

Vintage Bordeaux (Kirchhoff 87) AM Tet, Ev, H68cm (27in), F15cm (6in), E, Re, Ext Exceptionally sunfast, round, ruffled, very dark cherry-red, narrowly edged yellow in hot climates, red-tipped yellow filaments, lemon-green throat. In cooler climates the colour can appear more brown; it requires heat to open well. Slightly tender but because it is so vigorous it completely regenerates in cold-winter regions. Popular in Australia and New Zealand.

Vohann (Hager 86) Tet, Ev, H90cm (36in), F14cm (5½), E-M, Re Widely star-shaped, recurved, lightly ruffled, clear shimmering deep red, small lemon-green throat, raised midribs, red filaments. Very floriferous. Sunfast in hot climates; good branching and unusually tall scapes make it a valuable back of the border or landscaping daylily, as the shape is not as good as some.

Wally (Howard 91) Dip, Dor, H55cm (22in), F13.5cm (5¼in), Dd, M Consistently double, dark red, darker red eye. Vigorous with 4-way branching and a bud count of 20+. 'Best double red diploid on the market': Kevin Walek.

When I Dream (Yancey 79) AM Dip, SEv, H70cm (28in), F16.5cm (6½in), EM Eye-catching, slightly ruffled, blood-red, striking, large lemon-green throat fading to near white as it reaches the segments.

ALSO RECOMMENDED: 'Berlin Red', 'Bridget', 'Crimson Pirate', 'Drop Dead Red', 'Fire Music', 'Neon Flame', 'Obsession in Red', 'Southern Sunset', 'Stroke of Midnight'.

BLUE-RED (CHERRY) TO ROSE-RED

Charles Johnston (Gates 82) AM, PC Tet, SEv, H60cm (24in), F15cm (6in), EM, Re, Fra Wide, flat, ruffled, bright cherry-red self, yellow-green throat. Prominent lighter midribs. Noted for its unusual shade of red. Rather top-branched but a high bud count. After late, hard frosts or drought conditions, it may bloom within the foliage. Hardy in cold gardens although raised in the deep south. Appreciates some shade in hot humid conditions.

Cherries are Ripe (Hager 92) Dip, SEv, H70cm (28in), F6cm (2½in), Mini, M Round, cherry-red. Wiry multiple-branched scapes blooming over a long period.

Herman Apps (Apps 92) AM Dip, Dor (SEv in hot climates), H70cm (28in), F14cm (5½in), M Ruffled, flat, wide-segmented, cerise-red, green throat. Moderate bud count; excellent increaser, and, even though dormant, performs well in hot climates.

Little Maggie (Williamson 81) Dip, Ev, H30cm (12in), F7cm (3in), Sm, EE, Re Round, ruffled, recurved, lilac-influenced rose-red, with a misty burgundy eye and lemon-green throat, rose-pink filaments, brown anthers. Good substance and corduroy texture. Excellent foliage. Completely dependable and one of the first to bloom. Sometimes reblooms in English gardens.

Siloam Paul Watts (Henry 88) AM Dip, Dor, H45cm (18in), F11.5cm (4¾in), Ext Sunfast, round, nicely ruffled, deep rose to cherry-red of exquisite shape, green throat. Good substance and excellent foliage setting a new standard of refinement in form in this colour. Hardy in cold-winter regions and opens well. 'Harlem Nights' (Van Sellers) is very similar. 'Indy Spirit Walk' (Anderson) has all the same wonderful qualities but with larger flowers on a taller scape.

Tango Noturno (Reinerman 87) Dip, Dor, H50cm (20in), F10cm (4in), M Nicely rounded, evenly ruffled, recurved, rose-red, deeper rose-red halo, yellow throat blending into a green heart, yellow filaments. Well-branched, vigorous and hardy. A 'Siloam Dream Baby' (p.86) offspring raised in Europe.

Whooperee (Gates 88) AM Tet, Ev, H60cm (24in), F16.5cm (6½in), E, Re Recurved, round, bright rose-red with a slightly darker halo and veining, narrow yellow eye blending into a prominent green throat, red-tipped filaments, large red-brown anthers. Good substance, smooth velvety texture, well-branched and long-blooming. An early-morning-opener so a good performer in cooler gardens.

ALSO RECOMMENDED: 'Forever Red', 'Jesse James', 'Little Business', 'Little Fat Dazzler', 'Siloam Jim Cooper'.

CRANBERRY-RED TO RUBY-RED

Cranberry Baby (Croker 84) AG, FSC, AM Dip, Dor, H30cm (12in), F6.5cm (2¾in), EM, Ext Prolific, recurved, cranberry blooms with faint deeper ruby eye, lemon-green throat, on stout scapes. Excellent foliage exhibits a good mounding habit. Lovely in a large planting or mixed with creams such as 'Sugar Cookie' (p.44) or eyed varieties such as 'Water Witch' (p.93). A rapid multiplier.

Cranberry Cove (Stamile 85) HM Dip, Dor/SEv, H70cm (28in), F10.5cm (4¼in), Sm, EM, Fra Ruffled, translucent deep ruby-red self, green throat. Vigorous and a superb rich colour but the bud count is only moderate in some regions.

Jovial (Gates 87) HM Tet, Dor, H50cm (20in), F12cm (5in) M, Re, Ext, SNoc, Fra Full, ruffled, vivid ruby- to wine-red, narrow yellow throat, green heart, red-tipped lime-green filaments. Good growth and high bud count, weatherproof and opens well. The flowers lighten in strong sunshine to a beautiful violet-wine. Elegant, slender foliage. A superb parent but the wine pigment has proved to be dominant.

Little Red Warbler (Crochet 85) HM Dip, Dor, H45cm (18in), F9cm (3½in), Sm, EM, Re Distinctive, recurved, ruby-red, maroon eye, lemon-green throat. Opens perfectly in cooler climates, the blooms standing up reasonably well to hot sun. Floriferous and multiplies fast.

Pardon Me (Apps 82) DFM, AM Dip, Dor, H45cm (18in), F6.5cm (2¾in), Mini, M, Re, Noc, Fra Perfectly proportioned, ruffled, smooth, cranberry-red, lemon-green throat. Long-blooming, well-branched, floriferous and a bud builder. 'Siloam Red Toy' is similar. 'Little Ben' is Dar-

rel Apps' new introduction with wider petals and longer bloom season. Also a tetraploid conversion.

Pirate Bride (E. Salter 96) Tet, SEv, H70cm (28in), F9cm (3½in), Sm, M, Re Full, round, overlapped, tightly pleated, deep ruby-wine-red, rose-black to red-black band, slightly darker red edges, bright yellow throat, green heart, bright yellow filaments. Well-branched. Opens well in European gardens, well-branched.

Regency Dandy (E. Salter 92) Dip, Ev, H45cm (18in), F6cm (2½in), Mini, M, Re Round, full, recurved, smooth, rich ruby-red, tiny green heart. Well-branched scapes with multiple blooms. A rapid increaser and lovely in a clump. Fertile.

Siloam Red Velvet (Henry 75) Dip, Dor, H65cm (26in), F12cm (5in), ML, Re Wide, gently ruffled, velvety, ruby-red, glowing wide lime-green throat which lasts all day, cream midribs, red-tipped green filaments, dark brown anthers. Good substance and sunfast in high temperatures. Blooms late in the British Isles and opens fully by midday; slow to make clump strength although well worth the wait. Passes on its superb lime-green throat.

Siloam Showgirl (Henry 81) Dip, H45cm+ (18in), F11cm (4½in), Sm, M, Ext Ruffled, velvety, rich deep ruby-

The captivating, floriferous, green-throated ruby-red, miniture, 'Regency Dandy'.

to wine-red, deeper red eye, green throat, ruby-red-tipped, lemon-green filaments. Graceful, arching foliage.

Woodside Ruby (Apps 89) HM Dip, SEv, H85cm (34in), F11cm (4½in), Sm, M Round, lightly ruffled, vibrant, rich ruby-red self, lime-green throat. Only moderate branching but a good bud count and increases well.

ALSO RECOMMENDED: 'Little Cranberry Cove', 'Mallard', 'Oriental Ruby'.

WINE-RED TO PURPLE-RED

Little Grapette (Williamson 70) DFM, AM, RHS/HC Dip, SEv/Dor, H45cm (18in), F6cm (2½in), Mini, Her, M, Re Ruffled grape-purple, slightly deeper eye, yellow throat, recurved sepals. Vigorous and a prolific bloomer but needs warm nights to recurve well, although worthy of a place in any garden. Very hardy. A classic mini.

Little Wine Cup (Powell 69) Dip, Dor, H48cm (19in), F5cm (2in), Mini, Her, E, Re Recurved, lightly ruffled, deep wine-red, lighter midribs, lemon-green throat. Floriferous, vigorous and a reliable repeat bloomer in many areas including the British Isles.

Mojave Maroon (Guidry 83) Dip, SEv/Ev, H58cm (23in), F10cm (4in), Sm, Noc Slightly ruffled, recurved, deeply saturated velvety, rich wine-red self, lasting green throat. Little-known but superb, with excellent branching and wide leaves. Rain and sunproof, but fades to near-maroon in hot sunshine. Hardy and very popular in Europe. Not the typical circular Guidry form.

Siloam Grace Stamile (Henry 85) DFM Dip, Dor, H35cm (14in), F5.5cm (2¼in), Mini, EM, Ext, Fra Very round, ruffled, light wine-red, deeper red halo, lemon-green throat. A delightful, tiny daylily suitable for the front of a border or rock garden. Well-budded only in hot climates and poor branching but useful for its small size; frequently reblooms.

Siloam Royal Prince (Henry 83) Dip, Dor, H48cm (19in), F10cm (4in), Sm, M Ruffled, recurved, rich reddish-violet-purple, lemon-green throat, purple-tipped yellow filaments. Excellent form, good branching and bud count and very vigorous but needs a run of warm nights to open well.

ALSO RECOMMENDED: 'Double Grapette', 'Entransette', 'New Swirls', 'Royal Prestige'.

BLACK-RED

Africa (Kropf-Tankesley-Clark 87) Dip, Dor, H68cm (27in), F12cm (5in) ML, Re Open, narrow-tepalled, very dark red, bright tangerine-orange throat. The dark colour gives the illusion of being black and lasts all day. Multiplies very well. Highly recommended as being one of the blackest of the black-reds.

African Diplomat (Carr 92) Tet, Ev, 74cm (29in), F14cm (5½in), ML Ruffled, black-red-influenced deepest purple depending on the climate and time of day, sunburst diamond-shaped lemon-green throat. One of the nearest to black. Reasonably colourfast and performs well in severe climates.

American Revolution (Wild 72) Dip, Dor, H70cm (28in), F12cm (5in), E-EM Tapered, lily-shaped, velvety, black-wine-red self, yellow throat, small green heart, dark red-tipped yellow filaments. The flower buds are attractively coloured black-red. Hardy and very popular in English gardens.

Black Ambrosia (Salter 91) Tet, SEv, H75cm (30in), F12cm (5in), M, Re Triangular to rounded, ruffled, velvety-textured, midnight-black-red, intense lime-green throat, black-tipped ivory-lime filaments, black anthers. Usually black-red on first opening, gradually becoming nearer to purple-black later in the day but its colour varies from

'Siloam Royal Prince' is a subtle and unusual shade of red-violet. It requires heat in order to open fully.

region to region. Reblooms in hot climates into late summer. Reasonably hardy in most areas although foliage can get damaged in severe winters. Increases well; a true beauty and remarkably unfussy. Prodigious branching and bud count. Fertile.

Ed Murray (Grovatt 70) AM, AG, SSM, LAA Dip, Dor, H65cm (26in), F10cm (4in) M, Ext Sunfast, round, ruffled, recurved, maroon-black self, green throat. The petals are recurved and sometimes narrowly edged white. Very floriferous, vigorous, good substance. Foliage may be damaged in severe winters. The so-called 'Tet Ed Murray' can be crossed with both diploids and tetraploids: it is not a properly converted tetraploid as it produces 100% unreduced gametes. A classic. Found in the lineage of many of the best new reds-blacks although it is not an easy parent. One of only 3 red daylilies to be mentioned in the *National Arboretum Book of Outstanding Garden Plants*.

Jungle Beauty (Apps 90) HM Dip, Dor, H75cm (30in), F14cm (5½in), M Sunfast, rich black-red with a hint of violet, faint black halo, black veining. An outstanding performer with excellent branching and good bud count, opening early but slow to establish although well worth the wait.

Little Fred (Maxwell 77) Dip, SEv/Dor, H60cm (24in), F7cm (3in), Sm, EM, Re, Ext Heat-tolerant, open-formed, lightly ruffled, deepest black-red self, even darker eye, lemon-green throat.

Midnight Magic (Kinnebrew 79) AM Tet, Ev, H75cm (30in), F15cm (6in), EM, Ext Ruffled, very dark black-red, green throat. An early-morning-opener. Heavy substance but the petal edges can bleach to an unsaturated dark red in strong sunlight. Glossy green foliage. Well-branched, husky scapes. Increases rapidly, floriferous with scape proliferations. Not always reliably hardy in cold-winter regions. From 'Tet Ed Murray'.

Night Wings (Williams 85) HM Tet, Ev, H75cm (30in), F15cm (6in), E Rich, sooty-black-red self with blue-black sheen, lemon-green throat and pinched petals. Heavy substance. One of the nearest to black but slightly outdated in shape. However, it is a daylily I shall always treasure as it was given to me by the raiser Mrs June Williams who used her own popular dark red 'Dominic' as a parent. A superb performer with good branching and bud count. Fertile.

Siloam Plum Tree (Henry 78) Dip, Dor, H60cm (24in), F10cm (4in), Sm, EM, Re, Ext Very round, ruffled, very ribbed, deep burgundy-red to near black, lemon-green throat, burgundy-tipped filaments. It only fully recurves in very hot weather. Very floriferous and very popular in English gardens where it can rebloom. Looks superb with apricot dahlias.

Total Eclipse (Durio 84) Tet, Dor, H60cm (24in), F14cm (5½in), EM, Re Rounded, slightly ruffled, dark red-black self, striking green throat. Performs well in European gardens.

ALSO RECOMMENDED: 'Cinderella's Dark Side', 'Derrick Cane', 'Ezekiel', 'Jamaican Midnight', 'Obsidian', 'Serena Dark Horse', 'Siloam Sambo', 'Smith Brothers', 'Smoking Gun', 'Spanish Harlem'.

LAVENDER-PINK (ORCHID-PINK)

Catherine Woodbery (Childs 67) AM Dip, Dor, H60-75cm (24-30in), F15cm (6in), Her, ML, Ext, Fra Lightly ruffled, wide-open, orchid-lavender self, wide green throat. Because its colour was unusual at the time of introduction it was one of the most heavily used diploid parents of the 1960s. Although difficult to convert to a tetraploid it was eventually successful and was much used by other breeders, especially Bill Munson, for whom it became the foundation of his famous watermarked eyes, principally in mauve and purple. Probably the best daylily never to have be awarded the Stout Medal and still one of the most popular and sought after in the British Isles, despite its very poor foliage.

Frosted Encore (Guidry 89) Dip, Ev, H55cm (22in), F14cm (5½in), EM, Noc Opulent, wide, ruffled, slightly triangular, rose-lavender self, faint purple eye, very small faint yellow throat band, clear, rich green heart. After cool evenings the floral hue can be light rose-purple with a very subtle eye. Vigorous, wide 4–5-way branching. Can survive −14°C (5°F) and multiple frosts with little or no protection.

Luxury Lace (Spalding 59) LAA, AG, AM, SSM Dip, Dor, H75cm (30in), F10cm (4cm), Sm, Her, M, Re Dainty, frilled, slightly recurved, light lavender-pink, small yellow throat, lasting clear green heart. The pigment is very fugitive, it is only lavender-pink in cooler weather otherwise it is almost salmon-flesh. A vigorous daylily, now considered a classic; very popular in the British Isles.

Ocean Rain (Hanson 87) HM Tet, SEv, H65cm (26in), F12-15cm (5-6in), EM-ML, Noc Sunfast, full-formed, pastel orchid-lilac, lighter eye, prominent pearly-pink midribs, slightly paler sepals, lemon-green throat. Slightly recurved petals rimmed with gold (apparent in hot climates). Fully nocturnal in hot climates, the leathery-textured flowers are carried well above the lush, mounding foliage on beautifully branched scapes. Opens perfectly. Fertile. 'Ocean Rain' was Curt Hanson's first introduction and is truly a stellar performer.

Siloam Tiny Tim (Henry 84) Dip, Dor, H35cm (14in), F6.5cm (2¾in), Mini, M, Ext Ruffled, recurved, deep orchid-lavender, deeper veining, deeper grey to rose-purple eye, lemon-green throat, lighter pink midribs, yellow to mauve filaments, deep yellow anthers. Good substance and corduroy texture. Lovely near *Cercis canadensis* 'Forest Pansy'.

ALSO RECOMMENDED: 'Chicago Orchid', 'Chosen Love', 'Ice Cool', 'Lilac Chiffon', 'Luxury Lace', 'Mimosa Umbrella'.

LAVENDER-MAUVE

Aquamarine (Lambert 83) Dip, Dor, H70cm (28in), F17cm (7in), E-ML, Noc, Fra Large, trumpet-shaped, rare shade of pale bluish-lavender, bleaching to grey-lavender or near-white, ivory-white throat and white midribs. Healthy, lush foliage arching near the tips. Takes several years to settle down then produces multi-budded, top multiple-branched scapes for a long season. Reblooms in some regions if well tended. In 1996 it was voted the most beautiful cultivar by the Swiss Perennial Plant Society (GSS). Typical of the seemingly 'true blue' lavenders for which John Lambert was famed.

Charlie Pierce Memorial (Pierce 87) HM Dip, SEv, H60cm (24in), F15cm (6in), EM, Re, Ext Superb, round, ruffled, clear lavender, faint wine-purple eye, chartreuse throat. Appreciates some shade in hotter climates; free-flowering, opens well after cool nights. 'Graceful Eye' is similar but an older shape.

Lavender Memories (Stamile 90) Tet, SEv, H58cm (23in), F14cm (5½in), Ext, Noc, Fra Round, ruffled, clear lavender. There is virtually no branching but the plant produces multiple scapes per fan and the individual buds open in well-spaced succession. The flower looks best in dry weather; earwigs or heavy dew in its opening buds can destroy the top layer of pigment. Good tetraploids in pure lavender are rare so despite its faults it is well worth growing.

Lavender Stardust (J. Carpenter 91) Dip, Dor, H65cm (26in), F14cm (5½in), ML, Re, Fra Heavily ruffled, full lavender blend, striking green throat. Excellent branching and bud count. Rave reviews on the superb colour.

Metaphor (Gates 84) Dip, SEv, H55cm (22in), F15cm (6in), EM, Noc Wide to triangular, full-formed, stunning blue-lavender, lasting prominent green throat, wide pearly-white midribs, slightly paler sepals. Rather top-branched, with only moderate increase, but this is a lavender daylily that can be recommended for English and European gardens.

Prairie Blue Eyes (Marsh 70) AM Dip, SEv, H70cm (28in), F12cm (5in), M Star-shaped, lavender; bluish eye more prominent in hot weather, lemon-green throat. May produce polytepal blooms. Still grown in many gardens but superseded by newer varieties of better shape and clearer colour. Vigorous, floriferous and hardy. Some growers report that their plants differ from the registration details and would seem to be inferior.

Ra Hansen (Talbott 86) HM Dip, Dor/SEv, H65cm (26in), F11.5cm (4¾in), EM, Re Delicately ruffled, recurved, lavender to pale violet, wide light mauve-blue to near white eye, giving the impression of a lighter centre to the bloom, lemon-yellow throat. A lowish bud count but repeats well in hot climates with occasional proliferations; rain-resistant and an early-morning-opener. Vigorous and hardy but an autumn mulch is recommended for cold-winter regions. Hot, humid summer weather may be necessary to bring out the delicate gradations of colour.

Visual Pleasure (Gates 81) Tet, Ev, H50cm (20in), F12cm (5in), EM, Re, Fra Unusual and lovely lavender, slightly deeper lavender eye. It builds buds to give late bloom. Not a tetraploid although registered as one.

ALSO RECOMMENDED: 'Almost Indecent' (IMA, AM), 'Iridescent Jewel', 'Lavender Aristocrat', 'Lavender Illusion', 'Lavender Tonic'.

ROSE-VIOLET TO BLUE-VIOLET

Amethyst Art (Kropf 89) Dip, Dor, H45cm (18in), F12cm (5in), Dd, EM Nicely formed, hose-in-hose double, amethyst to rose-violet, large yellow throat flaring out onto the floral segments. Very slow to establish but doubles easily and readily.

'Grapes of Wrath', a full-petalled rich purple with a distinctive eye and contrasting pale yellow throat.

Glazed Heather Plum (Morss 90) Tet, SEv, H65cm (26in), F14cm (5½in), EM, Re, Ext Full, tightly pleated, wide, overlapped, bright rose-violet, purple halo, green throat, narrow yellow edge apparent in hot climates. Deep pink filaments, black anthers, prominent pearly-pink midribs. Well-branched scapes. Hardy in cold-winter regions and opens well; especially beautiful in early morning light.

Grapes of Wrath (Kirchhoff 93) Tet, Ev, H65cm (26in), F10cm (4in), Sm, EM, Re, Ext Full, overlapped, ruffled, sunfast bright purple, narrow deeper purple eye, very narrow yellow throat, green heart. Yellow to light purple filaments, deep purple anthers. Well-branched.

Meadow Sprite (E. Salter 79) Dip, SEv, H38cm (15in), F7cm (3in), Sm, M, Noc Round, recurved, lilac-purple, slightly deeper lavender-rose eye, wide bright green throat, rose-red-tipped lime-green filaments, black anthers. Well-branched but the blooms are bunched together as it is so floriferous. When dividing it does better if not cut up too small. Lovely with pale blue dwarf agapanthus.

Medieval Guild (Hanson 89) Tet, SEv, H75cm (30in), F12cm (5in), EM Wide, flat, deep scallop-ruffled, rose-lavender to pale violet, deeper halo, lemon-green throat. Heavy substance, excellent branching and bud count. Sometimes produces doubles. Needs hot weather to reveal the gold edge, otherwise a superb performer in cooler gardens.

Paint Your Wagon (Morss 95) Tet, Ev, H74cm (29in), F14.5cm (5¾in), M, Re, Ext Stunning, tightly pleated, full,

flat to recurved, deeply saturated rose-violet, slightly deeper halo, lemon-green throat, rose-tipped ivory-lime filaments, contrasting near-black anthers, white midribs. Well-branched and a consistent bloomer.

ALSO RECOMMENDED: 'Crayola Violet', 'Princess Blue Eye'.

DEEP PLUM-BURGUNDY-PURPLE

Barbary Corsair (Salter 80) Dip, SEv, H70-75cm (28-30in), F15cm (6in), Sm, M, Noc Beautifully proportioned, violet-plum, green-throated. Well-branched scapes display the weatherproof and perfectly opening flowers to perfection.

Catherine Neal (Carpenter 81) AM Dip, SEv/Ev, H70-75cm (28-30in), F15cm (6in), VL Ruffled, velvety, sunfast deep purple with vivid lime-green throat. Can produce polypetal blooms. Hardy in most areas. Registered as a VL but some growers report its first flower opening in M to ML. Much used as a parent for purples. 'Super Purple' (Dove 79) is very similar.

Gloucester Calling (Dickerson 88) Tet, Dor, H40cm (16in), F9cm (3½in), Sm, M, Re, Ext Rounded, tightly pleated, slightly recurved, deep burgundy-purple turning red-black, near-black veining, deep yellow throat and filaments, black anthers. A narrow white edge is apparent in hot climates. Heavy substance.

Grape Velvet (Wild 80) HM Dip, Dor, H60cm (24in), F11cm (4½in), Sm, M Ruffled, wide-petalled, overlapped, rich grape-purple, small lime-green throat, slightly paler raised midribs. Good branching and bud count and long blooming. Multiplies well and proliferates. Also a tetraploid conversion.

Purple Rain (Chesnik 85) HM Dip, Dor, H38cm (15in), F7cm (3in), Sm, EM, SNoc Round, recurved, ruffled, dusky deep plum-purple, near black eye, lemon-green throat. Healthy and vigorous. Excellent in containers or as a front of the border plant. Superb in all climates.

Royal Occasion (Apps 91) Dip, SEv, H65cm (26in), F10.5cm (4¼in), Sm, M, Re Unusually clear burgundy to burgundy-black, darker eye, dark green throat lasting all day. Hardy.

Solomon's Robes (Talbott 91) HM Dip, Ev, H75cm (30in), F15cm (6in), ML, Re, Noc, Fra Sun-resistant, nicely ruffled, flat, overlapped, rich royal-purple, sepals narrowly white-edged, jade-green throat. Probably the best branching and bud count of any purple self. An absolute must for collectors of this colour, but tender in cold-winter regions and needs good protection.

Strutter's Ball (Moldovan 86) AM Tet, Dor, H70cm (28in), F15cm (6in), M, Ext Lightly ruffled, deep violet-purple, sometimes a very narrow white watermark is apparent, lemon-green throat. One of the very best in this colour range although in cooler regions may assume a brownish tinge; appreciates a mulch in cold-winter regions. Recommended by many growers. An easy and productive parent.

ALSO RECOMMENDED: 'All American Plum', 'Dark Elf', 'Indigo Moon', 'Killer Purple', 'MacMillan Memorial', 'Olive Bailey Langdon', 'Pharoah's Treasure', 'Regale Finale', 'Silent Sentry', 'Ten to Midnight'.

BLACK-PURPLE

New Swirls (Wild 83) Dip, Dor, H75cm (30in), F14cm (5½in), Dd, ML Full, overlapped, cockatoo-double, bur-

A sultry black-purple small-flowered daylily, 'Night Beacon' is both sunfast and hardy in cold climates.

gundy-black, green throat, burgundy-tipped ivory-lime filaments, yellow anthers. The seersuckered surface texture needs shade in hot climates. Opens superbly in warmer European gardens.

Night Beacon (Hansen 88) Dip, SEv, H68cm (27in), F10cm (4in), Sm, EM, Re, Ext, Noc, SlFra Dark purple, black-purple halo, lemon-green throat, bisected by wide white midribs; the midribs are also apparent on the sepals, ivory-lime filaments. Virtually sunfast, hardy in severe climates, opens well. Vigorous with almost permanent rebloom in hot climates; also a good performer in the British Isles and Europe.

Nosferatu (Hanson 90) Tet, SEv, H65cm (26in), F15cm (6in), M, Fra Outstanding, full, broad, royal-purple to darkest purple self, triangular willow-green throat. 'Nosferatu' is a strong daylily with flowers of wonderful substance, and superb branching and bud count. It is a landmark in ruffled purple tetraploids. A top class performer in many climatic regions. Still very rare but becoming popular in Europe where it opens beautifully. Needs protection from afternoon sun.

Regent Street (Weston 89) Dip, Ev, H74cm (29in), F11cm (4½in), Sm, ML, Re, Fra Round, tightly pleated, very dark purple, black-purple eye, lemon-green throat, pale lavender filaments.

Tuscawilla Blackout (Hansen 92) Tet, SEv, H80cm (32in), F13cm (5in), Noc, Ext Rounded, recurved, narrowly ruffled to pleated, deepest lavender-rose to rich dark purple, raised midribs, lemon-green throat, burgundy-tipped yellow filaments, near black anthers. The surface has a soft velvety bloom, appearing almost black towards the segment tips. The general appearance is not as black as some other black-purples. Well-branched, floriferous and opens well in English gardens and, although reputed to be hardy in cold-winter regions, might be better protected with a winter mulch. The pigment can change and melt in very hot regions. Very fertile.

Tuxedo (K. Carpenter 87) Tet, Dor, H53cm (21in), F11.5cm (4¾in), EM, Re, Ext Sun-resistant, ruffled, velvety, darkest black-purple, vivid green throat flaring into the yellow midribs. Stoloniferous.

ALSO RECOMMENDED: 'Bela Lugosi', 'Midnight Raider', 'Nairobi Dawn', 'Swirling Water'.

****

The daylilies described in the following categories are so placed for their distinguishing features rather than their ground colour. For example 'Admiral's Braid' has near-white blooms but it is its gold-wire edging that makes it so remarkable. It is fully described under 'Yellow-gold Edges and Braids' (p.96).

SPIDERS AND SPIDER VARIANTS

These categories are fully described in Chapter 9, p.116.

CLASSIC SPIDERS

Cat's Cradle (Hager 85) Dip, Ev, H1m (3ft), F20cm (8in), EM, Re, Ext Spectacularly spider-like, diamond-dusted, rich yellow, very narrow segments, small maroon-dusted eye. Easily repeats in very hot climates into autumn. Scapes do not seem to bend in spite of very large blooms. Mulch in cold-winter locations. Ratio: 5.8:1.

De Colores (Temple 96) Dip, Ev, H70cm (28in), F21.5cm (8½in), E Striking, slender, recurved, bright yellow, bold red chevon-shaped eye on petals, lightly marked red chevon eye on sepals, large very green throat, red-tipped lemon-green filaments, elongated pistil. Subtle and intriguing. Well-branched. Not as hardy as once expected, therefore very slow to increase in many areas. Also a tetraploid conversion. Ratio:6.0:1.

Easy Ned (B. Brown 87) HM Dip, SEv, H1m (3ft), F16.5cm (6½in), VL, Fra Strap-shaped segments gently curl or twist out from the large very flat-open face of this green-throated chartreuse self. Seems to be only top-branched and very slow to establish but will flower over a 3–4 week period so it is valuable for its late bloom season. Opens well after cool nights, hardy. Ratio: 5.1:1, but segments may be wider in some gardens.

Garden Portrait (Bechtold 53) Dip, Dor, H70cm (28in), F15-17cm (6-7in), Her, M, Noc A masterpiece in linear elegance with soft yellow floral segments which are twisted and recurved. Perfectly-branched, displaying the slender spider-like flowers to perfection. Scapes rather thin and weak so good cultivation is needed to get the best from them. Hardy, rain-resistant and an early-morning-opener with some rebloom. Marc King rates it as the best branched and most harmoniously proportioned classic spider he knows. A definite spiderer. Ratio: 7.3:1.

Kindly Light (Bechtold 50) HO, HM Dip, SEv, Dor, H70cm (28in), F20cm (8in), M, Re Classic bright yellow

'Kindly Light', the archetypal Classic Spider daylily, has immense garden value.

spider, faint salmon-pink eye after cool evenings. The segments can be twisted and recurved when it is well grown. The stem may be weak often bending over and spoiling the effect. Narrow deep green foliage. Hardy, rain-resistant and an early-morning-opener, giving rebloom in some regions. Ratio: 7.7:1.

Lacy Marionette (Tarrant 87) Dip, Ev, H65cm (26in), F17cm (7in), Ext Perfectly presented, flat-open, yellow classic spider, very green throat with ruffled ripply edges. It blooms earlier than the mainstay of classic yellow spiders and is an important, showy, addition to this class; moderate branching and bud count but can be in flower for three to four weeks. Not totally hardy in cold-winter regions but well worth the extra care needed. Ratio: 5.11:1, but segments may be wider in some gardens.

Marked by Lydia (Temple 97) Dor, SEv, H74cm (29in), F21.5cm (8½in), E, Re, Ext Consistently formed, slender, twirling, pale to medium yellow, purple chevron-eye on petals, faintly marked rose sepals, huge lemon-green throat. Good substance with the colour holding well. More windproof than many spiders, on well-branched scapes with many buds. An important spider due to its hardiness. Ratio: 5.3:1.

Rococo (Biery 72) Dip, Dor, H50cm (20in), F10cm (4in), Sm, M, Ext Twisting and curling, medium yellow self. Shorter than most spiders, moderately good bud count, multiplies fast, hardy. Highly recommended although the stems can be weak until the plant is established. Ratio: 6.3:1.

Roger Grounds (King-Lamone 97) Dip, Dor, H60cm (24in), F15cm (6in), E-EM, Noc Bright burgundy-wine, chartreuse to yellow throat. The burgundy pigment of the tepals darkens slightly around the throat and then extends through the veins into the heart. Top-branched, medium bud count, hardy. Low growing and compact unlike most spiders; it blooms earlier than many. Ratio: 5.0:1.

Skinny Minny (Crandall 91) Dip, Ev, H80cm (32in), F15cm (6in), EM Narrow-segmented, greenish-yellow with pale cinnamon halo. An excellent performer with sturdy scapes. Ratio: 5.0:1.

Spiral Charmer (Dickson-Crandall 85) Dip, SEv, H90cm (36in), F14-15cm (5½-6in), M, SNoc Slender, trumpet-shaped in side view, soft pastel cream. Multibranched, high bud count, very beautiful in bloom. Hardy. Ratio: 5.0:1. Segments may get wider in some gardens.

Wildest Dreams (Temple 93) Dip, Ev, H65cm (26in), F25cm (10in), E, Re Extravagantly formed, coral-rose, huge olive-green to yellow throat radiating out onto the slender, looping floral segments, graceful drooping yellow filaments and elongated pistil. Still very rare. Ratio: 6.8:1.

ALSO RECOMMENDED: 'Aabachee', 'Dark Star', 'Fol de Rol', 'Fritz Schroer', 'Lavender Spider', 'Navajo Blanket', 'Scorpio', 'Stoplight', 'Tennessee Fly Catcher'.

SPIDER VARIANTS

Black Plush (Connell 56) Dip, Ev, H70cm (28in), F17cm (7in), Her, M Deep red-black near-spider (the floral segments could be wider apart and perhaps more slender for today's expectations), with narrow, recurved segments surrounding a small star-shaped golden-yellow throat. Unlike some early 'spiders' 'Black Plush' carries its blooms upright on well-branched sturdy scapes. Vigorous, rapidly

increasing. Foliage may be damaged in severe winters as it is somewhat tender. Also a tetraploid conversion; much used for breeding near-blacks. Ratio: 4.6:1.

Cerulean Star (Lambert 82) Dip, Dor, H80cm (32in), F17cm (7in), EM, Re, Noc, Fra Very slender, Unusual-open-formed, lavender-orchid with a clearly defined soft lemon-green, star-patterned throat. Wide-branching on slender scapes with moderate to good increase. Foliage dies down very early in autumn. Very unusual colour and form. Ratio: 4.0:1.

Divertissment (Hager 90) Dip, Dor, H1.1m (3½ft), F16.5cm (6½in), ML, Ext Slightly pinched and quilled, pale butterscotch-yellow, slight red-blush eye, tiny green heart. Strong supple scapes. Well-branched, a profuse bloomer, vigorous, hardy, easy to propagate and fertile. Ratio: 4.8:1.

Green Widow (Temple 82) HM, HO Dip, Ev, H65cm (26in), F16.5cm (6½in), E Upward-facing, fat, spidery, yellow-green self, very green throat radiating onto the segments. The segments can bleach to ivory-edged soft yellow in hot sun but the vivid green throat is constant. Multiple-clustered top-branching with the blooms held just above the foliage. Slow to establish but when growing well it flowers for approximately 3 weeks. Ratio: 4.1:1.

Lady Fingers (Peck 67) HO Dip, Dor/SEv, H80cm (32in), F15cm (6in), Her, M, Noc Graceful, twisted, delicate variant of spatulate shape, having a deep chartreuse throat fading to yellow, ivory-lemon filaments, orange-brown anthers. The slender scapes do not need staking. Rain-resistant and an early-morning-opener. Ratio: 4–5.8:1. (There are imposters in circulation which bloom early and are evergreen.)

Lavender Handlebars (Roberts 94) Dip, Dor, H90cm+ (36in), F21.5cm (8½in), M, Ext Huge, teardrop-shaped, lavender segments, lemon-green throat. Very well branched, hardy. Exotic and different. Still new and hard to find. Ratio: 4.3:1.

Lois Burns (Temple 86) Dip, Ev, H75cm (30in), F21.5cm (8½in), E, Re, Noc Elegant, yellow-green, strap-like flower, each bloom with variable crispation. The scapes are top-branched or with one side branch, moderate bud count. Needs protective cover in cold-winter regions. Ratio: 9.0:1.

Mountain Top Experience (Temple 88) HO, HM Dip, Ev, H74cm (29in), F19cm (7½in), E Stunning curled and twisted, yellow-green petals vividly marked with a purple chevron-eye, yellow-green sepals, matching filaments. Perfectly branched scapes. Good substance, well presented blooms. Many growers report that this daylily has very poor growth and bloom production other than in hot, humid climates. Ratio: 4.8:1.

Persian Pattern (Hardy 66) Dip, Dor, H75cm+ (30in), F17cm (7in), Her, M Open-formed, purple, deep purple-plum eye, lemon-green throat. Widely spaced branching on elegant, slender scapes in perfect harmony with the flowers, which start opening at daylight, taking a few hours in cooler weather, but in the end open well. Takes several years to start blooming. Ratio: 4.6:1.

Scarlett's Web (Reed Dip, Dor, H1.2m (4ft), F17cm (7in), EM, Ext Recurved, narrow-star-shaped, scarlet, yellow throat, lightly ruffled petals, tightly crimped sepals. Bud count approximately 11-15 on rather unbranched scapes. Ratio: 4.4:1.

Wilson Spider (Oakes 87) Dip, Dor, H70cm (28in), F19cm (7½in), M, Noc Bitone in purple with white eye, chartreuse throat extending into the midribs. Excellent vigour for a spider/spider variant but seems to be only top-branched. Ratio: 4.6:1.

ALSO RECOMMENDED: 'Boney Maroney', 'Ferris Wheel', 'Gadsden Light', 'Purple Arachne', 'Red Ribbons', 'Spindazzle', 'Sun Star', 'Yabba Dabba Do'.

UNUSUAL FORM

Asterisk (Lambert 90) Dip, Dor, H70cm (28in), F20cm (8in), EM-ML, Noc Large, flat spatulate open form of beguiling beauty; the asterisk-shaped segments change colour with temperature. After chilly evenings the floral hues are light rich lavender with a large lemon-cream star-shaped throat pattern, after warm weather they are almost white, blushed pale oyster-grey around the edges with a soft ivory-yellow throat. Top-branched with many buds which continue to open and build others over a long period and are elegantly displayed.

Brenda Newbold (King-Lamone 87) Dip, Dor/SEv, H70cm (28in), F15cm (6in), M, Noc, SlFra A ruffled, gently curved, twisting, pale pure pink star, lemon-green throat, green heart. With scapes producing 1–2 wide side branches, 'Brenda Newbold' is hardy and vigorous. Good substance. Fertile both ways.

Coburg Fright Wig (Brockington 90) Dip, Dor, H83cm (33in), F19cm (7½in), EM Large, spatulate, bicolour spider with diamond-dusted, maroon over yellow petals, large yellow throat, strong maroon eye, twisted and quilled sepals. Moderate branching and bud count, can proliferate, opens well. Fully hardy.

Dancing Summerbird (King-Lamone 87) Dip, Dor, H65cm (26in), F12cm (5in), EM, Noc, Fra An exceptional butterfly open form. Soft lilac-lavender, green throat turning chartreuse. Sweet fragrance in warm, humid weather. Top-branched to one side branch, moderate bud count. Hardy. A superb parent for Unusual-form daylilies and much sought-after by collectors.

Diabolique (Lambert 87) Dip, Dor, H90cm (36in), F19cm (7½in), EM, Noc Exceptionally formed spatulate of

'Asterisk' is a beguiling beauty whose palest lavender colour changes with fluctuation in temperature.

beautiful purple. Side-branching; average bud count is approximately 15–18.

Fuchsia Fashion (Webster 88) Tet, Dor, H70cm (28in), F22cm (9in), M, Fra Delicate, slender, salmon-rose self, pinched petal tips and curled back sepals, creating an attractive crispate shape. Its colours intensify once the root system adapts after transplanting.

Galaxy Rose (Webster 85) Tet, Dor, H80cm (32in), F24cm (9½in), M, Re, Fra Weatherproof, flat, star-shaped, rich, saturated rose self, pinched petal tips, recurved sepals. Top-branched to one, widely-spaced side branch, bud count approximately 25. Stunning display of very provocative open-faced flowers with lush rich deep green foliage. A rapid increaser.

Ghost Dancer (Schwarz 97) Tet, Dor, H1m (38in), F23cm (9in) M. Soft yellow, wide green throat. Double branched plus a terminal cluster – approximately 20 buds. A superb breakthrough in the tetraploid Unusual Form.

Golliwog (Wild 85) Dip, Dor, H63cm (25in), F15-20cm (6-8in), M, Noc Large, butterfly-formed, opulent pastel creamy polychrome to soft peach, elegant but sometimes untidy in shape. Floriferous, with many well-branched scapes. Its low-growing habit makes it an ideal companion for 'Mynelle's Starfish' (p.79). Hardy.

Hurricane Bob (Schwartz 97) Tet, Dor, H1m (40in), F28cm (11in) M Stunning, pinched and extravagantly curled, scarlet with sunburst yellow throat. Double branched plus a terminal cluster, 20+ buds on strong scapes. A real breakthrough for this shape in the tetraploid form.

Jan's Twister (Joiner 91) Dip, Ev, H70cm (28in), F28cm (11¼in) EM, Re Twisted, curled, spider-like, peach-pink segments fading towards the centre, flaring green throat, pink filaments, contrasting black anthers. The petals fold together at the centre and at times are only 1cm (½in) wide. Moderately well-branched, reasonable bud count.

Lady Neva (Alexander 70) Dip, SEv, H1.1m (42in), F22cm (9in), ML Attractive crispata with ruffled and pinched petal tips, sepals rolled and twisted. Buff to bright yellow, unsaturated rose-maroon markings and dots on all floral segments, but less on the sepals. Flaring yellow throat, maroon-touched yellow filaments, grey anthers, prominent yellow midribs. Well-branched and spectacular in a clump. Very popular in the British Isles.

Lake Norman Spider (K. Carpenter 81) Dip, Dor, H70cm (28in), F20cm (8in), M, Ext, Fra Huge, flat-faced, full, star-formed, silky orchid-lavender, cream water-marked eye with a lilac overlay, deeper veining apparent throughout the flower. The petals are pinched and the sepals twisted giving the impression of an open spider variant. Rather low bud count. A unique colour among Spider and Unusual Forms.

Lilting Lavender (Childs 73) Dip, Dor, H75cm (30in), F20cm (8in), ML, Re, Noc, Fra Full-formed, spidery-crispate, pure lilac-lavender, beautifully contrasting yellow throat. The sepals curl and twist attractively. A superb colour and thoroughly good performer in the British Isles and European gardens, blooming for many weeks. If well tended, will develop a better branching habit; moderate increase in the first two seasons, thereafter even better.

Lola Branham (Burkey 91) Dip, Dor, H96cm (38in), F19cm (7½in), ML Ravishing, lavender-edged, greenish-ivory, open-formed crispata with exquisite, corkscrew-twisting segments. Green throat turns greenish-cream as it seeps into the segments, ivory-tipped chartreuse filaments. 3-way branching and a bud count of approximately 23. Does not make large fans. Hardy.

Mico (Joiner 68) Dip, SEv, H111cm (44in), F25cm (10in), Her, M, Noc, Fra Huge soft golden-yellow flowers are displayed on top-branched scapes. Rather phototropic. Rediscovered through the research projects led by Rosemary Whitacre in the 1980s.

Moonlight Orchid (Talbott 86) Dip, SEv, H70cm (28in), F16.5cm (6½in), EM, Re, Ext, Fra Distinctive, spider-like, lavender bicolour, cream sepals. Superbly branched scapes, high bud count. Often produces white seeds and is a difficult parent to work with.

Mynelle's Starfish (Hayward 84) Dip, Dor/Ev, 50-63cm (20-25in), F25cm (10in), M, Noc, Fra Unusual, smooth, creamy-yellow self, contrasting dark anthers. This wide, rippled to ruffled-edged, starfish-like Unusual Form is best planted under or around taller spiders or spider variants or as a container plant on a terrace where its large flowers can be seen up close. Low bud count and unwilling to bloom in some cold-winter regions, although vigorous in hot climates, it may appreciate extra feeding to get it going. Its deep green foliage is on the low side.

'Lilting Lavender' needs time to establish but will make a garden-worthy daylily giving weeks of clear lavender flowers.

Open Hearth (Lambert 80) HM Dip, Dor, H65cm (26in), F22cm (9in), M, Noc Spectacular, spatulate, flat-faced, spider-like, red and copper bitone, ruby halo, large yellow throat, red-tipped filaments. Multiple top-branched, strong performer. Superb in its converted tetraploid form.

Peacock Maiden (K. Carpenter 82) Dip, Ev, H70-78cm (28-31in), F24-26.5cm (9½-10½in) EM-M, Noc Huge, Unusual-formed, rich reddish to purple-plum self, large star-shaped cream throat pattern extending to the tips of the tepals. Top-branched but flowers are produced slowly at the tips of the slightly leaning scape so no crowding occurs. Needs a few years to establish but can reward you with a tropical ambience. Requires some shade in hot climates. Hardy.

Planet Max (Reed 96) Dip, Dor, H106cm (42in), F17cm (7in), M-ML-L Ruffled, recurved, open star-shaped, spidery, rich blue-purple, lemon-white throat. Hardy and opens early in the morning.

Red Suspenders (Webster 90) Tet, Dor, H80cm+ (32in), F27cm (11in) M, Fra Flamboyant red self, the petals pinching and the sepals recurving. A beautiful presentation of open, slender floral segments.

Ruby Spider (Stamile 91) Tet, Dor, H85cm (34in), F22cm+ (9in), E Perfectly presented, widely spider- to star-shaped, intense, glowing ruby-red. The floral segments twist or pinch in warm weather creating a dramatic daylily – stunning in a border.

Satan's Curls (Crandall 89) Dip, Ev, H74cm (29in), F15cm (6in), EM Spider-type, red, edged yellow, floral segments twisting and curling. Excellent branching with 2-3 side branchlets and many buds. Colours sometimes fade and are not deeply saturated. Also a tetraploid conversion; yields exceptional, deep green throated curly and twisted Crispatas.

Starman's Fantasy (Burkey 91) Dip, Dor, H75cm (30in), F20cm (8in), M Slender, crispate, velvety, bright red. Huge lime-green throat extends from the heart flaring into the floral segments, where it is nearer to yellow, becoming yellow in the afternoon. The petals are pinched and the sepals twist creating a dramatic spidery effect. Erect scapes with 3-way branching, moderate bud count. Hardy.

Twist of Lemon (Brooks 85) HM Tet, Dor, H83cm (33in), F17cm (7in), EM One of the early slender-tepalled tetraploids, this robust, hardy ravishing beauty has cool yellow twisting and curling flowers, well-branched multiple scapes and a long-blooming season. Also a good parent in the gene pool for tetraploid spider breeding.

ALSO RECOMMENDED: 'Bimini Twist', 'Carolicolossal', 'Dune Needlepoint', 'Fire Arrow', 'Green Dolphin Street', 'Guten Omen', 'Lily Dache', 'Oklahoma Kicking Bird', 'Orchid Corsage', 'Puppet Lady', 'Starman's Quest', 'Windfrills'.

BICOLORS AND BITONES

Banned in Boston (Simpson 94) Dip, Dor, H65cm (26in), F11.5cm (4¾in), M, Re, Ext, Noc Rose and cream-pink bitone with cream to light lemon throat. An amazing combination of colour but in truth a hybridizer's plant. Do not overfeed with high nitrogen or it may produce lush foliage and new fans at the expense of blooms.

Blessing (Applegate 89) Dip, SEv, H55cm (22in), F13.5cm (5¼in), M Gorgeous, full, flat, ruffled, strawberry-rose petals, cream-pink sepals, striking pink veins, pearly-white midribs. Bud builds for a long bloom period if grown well. Fully hardy.

Brand New Lover (Brooks 87) HM Tet, SEv, H70cm (28in), F14cm (5½in), EM, Re Rounded, lightly ruffled, pale coral-rose with faint rose halo on petals, paler sepals, melon throat. Some faint gold edging is sometimes visible.

'Chocolate Dude' is a subtle and unusual chocolate to mahogany-brown coloured reverse bitone. It has great garden value when grown with blue or yellow perennials.

Floriferous, rapid increaser. Hardy. Performs well in most locations.

China Bride (Guidry 89) Dip, Ev, H60cm (24in), F15cm (6in), E, Re, Noc, Fra Round, ruffled, recurved, delicate rose-pink, deeper rose-pink veining, subtle rose halo, yellow eye blending into a deep green heart, cream-pink sepals. Usually magnificent branching with well-displayed large flowers, opening well for weeks on end and a good rebloomer, its only fault being somewhat thin foliage. Breathtaking. Very popular.

Chocolate Dude (Lewis 81) Tet, Dor, H70cm (28in), F12cm (5in), E, Noc, SlFra Open, ruffled, weatherproof khaki to light chocolate brown petals with mahogany-brown band flaring onto the middle of the petals, recurved mahogany-brown sepals, yellow throat blending into a faintly green heart. Thick substance and crêpy texture. A strange and unusual colour combination but has a definite place in the daylily garden among yellows, oranges and bronzes. Well-branched and a good increaser. Not everyone's choice but a favourite with me.

Eye-Yi-Yi (McKrosky 88) Tet, Ev, H75cm (30in), F14cm (5½in), E, Re Eye-catching, bronze, large red eye, yellow throat. Vigorous, can be divided sooner than most, average branching and bud count. Performs quite well even in harsh winter weather. Many growers are drawn to 'Eye-Yi-Yi' for its combination of colour and patterns, and it passes on good eye patterns in breeding.

Frans Hals (Flory 55) HM Dip, Dor, H60cm (24in), F11cm (4½in), Her, ML Distinctive, open, star-shaped, bicolor with fierce rust-red petals, creamy-yellow midribs, creamy-yellow sepals and matching filaments, black anthers. A classic and still popular in British gardens.

Pink Ambrosia (Stamile 95) Tet, Ev, H70cm (28in), F17cm (6¾in) E, Re, Ext Flat, deep, scalloped and ruffled bitone, with medium pink petals, very light pink sepals, deeper rose-pink veining, yellow throat, vivid grass-green heart, rose-pink-tipped ivory-green filaments. Excellent substance and smooth texture. Vigorous. Fertile both ways but a difficult pod parent. An offspring of 'Tet Barbara Mitchell'.

Royal Jester (Kennedy-Allgood 91) Dip, Dor, H60cm (24in), F15cm (6in), L, Fra Widely ruffled, slightly recurved bicolor, white-edged, deep rose-pink petals, cream-white midribs, slightly rose-blushed cream-white sepals, light green throat, cream-white to yellow filaments and anthers

matching the throat. A lovely bloom on a good plant; worth searching out.

ALSO RECOMMENDED: 'Affair to Remember', 'Best Kept Secret', 'Bombay Bicycle', 'Final Touch', 'Late Again', 'Pony', 'Tiny Tiki', 'Upper Crust Society'.

DARK BORDERS, LIGHT CENTRES

Angel Unawares (Mederer 70) Dip, Dor, H70cm (28in), F11cm (4½in), Sm, EM Ruffled, cream to pale yellow, lavender edges, chartreuse throat. Although an older variety, it performs like a trooper. Amazing bud-building quality gives it a very long bloom period. The last flowers are as large as the first ones, but the scape becomes quite tall due to the quantity of blooms, which continue until late in the season.

Antique Rose (Sikes 87) AM Dip, Dor, H63cm (25in), F14cm (5½in), M, Re Ruffled, clear, rich rose-pink petals fading to light rose in the centre, deeper rose edges, paler pink sepals, lemon-green throat. Good substance and fine form. Can be slow to increase but when established has a long bloom season.

Beautiful Edgings (Copenhaver 89) Dip, SEv, H75cm (30in), F15cm (6in), M, Re, Fra Wide, slightly recurved, ruffled, pastel cream to pale yellow, edged rose-pink (on some blooms only near the tips), pale yellow filaments. Good substance and smooth surface texture. 3-way branching with 12–15 blooms per scape. Increases moderately well and can be in flower for about 5 weeks. Hardy in cold-winter regions and is open before noon even on cloudy days, although it needs sun to open very early. A recurrent rather than a rebloomer. Good reports from western Canada. 'Forsyth Flaming Snow' (LeFever) is similar.

Emily Anne (Yancey 88) Dip, Dor, H70cm (28in), F11cm (4½in), Sm, Fra Ruffled, cream, edged coral to light strawberry-pink, yellow throat. Good branching and bud count. Smooth texture and elegant appearance. A beautiful daylily which deserves to be better known.

Mariska (Moldovan 86) AM Tet, Dor, H70cm (28in), F16.5cm (6½in), M, Re Exquisite, large, wide, pink with cream-lavender undertones. Lighter in the centre of the flower and noticeably darker at the edges in hot climates, although the colour can vary quite considerably. Delicate waffled texture. Great branching, many scapes but lowish bud count. Vigorous, survives period of severe frost, performing better in colder climates it also stands up to high temperatures. 'Ilonka', a sibling, possibly has a better colour, but is not such a good shape and has even thinner substance, increasing more slowly.

Raining Violets (Wild 83) HM Dip, Dor, H50cm (20in), F11.5cm (4¾in) ML, Re, Fra Open-formed to rounded, very ruffled, overlapping, flat diamond-dusted cream, with segments delicately edged palest red-violet. Sepals slightly recurved. Raised cream midribs run down into the green heart. Good substance and rainfast, well-branched, well-budded and vigorous. Can be delicate and die after transplanting.

Susan Weber (Branch 89) Dip, Dor, H65cm (26in), F15cm+ (6in) L, Ext Lightly ruffled, wide brushed rose-pink border on a near-white to ivory-pink base. Usually vigorous but sometimes slow to increase. A unique and beautiful daylily in a class by itself but only successful in cold-winter climates.

ALSO RECOMMENDED: 'Cameron Quantz', 'Fama', 'Princess Ellen', 'Unique Style'.

DARK CENTRES, LIGHT BORDERS

Avant Garde (Moldovan 86) Tet, Dor, H65cm (26in), F14cm (5½in), M, Ext Recurved, velvety, russet-amber, creamy-orange eye, segment edges and filaments. A good performer with excellent branching and bud count. A rapid increaser in European gardens, where, although not an early-morning-opener, it is perfectly hardy and a useful addition to this colour class.

Bubbling Brown Sugar (Weston 87) HM Tet, Dor, H68cm (27in), F14cm (5½in), M, Fra Yellow-edged, cinnamon-brown, brown eye, lemon-green throat. A very unusual colour but exquisite. Hardy.

Fortune's Dearest (Morss 94) Tet, Ev/SEv, H63cm (25in), F15cm (6in), E, Re Unique, full, overlapped, rich mauve-purple to wine-purple, dramatically edged buff to white in a shark's tooth pattern, paler watermark halo sometimes visible, vivid green throat. A well-proportioned plant with well-branched husky scapes. Opens easily but hot sunshine is needed to bring out the subtle colouration. New to the market so hardiness is yet to be determined. Extremely fertile.

Street Urchin (Kirchhoff 92) Tet, Ev, H63cm (25in), F14cm (5½in), M, Re Flamboyant, round, recurved, tai-lored, flat, velvety, russet-red, widely bordered cream-buff, lemon-green throat, contrasting red filaments. Well-branched, hardy in cold-winter regions and performs well in European gardens. Fertile. 'Pocket Change' (Crochet) is similar.

OVERLAYS AND BRUSHING
The blooms of daylilies in this category tend to spot easily and change colour with varying weather conditions.

Chestnut Mountain (Salter 91) Tet, SEv, H70cm (28in), F15cm (6in), M, Re Sumptuous, evenly ruffled, gold, overlaid with tan, giving the appearance of chestnut-copper, gold throat. Good substance and smooth texture. The colour varies from day to day depending on the weather. A gold edge can be apparent in hot climates. Well-branched scapes which carry multiple blooms. Popular in Australasia. Fertile.

Honey Jubilee (Pierce 80) Dip, SEv, H60cm (24in), F15cm (6in), M, Re Round, ruffled, soft cream and honey blend, giving the impression of warm brownish apricot with the honey hues concentrated near the ruffled edges of the flower. Petals nearly completely round, the sepals recurved creating a slightly triangular effect. This daylily looks lovely backed by a copper beech hedge or as part of an apricot border.

Moonlit Crystal (E. Salter 88) Dip, Ev, H50cm (20in), F9cm (3½in), Sm, M, Re Full, round, recurved, lightly ruffled, diamond-dusted, pale ivory-cream with palest amber highlights which can bleach to near-white in hot sun, vivid lime-green throat, matching palest amber filaments. Well-branched scapes, floriferous.

Seurat (Moldovan 91) Tet, SEv, H65cm (26in), F15cm (6in), M, Re, Ext Moderately ruffled, pale mauve-pink, overlaid with a deeper rose-pink dotting, intensifying towards the throat giving the impression of a slight eye pattern from a distance. Up to 4-way branching, vigorous, opens well. A good example of a vogue in daylily breeding for pointillist patterning in the manner of Seurat, covering the floral segments.

Smuggler's Gold (Branch 91) Tet, Dor, H60cm (24in), F15cm (6in), Ext, Very Fra Round, full, beautifully ruffled, recurved gold, randomly brushed and shaded bronze and tan (darker in cooler climates, possibly disappearing in very hot climates), accentuated by a circular pale yellow throat. Very heavy susbstance and can take up to 3 days to

The showy flowers of 'Cherry-eyed Pumpkin' are rich orange with a scarlet eye and a pale orange throat.

open but eventually it opens well. Vigorous with well-branched scapes and high bud count. Excellent but probably better for cold-winter regions. From 'Mary's Gold' (p.52).

Texas Toffee (Brooks 93) Tet, SEv, H58cm (23in), F15cm (6in), EM, Re Ruffled, light bronze with yellow sepals, brushed bronze. A most unusual colour, almost caramel.

Wildfire Tango (Kirchhoff 93) Tet, Ev, H65cm (26in), F15cm (6in), EE, Re, Ext, Noc Outstanding, wide, full, swept-back form, overlapping, intense orange overlaid bronze, green throat. Good substance and smooth texture. Fertile. Opens around midnight and remains open until

after dark the following evening so a valuable plant for cooler regions.

ALSO RECOMMENDED: 'Brushed With Bronze', 'China Veil'. 'Norwegian Woods', 'Wild One'.

LARGE, BOLD EYES, CONTRASTING WITH GROUND COLOUR
Daylilies in which the eye pattern is the distinguishing feature.

Beat the Barons (Hansen 91) HM Dip, Ev, H55cm (22in), F9.5cm (3¾in), L, Re, Ext, Noc Perfectly round, ruffled, light custard-yellow, strikingly contrasting vivid cherry-red eye, emerald green throat. Consistently good form and colour. Nice foliage, good branching and bud count, an early-morning-opener in cool climates, hardy in most areas if mulched, vigorous.

Ben Lee (Hansen 94) Dip, SEv/Ev, H50cm (20in), F10cm (4in), Sm, ML, Re Round, reflexed segment tips, ruffled, flat, light salmon-pink. Huge, sunproof, vivid violet-blue-cast eye virtually covers the face of the flower. The outer edge of the eye is rimmed with a feathered line of cranberry-red. The petals barely meet at the emerald throat. Trialled and proved hardy in cold-winter regions. Multiplies quickly and reblooms faithfully. Carries the genes for 'blue' eyes and will be a useful breeder's plant, especially when converted to tetraploid.

Center Ring (Riseman 90) Dip, Dor, H45cm (18in), F10cm (4in), Sm, M, Fra Fat, ruffled cream, grape-purple eye, green throat. Known to have over 70 blooms on a 5-year-old clump, 7 perfect, non-touching blooms on one scape with 6-way branching. Bred in an area of winter freeze/thaw cycles so should be hardy everywhere.

Cherry-eyed Pumpkin (Kirchhoff 92) HM Tet, SEv, H70cm (28in), F15cm (6in), EE, Re, Ext Showy, ruffled, full, slightly recurved, rich orange, bold scarlet eye, pale orange throat and matching filaments, tiny green heart. The petals can have a red picotee edging. 3-way branching, a bud count of 15-20 and an early-morning-opener at temperatures of 17°C (63°F); hardy and an excellent parent.

Cleopatra (Thomas 64) Dip, Ev, H85cm (34in), F12cm (5in), Her, E Unusual-spider-like, narrow, deep cream-melon petals and sepals, contrasting violet chevron eye on all segments. The pattern is larger and more pronounced on the petals, which are striped orange deep into the throat. Well-branched once established but the scapes are so slender that they can bend over. Pod and pollen fertile and dominant in passing on the distinctive eye pattern. Not reliably hardy everywhere so needs mulching in winter. Sought-after with the rise in popularity of spider-like daylilies.

Corsican Bandit (Salter 81) Dip, SEv, H45cm (18in), F9cm (3½in), Sm, ML Round, ruffled, pale ivory-cream with bold wedged eye of plum-purple forming a triangular pattern around the green throat. Fertile. A wonderful performer.

Cosmic Hummingbird (Kirchhoff 79) AM Dip, SEv, H60cm (24in), F9cm (3½in) EE, Re Round, overlapping petals of an unusual blend of peach, pink and honey, intense ruby-wine, wedge-shaped eye over a green throat. 3 or more blooms open at once, giving a bouquet-like effect. Hardy and vigorous.

Custard Candy (Stamile 90) AM, AG Tet, Dor, H60cm (24in), F10.5-12cm (4¼-5in), Sm, EM, Re Flawless, perfectly round, evenly ruffled, fully recurved, lemon-cream, vivid narrowish maroon eye, green throat. Opens well after cool nights and an excellent performer in most

'Eye of Newt' opens perfectly, displaying its bold, contrasting eye in Cor Govaerts' garden in Belgium.

climates. One of the very best of the 'Candys' with good branching and bud count, opening in a bouquet-like form.

Daggy (Joiner 93) Dip, Ev, H50cm (20in), F9cm (3½in), Sm, E, Re Showy, ruffled, yellow-ochre, bold dark maroon eye. The midrib penetrates the eye almost to the green throat. Well-branched scapes carrying 45 or more buds; broadish mid-green foliage. Can be tender in cold-winter regions.

Designer Image (Sikes 87) Tet, Dor, H50cm (20in), F14cm (5½in), M, Ext Very striking, round, wide-petalled, light lemon-beige, wide deep lavender eye, some deep lavender on the petal edges, yellow throat blending into a green heart.

Eye of Newt (E. Salter 91) HM Dip, Ev, H55cm (22in), F7cm (3in), Sm, M Bright gold, large velvety plum-black eye covering much of the flower, green throat. Good substance and smooth texture, the colour holding well. Well-branched scapes. A very showy garden plant but may be tender in cold-winter regions.

Femme Fatale (Talbott 85) Dip, SEv, H53cm (21in), F12cm (5in), E, Noc Round, ruffled pale melon, pearly-white midribs bisecting the vivid purple eye and chartreuse throat, chartreuse filaments. Well-branched. Hardy in cold-winter regions and opens perfectly in cool weather.

Fooled Me (Reilly 90) Tet, Dor, H60cm (24in), F14cm (5½in), EM, Ext Round, ruffled, hot orange-gold, vivid red eye, matching picotee edge, green throat. A long season bloomer and a superb performer in Europe, where it is perfectly hardy, but in cooler regions the red picotee edge is not apparent for at least 3 years.

Isle of Dreams (Morss 89) Tet, SEv, H55cm (22in), F15cm (6in), EM, Re, Noc Unusual-formed, cream to soft buff-yellow, bold, triangular violet-lavender sunburst eye, green throat. 5-way branching, high bud count, hardy and increases well. The main colour can become near-white in hot weather, thus creating an even stronger colour contrast. Needs long periods of hot weather to open well.

John Robert Biggs (Crochet 83) Dip, Dor, H38cm (15in), F9cm (3½in), Sm, EM, Re Round, ruffled, diamond-dusted, light beige-pink to deep cream (depending on the amount of heat), unsaturated rose-pink eye, yellow throat, tiny green heart, cream-yellow filaments, light brown anthers. Good substance and velvety texture. Well-branched, vigorous, opens well in British gardens.

Lambada (Kirchhoff 90) Tet, Ev, H75cm (30in), F16.5cm (6½in), M, Re, Ext, Fra Full, ruffled, light orange, bold red eye, tangerine throat, green heart. A red edge is sometimes apparent in hot climates. Well-branched and sturdy. Hardy in most areas.

Little Gypsy Vagabond (Cruse 79) Dip, Ev, H45cm (18in), F7cm (3in), Sm, EM Rounded, ruffled, light yellow, bold dark purple eye, green throat. An unusual colour combination in this size of daylily flower.

Little Show Off (Williamson 72) Dip, Ev, H40cm (16in), F6.5cm (2¾in), Mini, E Ruffled, cream, bold contrasting red eye, lemon-green throat. Just what its name implies.

Maleny Debutante (Alexander 94) Dip, Ev, H70cm (28in), F10cm (4in), Sm, E, Ext, Fra Exquisitely formed, ruffled, cream-pink, vividly contrasting narrow cerise-red eye, yellow throat, green heart, ivory-lime filaments. Raised in Australia and now popular in the US but needs long, hot summers to open well.

Mary Ethel Anderson (E. Salter 97) FSC Dip, SEv, H45cm (18in), F5.5cm (2¼in), Mini, M, Re Perfectly round, evenly ruffled, flat to gently recurved, crêpe-textured, pale pink, tinted alabaster-cream, vivid wide rose-red eye surrounding a tiny lime-green heart, petals narrowly edged rose-red in hot climates, rose-red-tipped lime-green filaments. Well-branched scapes carry multiple blooms. Fertile but not an easy parent.

Mokan Butterfly (Lenington 84) Tet, SEv, H89cm+ (35in), F14cm (5½in), E Graceful, airy, slightly triangular, unusual creamy-white to near-white, slender bluish-violet chevron eye, lemon-green throat. The foliage is thin and delicate. Can be slow to increase until well established.

Moonlit Masquerade (J. Salter 92) Tet, SEv, H65cm (26in), F14cm (5½in), EM, Re Eye-catching, ruffled, overlapped, smooth, alabaster-white, boldly contrasting, notched, darkest purple to near-black eye, prominent midribs, deep green throat, ivory-lime filaments, very conspicuous black anthers. Well-branched, vigorous, fertile. One of the most strongly contrasting bold-eyed daylilies, making a great impact in the garden.

Paige's Pinata (Hansen 90) HM Dip, SEv, H65cm (26in), F15cm (6in), EM, Re, Ext Bold, round, wide, ruffled, peach, around a striking wide fuchsia-pink eye, orange throat, green heart. Opens well in cooler regions and shouts across the garden. Out of 'Janice Brown' (p.90).

'Moonlit Masquerade' has a bold, wine-black eye that contrasts superbly with the alabaster-white ground colour.

Pandora's Box (Talbott 82) AM, AG Dip, Ev, H48cm (19in), F10cm (4in), Sm, EM, Re, Fra Ruffled, round, flat, ivory-cream, claret-purple eye, green throat. Moderately well-branched scapes. Performs well everywhere. A classic, winning many popularity polls. Excellent in containers.

Pug Yarborough (J. Carpenter 90) Dip, SEv, H50cm+ (20in), F16.5cm (6½in), E, Re, Fra Bold, ruffled, flat apricot-peach, rose-red eye and wide green throat. Good substance and ribbed texture. Hardy.

Pumpkin Kid (Spalding 87) Dip, SEv, H45cm (18in), F14cm (5½in), M, Re Ruffled, light pumpkin-orange, deeper orange veining, narrow red eye, wide green throat, light orange filaments, prominent cream midribs. Lush wide foliage; well-branched, floriferous but can be tender in colder climates.

Queensland (Trimmer 93) Tet, Dor, H63cm (25in), F10.5cm (4¼in), Sm, E, Fra Round, ruffled, ivory, burgundy-purple eye, green throat, narrow purple picotee edge to petals is often apparent. Beautifully branched, hardy. An outstanding 'Tet Siloam Virginia Henson' offspring which looks good every day but slow to increase. Can produce polytepal blooms. 'Winter Mint Candy' is similar.

Raging Tiger (Rasmussen 87) Tet, Dor, H63cm (25in), F15cm (6in), M Showy, ruffled, burnt-orange, bold wine-red eye, orange-yellow throat. Moderate branching and bud count; vigorous and fully hardy.

Raspberry Candy (Stamile 92) LP Tet, Dor, H65cm (26in), F11cm (4½in), Ext, Fra Round, ruffled, recurved, warm ivory-cream, diamond-shaped raspberry-wine eye, lemon-green throat and filaments, dark grey anthers. Excellent performer which multiplies well, has good branching and bud count. Superb in many European gardens.

Roswitha (Trimmer 92) Dip, Dor, H35cm (14in), F8.5cm (3¼in), Sm, Dd, EM Tightly ruffled, full, peach, bold contrasting purple eye. Multiplies fast. One of Dan Trimmer's popcorn doubles. Breathtaking as a clump.

Russian Easter (Kirchhoff 92) HM Tet, H75cm (30in), F16.5cm (6½in), M, Re, Fra Distinctive, flat, tightly ruffled, wide-segmented, cool pale yellow, slightly deeper yellow veining, wide pastel-rose unsaturated eye, which is almost a watermark, narrow yellow throat blending into a wide electric-green heart, ivory filaments. Narrow, ruffled, recurved sepals. Firm substance and soft, crêped texture. Vigorous and very hardy. Fertile.

Siloam Baby Doll (Henry 81) Dip, Dor, H50cm (20in), F7cm (3in), Sm, M, Ext Rounded, ruffled, apricot, light rose-pink eye, green throat. Very popular in British and European gardens.

Siloam Doodlebug (Henry 86) HM Dip, Dor, H45cm (18in), F8.5cm (3¼in), Sm, EM Ruffled, cream, touched icy-lemon, striking black-purple eye, green throat. An outstanding garden plant and one of the best of the 'Siloams' but needs moisture to keep up its heavy blooming capabilities.

Siloam Dream Baby (Henry 80) Dip, Dor, H45cm (18in), F9cm (3½in), Sm, EM, Ext Ruffled, creamy-apricot, distinctive dark red-purple eye band, green throat. Lovely with dark red and purple foliage plants.

Siloam Ethel Smith (Henry 81) Dip, Dor, H50cm (20in), F8.5cm (3¼in), Sm, M Ruffled, beige, attractively contrasting narrow scarlet eye, green throat. Good branching and bud count and a rapid increaser. 'Siloam Ethel Smith' is a small-flowered daylily with flowers in a distinctive and unusual colour combination.

Siloam Ladybug (Henry 83) Dip, Dor, H50cm (20in), F7cm (3in), Sm, EM, Ext Round, gold-yellow, maroon-brown eye, green throat. Rain-resistant and an early-morning-opener in most gardens. Rather a stiff habit but very eye-catching.

Siloam Ury Winniford (Henry 80) HM Dip, Dor, H50cm (20in), F8.5cm (3¼in), Sm, EM, Re, Noc Very ruffled, diamond-dusted, rich ivory-cream, light cream midribs bisecting the claret eye and green throat. A hint of claret on the petal tips and the narrow, recurved, flat-edged sepals, filaments cream, touched claret. A superb garden plant which is rain-resistant and an early-morning-opener. 'Siloam Penny', cream-buff with a washed claret eye and green throat, is similar and just as good, but less well known. Both rebloom in cooler climates.

Siloam Virginia Henson (Henry 80) Dip, Dor, H45cm (18in), F10cm (4in), Sm, EM Perfectly round, recurved, light buff-pink to pale cream-pink, ruby-red eye, green throat. Foliage may be damaged in severe winters and it does not always open well in cooler regions. A parent or grandparent of the 'Candy' series in its tetraploid form, which arose from a successful chance conversion. The 'Candy's are particularly useful in hot climates where the Siloams are generally not good performers but some of the 'Candys' have inherited 'Siloam Virginia Henson's inability to open perfectly. Slow to increase in English gardens.

Svengali (Moldovan 89) Tet, SEv, H75cm (30in), F16.5cm (6½in), M, Ext Ruffled, recurved, bold lavender-influenced, buff-pink to pale melon, bold plum eye, light green throat, buff-pink filaments, black anthers. Good substance and smooth texture. Makes a magnificent clump. Hardy and opens well in cooler climates.

Tiny Talisman (E. Salter 82) Dip, SEv, H40cm (16in), F5.5cm (2¼in), Mini, M, Re Very full, round, recurved, overlapping, smooth, buff-ivory, soft subtle triangular light raisin plum eye, intense lime-green throat. Recommended for British gardens.

Tiny Temptress (E. Salter 84) Dip, H38cm (15in), F6.5cm (2¾in), Mini, ML, Re Ruffled, soft pale pink-rose (buff-pink in cooler climates), intense bold, triangular, deep rose-red eye pattern enhanced by a bright lime-green heart. Well-branched. Recommended for British gardens but may need winter protection in severer climates.

True Grit (Stamile 92) Tet, Dor, H53cm (21in), F12cm (5in), ML, Ext Ruffled, strong, mid-pink, purple eye, green throat. Good branching and bud count, vigorous and hardy. The largest flower from Patrick Stamile's 'Tet Virginia Henson' crosses.

Tuscawilla Dave Talbott (Hansen 91) HM Dip, Ev, H65cm (26in), F10cm (4in), Sm, EM, Re, Ext, Noc Round, ruffled, ivory overlaid with unique diamond-dusted, bronze-lavender glow, wide dark raisin-plum eye, intense green throat. Widely branched, superb bud count, extremely vigorous, a rapid increaser and opens early in cooler climates. Although reasonably hardy it is well worth the effort of a light mulch in winter.

Wineberry Candy (Stamile 90) AM Tet, Dor, H55cm (22in), F11.5cm (4¾in), Ext, Fra Ruffled, gently recurved, palest orchid, vivid burgundy-purple eye, small green throat, burgundy-tipped ivory-lime filaments, dark anthers, slightly raised midrib. Sturdy habit and substance and ribbed texture. 'Peach Candy' is an outcross from 'Wineberry Candy'.

Wings of Chance (Spalding 85) Dip, Ev, H40cm (16in), F14cm (5½in), M, Ext Prolific blooming, round, superbly ruffled, lemon-yellow, bold virtually round cherry-red halo, lemon-green throat. A typical Spalding low-grower, it produces an abundance of scapes so its lack of branching in some regions is not noticeable. Proliferates, usually a rapid increaser, hardy and reliable.

ALSO RECOMMENDED: 'Arthur Vincent', 'Baronet's Badge', 'Duke of Durham', 'Erica Ekstein', 'Fairy Rings', 'Forsyth Ridge Top', 'Goodnight Gracie', 'Making Double Time', 'Maleny Bright Eyes', 'Radiant Ruffles', 'Siloam Dream Baby', 'Violet Explosion'.

EYES DEEPER-TONED THAN GROUND COLOUR

Where the eye enhances the daylily as a whole.

Always Afternoon (Morss 89) DS, AM, SSM Tet, Ev, H55cm (22in), F14cm (5½in), E, Re Distinctive, round, ruffled, recurved, smooth-textured, saturated lavender-mauve with midnight-purple eye, narrow yellow throat, green heart, finely edged in gold in hot climates. Well-branched, floriferous to the point of overproduction, strongly reblooming, hardy, although the superb foliage can be damaged in severe winters. Fertile. A consistent performer, destined to become a classic everywhere.

Autumn Shadows (Rasmussen 85) Tet, Dor, H70cm (28in), F15cm (6in), ML Ruffled gold, reddish-bronze eye, yellow-gold throat. Adequate branching but can finish flowering rather too quickly. A Marker for Late Flowering daylilies.

Baby Blues (G. Stamile 92) Dip, Dor, H50cm (20in), F6.5cm (2¾in), Mini, Ext, Fra Round, full-formed, diamond-dusted, pale lavender, blue-grey eyeband, green throat. Fine foliage. Increases well and produces a succession of flowers.

Borgia Queen (Munson 87) HM Tet, Ev, H65cm (26in), F12cm (5in), ML, Re Ruffled, slightly recurved, silvery lavender-mauve bloom with bold slate-grey to deeper mauve eye, lemon-green throat. A good performer in English and European gardens.

Bowl of Cherries (Moldovan 95) Tet, Dor, H74cm (29in), F9.5cm (3¾in), Sm, M, Re Ruffled, darker-veined, deep pink, orchid-influenced cherry-red eye, glowing green throat. Well-budded scapes. The scape height in relation to the foliage is picture perfect. Hardy.

Bronze Eyed Beauty (J. Carpenter 94) Dip, Dor, H60cm (24in), F15cm (6in), ML, Re, Fra Distinctive, ruffled, flat, buff-influenced, rich bronzy-orange, dark mahogany eye, narrow yellow throat, small dark green heart, cream-yellow filaments, raised midribs. Reblooms well in colder climates.

Buffy's Doll (Williamson 69) Dip, Dor, H30cm (12in), F7cm (3in), Sm, Her, M, Re, Ext Round, recurved, buff-pink, prominent rose-wine eye, yellow throat shading to a green heart. A good performer in most areas and ideal for containers.

Candide (Crochet 86) Dip, SEv, H45cm (18in), F9cm (3½in), Sm, EM, Re Ruffled, pale terracotta-rose, deeper fuchsia-rose eye, gold throat, tiny green heart, rose-tipped yellow filaments, narrow pearly-pink midribs. Good substance and smooth texture. Long season of flower.

Carpenter's Shavings (Kropf 76) Dip, Dor, H53cm (21in), F10cm (4in), Sm, Dd, M, Re, Ext, Fra Star-shaped, pom-pom double, ruffled, cedar-brown, darker brown eye, yellow throat. Moderate bud count. Narrow, grass-like foliage. Very hardy.

Chorus Line (Kirchhoff 82) AM, AG, LAA, LP Dip, Ev, H50cm (20in), F9cm (3½in), Sm, M, Re, Fra (in hot climates) Salmon-influenced, pale to mid-pink, rose eye, yellow-throat, green heart. Scapes tend to be somewhat rigid and upright. Probably a better performer in hotter climates though still popular everywhere in spite of the early blooms being less good than those appearing later. Also a converted tetraploid, of which there are now similar forms,

PLATE VI
SMALL-FLOWERED DAYLILIES

H. 'Little Maggie'

H. 'Siloam Plum Tree'

H. 'Dazzle'

H. 'Purple Rain'

H. 'Little Monica'

H. 'Little Toddler'

H. 'Water Witch'

H. 'Meadow Sprite'

H. 'Mini Pearl'

H. 'Siloam Ribbon Candy'

All flowers are shown at approximately ¼ size

H. 'Little Business'

H. 'Tootsie Rose'

H. 'Siloam Showgirl'

H. 'Pudgie'

H. 'Siloam Ury Winniford'

H. 'Green Glitter'

H. 'Custard Candy'

H. 'John Robert Biggs'

H. 'Pandora's Box'

H. 'Lullaby Baby'

for example 'Chorus Line Kid' (Stamile) and 'Chorus Line Lady' (Kirchhoff), although the original introduction is still the most popular and the better garden plant.

Cimarron Knight (J. Salter 90) Tet, Dor, H55cm (22in), F15cm (6in), M Ruffled, wide, full, flat, intense dark burnt-sienna, bold raisin-plum to black-plum eye. Well-branched, erect scapes, vigorous. Ideal for a hot-coloured border.

Dazzle (Hansen 93) Dip, SEv, H55cm (22in), F9cm (3½in), Sm, L, Re, Ext, Noc Perfectly round, flat, lightly ruffled, orchid-lavender, wide vivid purple eye, green throat. The colours can alter significantly in differing growing conditions. Well-branched, good bud count, vigorous and a rapid increaser. 'Dazzle' has proved successful in warmer parts of Europe.

Decatur Cherry Smash (Davidson 81) Tet, Dor, H65cm (26in), F10cm (4in), Sm, M, possible LRe Outstanding, saturated rose-pink, wide cherry-red eye. Excellent blue-green foliage. 4-way branching, high bud count, blooms well above the foliage and open well into the evening. Outstanding vigour, thoroughly reliable.

Designer Jeans (Sikes 83) LAA, AM Tet, Dor, H85cm (34in), F16.5cm (6½in), M Graceful, recurved, lightly ruffled, pale mauve-pink, with darker eye, yellow throat, green heart. Petals lightly touched with a picotee edge. Well-branched, opens well, vigorous and hardy.

Dragon's Eye (E. Salter 92) AG Dip, SEv/Dor, H55cm (22in), F9cm (3½in), Sm, ML Round, full, overlapped, ruffled, palest cream pink to rose-pink; narrow, depressed pearly-pink midribs bisect the rose-red eye, which has a startling intensity and covers most of the petal area; lime-green throat, pink-tipped lemon-green filaments, light brown anthers. Well-branched scapes and good bud count, proliferates and multiplies fast. Hardy, even in regions of winter freeze/thaw cycles. A wonderful colour combination and a good parent for eyed daylilies.

Eleanor Marcotte (Guillory 82) Dip, Ev, H50cm (20in), F10cm (4in), Sm, Ext, Fra Weatherproof, ruffled, lavender, purple eye, green throat. Highly recommended by Jan Wyers, see collections (p.127).

Emperor's Dragon (Munson 89) HM Tet, Ev, H65cm (26in), F12cm (5in), ML, Ext Broad, overlapping, triangular, silver-mauve, triangular raisin-plum eye. Smaller eyes on the sepals project beyond the eye of the petals forming an exotic geometrical design; lemon-green throat topped by a lighter pink shading before merging with the huge eye pattern. Can be slow-growing in cooler regions.

Janice Brown (E. Brown 86) AG, DS, AM, SSM Dip, SEv, H55cm (22in), F10.5cm (4¼in), Sm, EM-ML Sunfast, full, round, recurved, widely and deeply ruffled, diamond-dusted, buff-influenced, pale pink, enhanced by an unsaturated, wide rose-red eye, chartreuse throat, light rose-pink-tipped chartreuse filaments, pinkish-brown anthers, pearly-lavender midribs. Well-branched with lush, arching foliage, floriferous and hardy. Dependable and opens well after cool nights. Resents being divided and a little difficult to establish but vigorous when it gets going. Newly planted divisions are best kept shaded for several days, especially in hot climates. Ra Hansen advises that pods should not be set on new plants until the second year. One of the most popular daylilies ever raised. Chosen for the cover of *Daylilies – A Fifty Year Affair* (American Hemerocallis Society). Also a tetraploid conversion.

Jedi Codie Wedgeworth (Wedgeworth 90) Dip, SEv, H65cm (26in), F15cm (6in), EM, Ext, Fra Rounded, ruffled, lavender-pink, wide, pearly-lavender midribs bisect the vivid narrow maroon eye, bright lime-green throat, ivory-lime filaments.

Katie Elizabeth Miller (Crochet 85) HM Dip, Dor, H40cm (16in), F10cm (4in), Sm, M, Re Wide-segmented, recurved pastel-pink, dark pink eye, green throat. Opens well, sometimes reblooms in cooler climates and a rapid increaser.

Marilyn Siwik (Kirchhoff 95) Tet, Ev, H70cm (28in), F17cm (7in), EE, Re Full, wide, overlapped, nicely ruffled, fiery deepest orange to bronze, vivid red eye, orange throat, small olive-green heart, orange filaments, brown anthers. Lush, arching foliage, well-branched scapes and opens well. Hardy. Fertile.

Navajo Princess (Hansen 92) HM Dip, SEv, H60cm (24in), F11cm (4½in), Sm, ML, Re, Ext, Noc Distinctive, round, ruffled pale cream pink to mid-pink (depending on climate). Vivid, diamond-shaped eye, covering nearly the entire face of the bloom, resembles a feathered Indian design and gives a triangular effect; chartreuse to green heart, creamy-green filaments, dark anthers. Tender; protect in cold climates. Out of 'Janice Brown' (above).

Oceanside (Yancey 86) Dip, SEv, H50cm (20in), F14cm (5½in), M, Noc Ruffled, blue-influenced, light orchid-lavender, diamond- to chevron-shaped vivid plum-wine eye, faint watermark blending into light lime-green heart, pale mauve filaments, dark grey anthers, wide pearly-white midrib. Rather thin substance but worth growing in cooler areas for its beautiful colour and hardiness.

Outrageous (Stevens 78) Tet, Dor, H55cm (22in), F12cm (5in), M Eye-catching, open-form, burnt orange with vividly contrasting wide, dart-shaped intense mahogany-red eye, tangerine-yellow throat, matching tangerine-orange filaments, contrasting black anthers. Lighter yellow midribs. Rather top-branched but good scape production, moderate to good bud count. Healthy and vigorous.

Pastilline (G. Stamile 91) Dip, Dor, H35cm (14in), F6.5cm (2¾in), Mini, M Ruffled, pastel-lavender-pink, creamy-blue-grey eye. A rapid increaser with abundant, narrow foliage. Has a strong 'Siloam' background and is reminiscent of 'Siloam David Kirchhoff' (p.95). Ideal for the front of a border or a container. Recommended by many growers.

Piccadilly Princess (E. Salter 90) HM Tet, Ev, H45cm+ (18in), F7cm (3in), Sm, M, Re Full-formed, lightly ruffled, extremely overlapped, delicate peach-pink, pale rose eye pattern, green throat. Opens well on well-branched scapes and is a bud builder. A good, free flowering garden plant; very vigorous. Extremely fertile.

Pink Cotton Candy (Stamile 92) HM Tet, Dor, H58cm (23in), F12cm (5in), ML Round, ruffled and pleated, peach to clear pink, narrow rose-red halo, very ruffled gold edges, the ruffling can go down into the lemon-green throat, ivory-pink filaments, light brown anthers, pearly-pink midribs. Excellent branching and bud count; always opens well, vigorous and fertile. 'Sweet Sugar Candy' (Stamile) is similar, but a more subtle colour.

Preppy Paige (Hansen 89) Dip, SEv, H60cm (24in), F10cm (4in), Sm, E, Re Fully recurved, orchid-rose, deeper veining, wide fuchsia eye, depressed lavender midribs, small green heart, deep cream filaments, fuchsia-tipped style. Should do well in cooler gardens as it is a child of 'Pyewacket' (Salter), rose with a plum eye, and 'Siloam Ury Winniford' (p.86).

Priscilla's Dream (Shooter 94) Dip, Dor, H68cm (27in), F9.5cm (3¾in), Sm, M, Re Rounded, recurved, grey-ish-violet-purple, attractive magenta-purple and lavender eye, gold throat. Vigorous. Can produce proliferations.

'Piccadilly Princess', a delicate peach-pink, opens well and is a good performer in cooler gardens.

Priscilla's Rainbow (Spalding-Guillory 85) Dip, Ev/Dor, H55cm (22in), F15cm (6in), M, Ext Rounded, ruffled, pink-lavender with rainbow halo made up of layers of dark lavender-violet pigment, intense lemon-green throat. Very low-growing. Sometimes proliferates. Hardy in cold-winter regions and must have winter chill to perform well. Resents division and takes some time to re-establish.

Real Wind (Wild 78) HM Tet, Dor, H16.5cm (6½in), F15cm (6in), M-L Distinctive, recurved, lightly ruffled, pink-influenced melon, deeper rose-pink eye, bisected by light orchid-lavender midrib going deep into the gold-green heart, melon filaments, contrasting dark anthers. A striking daylily of good substance but has the stiffness associated with the earlier tetraploids. The spent blooms die ungracefully and need removing promptly. A Marker Daylily for ML.

Siloam Baby Talk (Henry 82) Dip, Dor, H38cm (15in), F6cm (2½in), Mini, EM, Ext Rounded, ruffled, pastel-cream-pink, slightly washed plum-purple halo, vivid green heart. Vigorous and floriferous, its only fault being a tendency for the flowers to sit in the foliage mound.

Siloam Bertie Ferris (Henry 82) Dip, Dor, H40cm (16in), F6.5cm (2¾in), Mini, EM Round, ruffled, shrimp-rose-pink-copper, darker eye, green throat. A subtle, unusual colour combination.

Siloam Bill Munroe (Henry 85) Dip, Dor, H40cm (16in), F8.5cm (3¼in), Sm, Ext Ruffled, pink, red eye. Rain-resistant and an early-morning-opener. Hardy.

Siloam Bo Peep (Henry 78) Dip, Dor, H45cm (18in), F11cm (4½in), Sm, EM, Ext, Fra Ruffled, subtle orchid-pink, deep plum-purple eye, green throat. Excellent branching, bud count and multiplies well.

Siloam Bye Lo (Henry 80) HM Dip, Dor, H40cm (16in), F8.5cm (3¼in), Sm, EM Round, frilly, rose, rose-red eye, lemon-green throat.

Siloam Fairy Tale (Henry 78) Dip, Dor, H45cm (18in), F6cm (2½in), Mini, M, Ext Rounded, ruffled, frosted pale pink, deep orchid-pink eye, green throat.

Siloam Gum Drop (Henry 85) Dip, Dor, H45cm (18in), F8.5cm (3¼in), Sm, EM, Ext, Fra Ruffled, pink, red eye, green throat. Multiplies rapidly. Also a tetraploid conversion and much used by Dan Trimmer in his breeding programme.

Siloam Leo Sharp (Henry 86) Dip, Dor, H45cm (18in), F6.5cm (2¾in), Mini, Ext Ruffled, orchid, darker eye. Rain-resistant and an early-morning-opener.

Siloam Little Girl (Henry 76) HM Dip, Dor, H45cm (18in), F9.5cm (3¾in), Sm, M Delicately ruffled, shrimp-pink, lightly marked with a deeper rose-pink eye, green-gold throat. Well branched, multiple scapes. Sometimes produces polytepal blooms and opens too many flowers at the same time so the bloom season is short. A subtle but difficult colour combination to fit into a garden border.

Siloam Merle Kent (Henry 85) AM, AG Dip, Dor, H45cm (18in), F9cm (3½in), Sm, M Well-formed, beautifully ruffled, orchid-pink, dark purple eye, green throat. Good substance. Very high bud count, good growth habit and increases well. Good proportions of flower size to bloom scape. One of the most popular 'Siloams'.

Siloam Wendy Glawson (Henry 87) HM Dip, Dor, H40cm (16in), F6.5cm (2¾in), Mini, M Round, lightly ruffled blush-pink, vivid burgundy eye.

So Excited (Hansen 87) AM Dip, SEv, H65-70cm (26-28in), F14cm (5½in), ML, Re Vibrant, round, recurved, hot rose-pink, huge raspberry-pink eye covering most of the base colour, green throat, lime-green filaments. Good substance, proliferates and does well in most regions. Runner-up for several awards and one of the first two of Ra Hansen's large-flowered introductions.

Someplace Special (Sikes 90) Dip, SEv, H63cm (25in), F15cm (6in), M, Re, Ext Ruffled, recurved, bright rose-pink blend, striking diamond-shaped rose-red eye, huge, vivid green throat. Multiplies fast, blooms outstandingly well and may produce polypetal blooms.

Strawberry Candy (Stamile 90) AM, STG Tet, SEv, H65cm (26in), F10.5cm (4¼in), Sm, EM, Re Perfectly round, tightly ruffled, bright strawberry-pink, rose-red eye, partial red picotee edge (inherited from Munson's 'Panache', a purple-eyed peach with a strong picotee edge). Good branching and bud count. The best-known of the 'Candy' series although, probably because of its heavy substance, the blooms require long periods of heat to produce perfectly opened flowers. Very hardy and consistently reblooms in most areas.

Tante Ju (Reinerman 87) Dip, Dor, H50cm (20in), F10cm (4cm), M Nicely ruffled, full, overlapped, light rose-pink, darker veining, bold dark purple eye and green throat, bisected by a white midrib, ivory-lime filaments. Well-branched, floriferous and completely hardy. An off-

'Trahlyta', a near Unusual-form daylily, is enjoying renewed popularity as this flower shape is becoming much in demand.

spring of 'Siloam Dream Baby' (p.86) from one of Europe's top breeders.

Tiger Kitten (G. Stamile 92) Tet, Dor, H55cm (22in), F8.5cm (3¼in), Sm, M Sunfast, delicately ruffled, clear light orange, striking red eye. Makes a stunning clump.

Trahlyta (Childs 82) Dip, Dor/SEv, H75cm (30in), F16.5cm (6½in), EM, Fra Recurved, star-shaped subtle smoky-purple, unique chevron-shaped clear violet-mauve eye above a vivid lemon-green throat. Perfect balance between the eye and the outer segments, but the colour can change from day to day. Flowers and multiplies well and is a good performer in cold climates. Also a tetraploid conversion and, although not a Spider or Unusual Form, is much used for breeding for this category.

Unloosed Dreams (Kirchhoff 92) Tet, Ev, H68cm (27in), F8.5cm (3¼in), Sm, Re, Ext Round, full-formed, ruffled, sunfast, salmon-pink, bright rose-red eye, yellow throat, green heart. Pink filaments, dark brown anthers. Narrow, pointed, flat-edged sepals. Well-branched. Hardy in most climates and recommended for European gardens.

Victorian Violet (Salter 88) Dip, SEv, H50cm (20in), F7cm (3in), Sm, EM, Re Full, round, greyish-violet, deeper violet to slate-blue eye, small lemon-green throat. Well-branched scapes bearing multiple blooms.

Water Witch (E. Salter 79) Dip, Dor, H35cm (14in), F9cm (3½in), Sm, M Roundish, pointed-tipped, recurved, narrowly ruffled, pink-lavender, deeper rose-pink veining, plum-wine halo, contrasting chartreuse throat. Pink filaments, grey-brown anthers. A blue cast to the healthy foliage. Good substance and smooth texture. One of the first of this colour to flower, which it does for many weeks.

ALSO RECOMMENDED: 'Addie Branch Smith', 'Bug's Hug', 'Just Whistle', 'Lady Blue Eyes', 'Mambo Maid', 'Mendocino', 'Monrovia Gem', 'Night Dreams', 'Pyewacket', 'Stoke Poges', 'Watermill Blush', 'Will Return'.

WATERMARKS AND WASHED, VEINED OR ETCHED EYES

The colour definition of the daylilies listed below is usually more obvious in hotter climates.

Alpine Mist (Salter 88) Dip, Dor, H45cm (18in), F7cm (3in), Sm, M Round, overlapped, recurved rose-violet to lavender-mauve, bright lavender-purple washed eye, large lemon-green throat. Well-branched scapes with multiple blooms, good rebloom. Performs well in poor weather conditions and is highly recommended for cooler climates.

Apollodorus (Munson 85) HM Tet, H70cm (28in), F11-12cm (4½-5in), Ev, ML-L Full, triangular, lightly ruffled, overlapping, wide-segmented velvety, light rose-purple to violet-purple of beautiful clarity. The colour is rich and saturated. A dark rose-chalky eye radiates onto the petals in hot weather, bright lemon-yellow throat. Rose-red-tipped yellow filaments. Moderately vigorous, superb multiple branching, bud count approximately 25–30. Cool nights can affect the first flowers to open. Fertile.

Benchmark (Munson 82) AM Tet, Ev, H75cm (30in), F16.5cm (6¾in), M, Re Broad-petalled, near triangular, lightly ruffled, pale lilac-lavender with recurved petals, white midrib appearing on inner section of petals only, shimmering ivory-chartreuse throat. A prominent light violet-purple washed eye often appears. Husky scapes. Very vigorous. Fertile and a good parent. A landmark in lavender breeding. Can produce polytepal blooms.

Cameroons (Munson 84) Tet, Ev, H70cm (28in), F15cm (6in), EM, Re Sunfast, ruffled, fluted, recurved, clear dark rose-claret to wine-violet, chalky-light pink eye, narrow yellow throat, green heart, purple-tipped yellow filaments, near black anthers, twisted and flaring sepals. Vigorous, high bud count, proliferates and fertile. One of the very few of the Munson watermark-eyed daylilies of Unusual Form having squilled and pinched sepals. Similiar to 'Morticia' (Munson) and tends to produce spider-like offspring.

China Lake (Munson 87) HM Tet, Ev/SEv, Tet, Ev, H70cm (28in), F15cm (6in), EM, Re Elegant, broad, flat, slightly ruffled, sunfast, waxy-textured orchid-lavender, chalky-pale lavender watermarked eye, small lemon-green throat. Well-branched, fertile, and an excellent parent. Not always a fast increaser. Opens well after cool nights.

Chinese Cloisonne (Munson 85) HM Tet, SEv, H65cm (26in), F12cm (5in) EM, Re Unusual creamy-melon with veined eye of pale blue-violet shaded violet-plum. Light tangerine throat, green heart, black anthers. The petals overlay the sepals and are raised in the throat area giving the impression of ruffles extending into the throat. Full form with recurved sepals and flaring petals. A complicated flower that needs heat to reveal its full beauty.

Court Magician (Munson 88) HM Tet, Ev, H65cm (26in), F14cm (5½in), M, Re Round, ruffled, overlapped, recurved, deepest lavender-purple, chalky-ivory-lavender watermarked eye, yellow-green throat. May need afternoon shade in hot climates. Scapes, strong, erect and well-branched, but the bud count can be lowish. Increases and flowers well in southern England. A very good parent.

Dark Mosaic (E. Salter 97) Dip, Ev, H58cm (23in), F10cm (4in), Sm, EM, Re Ruffled, flat-faced, bright burgundy-purple, slightly deeper red halo above very distinctive horizontally-rippled white watermarked echo eye, around a vivid green throat, bisected by greenish to white midrib, red-tipped green filaments. Well-branched scapes. A stunning new development in the quest for ever more distinctly marked eyed blooms by one of the leading exponents of this type of daylily. An excellent performer in regions of winter freeze/thaw cycles.

Devil's Footprint (E. Salter 94) Dip, SEv, H45cm (18in), F7cm (3in), Sm, EM, Re Full, lightly ruffled, creamy-yellow, multiple washed pale eye of lavender and purple punctuated by a series of pale frosted spots which line up with the lighter midribs, these spots also appearing on the sepals, green throat. Well-branched scapes and good bud count. Vigorous grower and excellent bloomer in hot climates and a good performer in regions of winter freeze/thaw cycles but may need winter protection. The eye pattern can be more apparent in cloudy weather. Fertile.

Dragon Dreams (E. Salter 92) Dip, SEv, H55cm (22in), F9cm (3½in), Sm, ML, Re Round, full, overlapped, pale lavender, ethereal etched eye of washed blue-lavender, deep green heart. Well-branched scapes. Some doubling in hot climates. Fertile.

Earth Music (Hanson 92) Tet, Dor, H70cm (28in), F17cm (7in), EM Sumptuous, full, wide, gently recurved, heavily ruffled, dark burgundy-maroon becoming bright rose-claret in warm humid weather, subtle rose-amber watermark accented by thin white chevrons leading towards a lemon-green throat. Heavy substance and matt surface texture. Consistently opens well in low temperatures. 3-way branching on tall, erect scapes and a substantial bud count. One of the roundest of the purples and ideal for cold-winter regions but rather slow to increase.

Etched Eyes (Kaskell 94) Tet, Ev/SEv, H70cm (28in), F14cm (5½in), E Ruffled, flat-opening, pale yellow, etched pencil eye in raspberry-red fading to pale lavender. Wiry scapes. An early-morning-opener even after cool nights; in hot climates at its best early in the day. Hardy, well-branched, high bud count, multiplies rapidly even in cold-

A new break in breeding for unusual eye patterns, small-flowered 'Devil's Footprint' has frosty spots on the midribs.

winter regions. Makes an airy and graceful display. From 'Paper Butterfly' (p.95).

Exotic Echo (Sellers 87) AM, AG Dip, Dor, H40cm (16in), F7cm (3in), Sm, M Ruffled, pink-cream blend, triple burgundy eye, green throat. Blooms until moderately late; often produces attractive doubles. Superb branching and high bud count. Hardy even in areas of freeze/thaw cycles. Also a tetraploid conversion, which is striking but its colour can fade in hot sun. One of the first of the 'echo-eyed' daylilies.

Jason Salter (E. Salter 87) AG, AM, DFM, DS Dip, Ev/Dor, H45cm (18in), F6.5cm (2¾in), Mini, EM Full, round, overlapped pale to light buff-yellow, washed raisin to lavender-purple eye, darker pencilled edge, green throat. Good foliage, well-branched, a high bud count, very vigorous growth. Although usually hardy it can suffer in severe winters and is reportedly not a good performer in all gardens. It can be quite a drab colour in cooler regions where the washed eye is unlikely to be apparent. A parent of many of Elizabeth Salter's daylilies with washed eyes.

Magic Carpet Ride (Kirchhoff 92) HM Tet, Ev, H70cm (28in), F15cm (6in), EM, Re, Ext Round, recurved, velvety, deep, rich scarlet, lighter coral-orange chalky eye, yellow throat, green heart. Yellow midribs apparent on the eye, red-tipped filaments, dark brown anthers. Good substance, the colour holding well given a little shade in hot regions. A rapid increaser with well-branched scapes. Very fertile. Opens well early in the morning.

Malaysian Monarch (Munson 88) AM Tet, SEv, H60cm (24in), F15cm (6in), EM, Re, Fra Broad, full, over-lapped, velvety, burgundy-purple, vivid chalky-lavender eye, ivory-lemon throat, tiny green heart. Lavender-touched, ivory-lime filaments, grey-brown anthers, prominent light purple midribs. Well-branched scapes, low foliage. Opens beautifully even after cold nights; may need some shade in hot climates. Fertile but difficult pod setter.

Nile Plum (Munson 84) Tet, Ev, H50cm (20in), F12cm (5in), EM, Re Rounded, ruffled, velvety, plum-purple, wide chalky-red watermarked eye, small lemon green throat. Spotless blooms which always open well in rainy weather.

Nivia Guest (Munson 90) HM Tet, Ev, H60cm (24in), F12cm (5in), M Broad, triangular, ruffled, burgundy-red, narrow chalky-red watermarked eye, lemon-green throat, burgundy-red filaments, white midrib fading halfway up the petals, wide, recurved sepals. Well-branched, strong scapes, floriferous, but the colour does not hold as well as some. Fertile. 'Caruso' (Salter) is very similar.

Paper Butterfly (Morss 85) AM Tet, H60cm (24in), F15cm (6in), SEv, EM, Re Open, tapered, creamy-peach, exotic starburst-patterned broad blue-violet eye, yellow throat, olive heart, dark anthers. Graceful foliage and wiry scapes. Needs very good drainage but vigorous and a good rebloomer in hot climates although it can perish in prolonged periods of heavy freeze. Does not open well after very cool evenings. Legendary parent for exotic eyes.

Patchwork Puzzle (Salter 91) HM Dip, Ev, H45cm (18in), F6.5cm (2¾in), Mini, EM Round, full, overlapped, pale ivory-lemon, purple pencil-etching surrounds a washed eye of pale ivory, lavender and lemon, tiny green throat. Well-branched scapes. Needs time to adjust to cooler climates then it opens well. Fertile.

Prince of Midnight (Salter 92) Tet, SEv, H70cm (28in), F14cm (5½in), EM, Re Uniquely twisting and curling, full-formed, deep black-purple, narrow chalky-pink watermark, striking pale yellow throat, small green heart, bisected by pearly-white midribs reaching to the segment tips, yellow touched palest pink filaments. Heavy substance with the colour holding well. Vigorous, quickly forming clumps. Fertile. The very green-tipped narrow sepals indicate that it requires warm nights to open well.

Ruffled Carousel (Brown 85) Dip, SEv, H58cm (23in), F9.5cm (3¾in), Sm, E, Re, Ext Very ruffled, cream, apricot pencilled eye. Hardy, good rebloom.

Siloam David Kirchhoff (Henry 88) AM, DS, AG Dip, Dor, H40cm (16in), F9cm (3½in), Sm, EM, Re, Ext Superb, rounded, ruffled, delicate orchid-lavender, narrow deep cerise pencil-thin eye (almost a washed eye), green throat. Lowish bud count and blooms inconsistently.

Siloam New Toy (Henry 86) Dip, Dor, H45cm (18in), F7cm (3in), Sm, EM, Ext, SlFra Round, ruffled, recurved, diamond-dusted, dark orchid-lavender, deeper rose-plum veining, washed plum-purple eye, chartreuse heart bisected by pale pink midribs, Light brown anthers. Good substance, ribbed texture. An attractive container specimen.

ALSO RECOMMENDED: 'Bittersweet Holiday', 'Forgotten Blues', 'Gerda Brooker', 'Gilded Masterpiece', 'Irving Schulman', 'Jackie's Choice', 'Mandala', 'Nordic Night', 'Respighi', 'Shishedo', 'Song of Singapore', 'Witch Stitchery'.

PICOTEE EDGED

There are daylilies with edgings in 3 or 4 different colours from the basic petal colour, but the norm is purple.

Canadian Border Patrol (Salter 95) Tet, SEv, H75cm (30in), F14cm (5½in), M, Re Full-formed, warm ivory, vividly contrasting deep purple eye, small lime-green throat, ruffled wide deep purple petal edges, purple-tipped ivory-lime filaments. Heavy substance and smooth texture holding well in hot sun. A great performer in many

'Gerda Brooker', a glamorous new spideresque introduction, has a veined eye of lavender chased with edges of red-violet.

cold-winter and cooler climates as it opens well, is fully hardy and a rapid increaser. The well-branched scapes are erect but slightly too tall for perfect proportion. Fertile. From the renowned 'Pirate's Patch' (below).

Creative Edge (Stamile 93) Tet, SEv, H58cm (23in), F15cm (6in), M, Re, Fra Superb, ruffled, lightly recurved, cream-lavender, bold purple eye, lemon-green throat heavily edged in purple and gold braid. A breakthrough in 2-colour edges with 'Royal Braid' (below).

Daring Dilemma (Salter 93) Tet, SEv, H60cm (24in), F12cm (5in) M, SlFra Full, round, ruffled, overlapped, pale ivory-pink to palest light peach, circular plum-purple eye, purple picotee edge among the ruffles, sepal tips blushed plum, small yellow-green throat. A vigorous grower with well-branched scapes, and produces proliferations. An excellent parent for picotee edges. Needs consistently hot weather to perform well. Popular in Australia and New Zealand.

El Desperado (Stamile 91) Tet, Dor, H70cm (28in), F10.5cm+ (4¼in), Sm, L, Ext Ruffled, mustard-yellow, bold, wine-black eye, matching picotee edges, green throat. Reported by many growers to be an excellent performer, even in cold-winter regions. Valuable as a late-bloomer. Fertile.

Pirate's Patch (Salter 92) Tet, SEv, H70cm (28in), F14cm (5½in), M, Re Full, ruffled, bright cream to ivory (in very hot climates), vivid plum-black eye and matching picotee edge encircling the petals, which are bisected by pearly midribs, green throat. Fertile. Needs frost protection in cold-winter regions and freeze/thaw cycles. There are good reports on its excellent performance in Britain.

Prize Picotee Deluxe (Klehm 87) Tet, Dor, H65cm (26in), F12cm (5in), E Magnificently ruffled, tightly crimped, creamy-yellow, striking purple eye and edging, lemon-green throat. Well-branched, vigorous. Does well in cooler climates, as does the similar 'Prize Picotee Elite'.

Royal Braid (Stamile 94) Tet, SEv, H63cm (25in), F12cm (5in) M, Re, Fra Pristine, recurved, cream-lavender blend, bold royal-purple eye, chartreuse throat, lavender-tipped filaments, black anthers. Petals braided with purple picotee and silver edge. 5–6-way branching, high bud count; needs heat to open well. 'Regal Braid' (Stamile), which has a wide purple braid, is best as a breeding plant.

Tigerling (Stamile 89) Tet, Dor, H63cm (25in), F9.5cm (3¾in), Sm, M, Re, Fra Round, ruffled, pleated, chalice-

shaped, vivid orange-gold, bold maroon eye and matching edge extending out from the eye, green throat, light orange filaments, contrasting black anthers. A superb, well-branched, floriferous daylily suitable for most climates which has 'Tet Siloam Virginia Henson' as a parent.

ALSO RECOMMENDED: 'Booroobin Magic', 'Mort's Masterpiece'.

YELLOW-GOLD EDGES AND BRAIDS

Admiral's Braid (Stamile 90) Tet, Ev/SEv, H53cm (21in), F14cm (5½in), M, Re, Fra Ruffled, overlapped, ivory, touched creamy-pink on sepals, widely fringed and ruched gold-wire edge on petals, green throat. Good substance but can fade in hot sun. An acclaimed pollen parent. Takes several seasons to become well-established in colder regions and for the braided edge to expand to its full width. Only the second near-white with gold braided edges. Not a vigorous daylily. Should not be overfed with high nitrogen fertilizer or it may produce lush foliage at the expense of blooms; the flowers can also be down in the foliage. Will need frost protection in cold-winter regions.

Ben Adams (Salter 95) Tet, Dor, H65cm (26in), F14cm (5½in), EM, Re Full, overlapped, fine flower of ivory-cream to cream-yellow, extravagant piecrust ruffling with gold-wire edges, small lime-green throat. Smooth substance, opens well, vigorous, holding its colour throughout the bloom period. Good branching and bud count. An excellent performer which should do well everywhere. Fertile.

Edge of Eden (Petit 96) Tet, Ev, H55cm (22in), F14cm (5½in), M Dramatic, wide-petalled, looped, ruffled, deep black-red to deep black-purple, pronounced gold-bubbly edging, green throat, ivory-green filaments, black anthers. Requires shade in very hot climates; hardy and a good performer in cold-winter regions. Out of 'Midnight Magic' (p.71).

Enchanted April (Trimmer 95) Tet, Dor, H60cm (24in), F14cm (5½in), ML Ruffled, fluted, lavender-pink, embroidered, bubbled and looped gold edge. Beautifully branched, with up to 60+ blooms per scape, opens well and very winter-hardy so promises to be a good performer in colder regions. Possibly a clearer colour than similar 'Ida's Magic' (below). ('Techny Peach Lace' × 'Wedding Band').

Etched in Gold (Peck 71) Tet, Dor, H50cm (20in), F12cm (5in), EM Tightly frilled blend of primrose-yellow and pink, embossed gold edges, yellow throat, matching filaments, contrasting large black anthers. On introduction the gold edges were not remarked on since the fashion for them did not materialize until the late 1980s and early 1990s. Known to have the defect of cracking scapes.

Ferengi Gold (Petit 94) Dip, SEv, H48cm (19in), F14cm (5½in), EM Round, very ruffled and pleated, cream-yellow, overlaid pink, the flower sometimes appearing as light cream-pink depending on the weather. Cream-yellow watermark, green throat, thick ruffled gold edge. Excellent form and substance and increases well. 5-way branching, good bud count. Opens flat by dawn even on cold nights. Should perform well in a wide climatic range although the colouring may not always be as registered. Very fertile.

Gentle Country Breeze (Klehm 88) Tet, Dor, H58cm (23in), F14cm (5½in), ML Wide-petalled, rounded, gently recurved, ruffled, cream-pink, golden-green throat, delicate gold edging apparent even in cooler climates. An excellent, free-flowering garden plant with healthy foliage.

Ida's Magic (Munson 88) Tet, Ev, H70cm (28in), F15cm (6in), EM, Re Round, rose-lavender to drab mauve (depending on the climate) wide amber-peach eye, green throat, heavily ruffled gold-wire edges. Opens well provided night and day temperatures are evenly warm, otherwise a dominant lower petal will appear, a trait that is passed on to its seedlings. This exquisite daylily is in the main a breeder's plant as it passes on its gold edges and is very fertile. Good increase. Still quite expensive.

Moonlit Caress (J. Salter 96) Tet, SEv, H65cm (26in), F14cm (5½in), ML, Re Round, recurved, heavily ruffled and prominently braided yellow-gold, pale ivory to creamy-white, dark lime-green throat. Good substance, the colour holds well, vigorous. In cooler weather a pink blush is apparent. Highly recommended by many US growers and has the vigour to cope with cold-winter weather.

Rondure (Kirchhoff 95) Tet, SEv/Dor, H60cm (24in), F10cm (4in), Sm, E, Re, Ext, Noc, Fra Perfectly round, slightly recurved, cream-influenced, sunshine-yellow self, small green heart, edges ornately ruffled in gold hooks and knobs. Heavy substance and ribbed texture. Sunfast, well-branched, hardy and fertile. Excellent for colder European gardens although can be slow to increase.

Sherry Lane Carr (Carr 93) Tet, Ev, H58cm+ (23in), F15cm (6in), EM, Re, Ext, Fra Very wide, slightly recurved, overlapping, light to medium yellow-apricot blend (which darkens slightly later in the day), extending deeply into the small lime-green throat. Heavy substance, surface is textured with ridges between the veins extending into the throat. Thick, upright scapes and dark green foliage. Well-branched with a high bud count; flowers presented in a bouquet-like form. Opens well in all weathers in spite of its heavy, often bubbled, apricot-gold edge; reported to be performing brilliantly in the US from the cooler Pacific North West to East Coast gardens and there are positive reports on its cold-winter hardiness.

Spiritual Corridor (Hanson 93) Tet, SEv, H63cm (25in), F15cm (6in), EM, Fra Consistently good, ruffled, full-formed, flat, clear orchid-lavender, bold round palest creamy-orchid watermark, lime-green throat, distinct evenly-spaced knobbed gold edges. Tall, erect, well-branched and budded scapes. Vigorous, hardy, very fertile.

Techny Peach Lace (Reckamp-Klehm 88) Tet, Dor, H68cm (27in), F12cm (5in), L, Fra Widely star-shaped, amber-peach blend, bright yellow throat flaring out onto the floral segments, prominent pearly-lavender midribs, gold-fimbriated edges. Heavy substance and ribbed texture. High bud count (although there can be some bud drop), close branching, moderate increase and a short season of flower. Opens well in cooler climates. Known as 'the poor man's 'Ida's Magic'. An unusual beauty.

Techny Spider (Reckamp 87) Tet, Dor, H53cm (21in), F17cm (7in), ML, Fra Open, Unusual-form, crimped, ruffled, spider-like, pale yellow and pink blend, creamy-pink midribs, green throat. The petal edges have a thick golden-yellow border, which is apparent in cooler regions, where it opens perfectly. This unusual, line-bred daylily will appeal to growers seeking a change from round, ruffled forms. Slow to increase and to bloom.

Wedding Band (Stamile 87) SSM Tet, SEv, H65cm (26in), F14cm (5½in), M, Re Rounded, ruffled, ivory to warm cream, consistent but not gaudy gold-wire edge, flaring yellow throat reaching halfway up the sepals, ivory filaments, dark anthers. Opens well in cooler temperatures. 3–4-way branching (show branching) and makes nice clumps. The first near-white daylily with a gold edge. Reported by Scott Alexander to be a great parent for introducing edges in a wide range of colours.

ALSO RECOMMENDED: 'Alpine Snow', 'Barbara Dittmer', 'Chris Salter', 'Ed Brown', 'Gold Reef', 'Joe Marinello', 'Magic Filigree', 'Miss Aloha', 'Spacecoast Starburst', 'Tropical Triumph', 'Uppermost Edge', 'Wisest of Wizards'.

6
DAYLILIES IN THE GARDEN

Daylilies are so collectable that it is easy to forget that the great majority are also good garden plants, and that there are many different ways of using them. Some gardeners like to segregate them in a part of the garden devoted only to daylilies, believing that the best way to enjoy the beauty of each individual bloom is without the distraction of other flowers; others prefer to grow them with other perennials or shrubs, thinking that this shows them off to best advantage; and yet others think they make most impact when grown in large drifts of single varieties, or when allowed to naturalize in the wilder reaches of the garden. With thousands of varieties to choose from there is room for all these differing points of view and no doubt many others. I should like to add some observations of my own.

COLOUR IN LATE SUMMER BEDS & BORDERS
By far the most important attribute of the daylily is that it provides a boost of brilliant colour in our flagging beds and borders from midsummer onwards, after the majority of the roses and many of the early-season perennials have passed their first flush of bloom. They also associate well with the more exotic of the late summer flowers, such as agapanthus, kniphofias in all colours, crocosmias, galtonias and hardy lobelias.

Agapanthus, with their spheres fashioned from single small florets in all shades of blue to white, are the perfect contrast in flower form and colour, not only with daylilies in yellow, orange, ginger and bronze, but with the pinker colours, such as 'Barbara Mitchell', 'Delightsome' or 'Jedi Brenda Spann', whose pastel tones emphasize the rich navy-blue of *Agapanthus* 'Lilliput', 'Dark Navy Blue' and 'Super Midnight Star'.

'Yazoo Mildred Primos' is very effective in a mixed border planted along with *Spiraea bumalda* 'Goldflame' and *Salvia farinacea* 'Victoria'.

Again on the blue-pink side of the spectrum, selections of *Phlox paniculata*, relishing the same conditions – full sun and moist soil – demanded by daylilies, offer many combinations of colour and colour echoes in paler or deeper tones. Bold eyed daylilies, such as 'Designer Jeans' or 'Jedi Codie Wedgeworth', lovely as individuals, acquire a sumptuous richness when their eye patterns are echoed by the tiny eyes that are the hallmark of many of the hybrid phlox. *Phlox paniculata* 'Amethyst' would enhance some of the claret-purple-toned daylilies with negative or watermarked eyes, such as 'Respighi' or 'Nordic Night'. Equally, lavender-blue phlox 'Blue Boy', 'Cool of the Evening' or 'Prospero' would almost exactly match the daylilies 'Graceful Eye' and 'Metaphor', neither of which possesses the rosy flush that accompanies many of the so-called lavender-coloured daylilies. The latter would assort better with the large globes of allium species and cultivars. Another lovely combination is *Phlox paniculata* 'Blue Ice' or 'Europe', their tiny, deep carmine eye exactly echoing the bolder eye of *Hemerocallis* 'Pandora's Box', also on an almost white ground colour.

Late summer perennials are often flamboyant or even garish, usually flowering in the hotter reds or burntoranges. We plant red Spider and Spider Variant daylilies, such as 'Open Hearth' and 'Ruby Spider', with crocosmias 'Mrs Geoffrey Howard' (syn 'Mrs Morrison') and 'Vulcan', with *Oenothera glaber* at their feet, repeating the sunburst yellow throats of the daylilies. Rich autumnal tapestries of colour can also be created with the crocosmias 'Emily McKenzie' and 'His Majesty', brown heleniums and ginger and copper daylilies, such as 'Autumn Shadows' and 'Tawny Gold'.

Shrub and Mixed Borders
In shrub and mixed borders, the large-flowered daylily comes into its own: a mature clump can be some 1m (3ft) across. Daylilies with flowers in vinous colours, or those

'Purple Rain' picks up the burgundy-purple of *Cercis canadensis* 'Forest Pansy', the focal point of this border.

A multi-stemmed *Cercis canadensis* 'Forest Pansy' is the focal point in our purple, rose-pink and pink daylily border, and it enhances the daylilies in different ways: underlining the rich heavy burgundy-purple of 'Catherine Neal' and 'Strutters Ball', echoing the eye in 'Siloam Merle Kent', lightening the lavender of 'Lavender Memories', and compounding the richness of 'Silken Touch'. Any possible heaviness in this scheme is counteracted by a foliage border of sub-tropical ambience across a narrow grass path, into which is woven a tapestry of purple and mauve Spider daylily forms such as 'Persian Pattern' and 'Roger Grounds'. Although quite different in concept, the borders are linked by the daylilies.

Shrubs with lime-yellow or golden-yellow leaves are equally good companions for daylilies, either as a foil or as a deeper or lighter-toned colour echo or complement. The humble privets (*Ligustrum*), when selected in their yellow-leafed forms, are very acceptable foliage backdrops. *Ligustrum ovalifolium* 'Aureum', the vigorous form, 'Vicaryi', and the tiny-leafed old-gold *Lonicera nitida* 'Baggesen's Gold', make an excellent background for creamy-lemon *Hemerocallis* 'Alec Allen' and 'Brocaded Gown' or provide a contrast for 'Carpenter's Shavings' or 'Mahogany Magic'. The golden forms of *Philadelphus* and *Sambucus*, having, as Graham Thomas points out, the good taste to provide demure white flowers, can be combined with daylilies in purple, mahogany-red and all shades of brown; I would use 'Bronze-eyed Beauty' or 'Texas Toffee'. Apricot-melon 'Fall Guy' looks stunning in front of *Sambucus nigra* bronze form, with bronze-leaf fennel, purple sage, *Heuchera* 'Chocolate Ruffles' and *Ajuga* 'Braunherz'. *Hemerocallis* 'Chocolate Dude' is another suitable companion.

A COTTAGE GARDEN THROUGHOUT THE SEASONS

For me, and many other English gardeners, it is the older *Hemerocallis* hybrids and the most gardenworthy of the species that consort particularly well in cottage gardens with other similar simple-structured, old-fashioned flowers. In such gardens, where every square inch of soil must pay its way, their importance derives from their singularly long season of interest. Daylilies are usually among the first plants to start into growth, their foliage (if it ever stopped growing) looking clean and glossy as winter gives way to early spring. The fresh leaf spikes appear with the very first of the spring flowers, like the pink clusters of the bulky, leathery-leafed bergenias, the snowdrops and winter aconites, and the earliest of the species daffodils. A month or so later the new daylily foliage is contributing its own glaucous, green or yellowish tones to the richer colours, often livid puce, of young peony foliage. Added to this are the showy flowers and foxy

having bold contrasting eyes of plum, wine and maroon, such as 'Wineberry Candy' and 'So Excited' are key players in a wealth of colour schemes. They mix particularly well with purple-leafed shrubs of strong or intricate leaf shape, such as *Berberis*, *Cotinus*, the cut-leaf maples (*Acer palmatum*), allowing for the fact that 'horticultural purple' can vary from bronzy-brown, through mahogany-red to the most sombre purple. There are daylilies with bold eyes to pick up all these gradations. The little, bold-eyed Siloam daylilies are ideal used between such shrubs if space is at a premium.

Purple and apricot look good together too, and 'Siloam Dream Baby', with its apricot ground, makes a wonderful picture in front of the Japanese maple, *Acer palmatum* 'Garnet', especially when grown along with the taller, dusky purple-black 'Siloam Plum Tree' which, on its rebloom, just coincides with the peachy-apricot toned dahlias 'Apricot Jewel' and 'Shandy'. *Ajuga reptans* 'Multicolor' carpets the foreground nicely.

fragrance of crown imperials (*Fritillaria imperialis*) amid a carpet of sky-blue forget-me-nots.

H. lilioasphodelus, 'Queen of May', 'Earlianna' and smaller sorts, like 'Little Bronzene' and 'Little Dart', are typical of those daylilies that bloom in earliest summer, when the first of the hybrid peonies come into flower. The two counterbalance each other well: the big, often startlingly bright chalices of the peonies offering a complete contrast to the sheer simplicity of the daylilies' slender trumpets and narrow, grassy leaves. The picture can be enlarged by adding irises, such as the Siberian irises (*Iris sibirica*), in shades of purple, blue and yellow with erect, spiky foliage, or the inky-blue-stemmed, near navy-blue 'Gerald Darby' and the brown-veined 'Holden Clough', and the whole scene set off by rounded mounds of *Geranium × magnificum*.

The tawny fulvous daylily, *H. fulva*, now much maligned and often dismissed as too invasive, can be left to increase and bloom undisturbed in the wilder parts of the cottage garden, perhaps in a ditch or an orchard or, as William Robinson advocated, colonizing a river bank, intermingled with the male fern (*Dryopteris felix-mas*).

ECOLOGICAL PLANTINGS

Increasingly, as gardens are seen more and more as the last refuge of wild plants from Man's destruction of his natural world, they are being planted to, quite literally, imitate nature. Such gardens are viewed strictly as habitats and the aim is to assemble in them such plants as would naturally grow in this or that particular habitat. The classic example of such planting is Rosemarie Weisse's pioneer scheme at Westparc in Munich in which daylilies have their place. Here, as elsewhere, they are particularly effective as a ribbon of colour threading through grasses and other tall perennials. Obviously the species and those hybrids that most nearly resemble the species in the simplicity of their flower form will look at home in such plantings. The natural companions of daylilies, viewed from a habitat point of view, are grasses, such as miscanthus and molinia, and polemoniums and veronicas, particularly *V. longifolia*.

Piet Oudolf, a leading European garden designer and plantsman, well-known for his naturalistic plantings is now using daylilies to form blocks or ribbons of late-summer colour along with eupatoriums and sedums, as a contrast to ornamental grasses. He has combined the acid yellow of *Hemerocallis* 'Green Glitter' with the warm magenta of 'Lady Blue Eyes' to great effect.

WATERSIDE

It has always been thought that daylilies will not do well in bog conditions, where the water is stagnant and anaerobic, or when planted beside a pond in such a way that the crown is almost submerged. However, 'Amadeus', 'Lullaby Baby' and 'Viracocha', among others, will survive swamp conditions, and, in recent years, there have been some successful experiments in growing certain types in submerged pots for the summer season. Obviously there is room for further experimentation.

In damp ground at the water's edge, daylilies associate well with the fuzzy, flame-shaped flower plumes of astilbes, either large or small and in every imaginable shade of pink, mauve, red and white, and with aruncus. They also look good with irises, grown as much for their ascending, sword-like leaves as for their flowers, and with moisture-loving umbellifers, such as *Angelica archangelica* or *A. gigas*, as well as large ferns like *Matteuccia struthiopteris* and *Osmunda regalis*. Moisture-loving grasses, such as glyceria, can be used to complete the grouping, with calamagrostis and molinias to give height.

A supreme example of this kind of daylily planting can be seen at Longstock Water Garden in Hampshire.

SUB-TROPICAL EFFECTS

For the majority of daylily growers whose gardens are not in sub-tropical regions, a surprising number of daylilies lend themselves remarkably well to exotic-looking plantings that create a tropical ambience. Again with the help of ornamental grasses, this time emphasized with clumps of

Daylilies 'Mokan Butterfly', 'Pony' and 'Prairie Blue Eyes' with *Geranium pratense* 'Mrs Kendall Clark', *Ageratum* 'Blue Horizon', and *Salvia farinacea* 'Victoria'.

bamboo, it is possible to put together such an effect using daylilies. Marc King does this to perfection in his Italian garden, Casa Rocca. Backed by steep terraces, the garden beckons one down narrow, winding paths planted, not only with Spider and Unusual Form daylilies, but also with those whose blooms are spectacularly large, over 16cm (6in), and which, as such, could be out of place in a traditional border.

All the plants at Casa Rocca have to be winter hardy since the temperatures can go down to −10 to −12°C (10–14°F), sometimes −15°C (5°F) in winter. However, surprisingly luxuriant effects can be created with the graceful, spider-like daylilies in contrast with ginger lilies (*Hedychium*), the only hardy banana, *Musa basjoo*, the hardier kniphofias and billowing mounds of miscanthus, from the tallest M. 'Silberturm' at 3m (10ft) to the smallest 'Little Kitten' at 45cm (18in).

Marc King plants the canna lilies, with their sombrely marked bold leaves and ebullient floral spires in red, orange and coral, to take over from the daylilies in late August, using the solid oval canna leaves as a foil to the narrow segments of the more Unusual-form daylilies, like 'Trahlyta' and 'Isle of Dreams'. The glossy palmate leaves of *Fatsia japonica* with the hardy evergreen Chusan palm (*Trachycarpus fortunei*), create a magnificent backdrop. *Yucca gloriosa* and Y. 'Vittorio Emmanuele II', contribute bold linear lines. For gardens where phormiums will not survive, one might use the deciduous *Iris pseudacorus* 'Variegata' or *I.* 'Berlin Tiger' with its massive, dark husky leaves. Other winter-hardy shrubs with exotic leaves include *Aucuba* species and variegated cultivars, mahonias and the large-leafed *Magnolia delavayi*.

LANDSCAPING WITH DAYLILIES

Daylilies excel when massed. The South American designer Roberto Burle Marx, who seems at times to have regarded his plant materials merely as a means of providing colour to fill a pattern, was fond of using massed plantings of a single colour of daylily. Usually these were employed as part of an overall scheme the other elements of which were bands of other plants massed in single colours like *Setcreasea purpurea*, *Chlorophytum comosum* 'Variegatum', coleus, *Eragrostis curvula* and *Crinum americanum*.

Daylilies are also often a major element in the New Wave gardens of landscape architects Oehme and van Sweden, though their preference seems to be for mixed colours, as in the gardens of the International Centre in Washington, DC. They usually use them in association with achillea and rudbeckias and, of course, with the grasses for which their gardens are so famous, particularly varieties of calamagrostis and pennisetum, which enjoy the same moist, nutrient rich soils as the daylilies.

The Royal Horticultural Society's Garden at Wisley in Surrey, has daylilies in large sweeps and drifts in the less formal areas of the 200 acre site. A spectacular planting in Seven Acres, forming conspicuous drifts of mainly cool colours, can be seen across a wide expanse of grass from the restaurant. A narrow path of stepping stones winds between their waist-high blooms – allowing visitors to experience their beauty close at hand. Many of the cultivars used have been growing at Wisley since they were raised or were planted in the gardens having first taken part in the permanent daylily trials. Some are late mid-century US hybrids like 'Ava Michelle', 'Bejewelled', 'Perennial Pleasure' and 'Tetrina's Daughter', others are German introductions from Tomas Tamberg – 'Berlin Lemon', 'Berlin Red Velvet' and 'Helle Berlinerin' – many of which have won awards from the Royal Horticultural Society. Yet others represent the work of the English hybridizers Lady Carew Pole, Leonard Brummitt and Harry Randall. The vast collection is always being updated and now includes some of the most modern introductions from the United States and Australia. Among these, visitors can now see Mort Morss's 'Mendocino' and 'Always Afternoon', a recent Stout Medal Winner, a good representation of the cultivars raised by the Guidry family and some of the last introductions of Brother Charles Reckamp.

Perhaps the most important single factor to consider in landscaping with daylilies is whether the light will be falling on them or will be beyond them, causing them to glow, seemingly from within, like a glass of wine held up to the light. On the whole, it is the paler colours that look best with the sun beyond them: the whites, creams, pale lemon-yellows, the blushes and pale pinks. Heavier colours, the true reds, rich yellows, purples and all those shades that lean towards blackness are best with the light falling on them. In this context, backgrounds are particularly important. Dark colours lose themselves against dark backgrounds, but pale colours look all the better for a dark backdrop, and appear positively luminous in this situation if also lit from the side.

In some countries daylilies are used for landscaping schemes around buildings and, here again, large blocks of one colour are the most effective. Or one could use a large-flowered bold eyed cultivar such as 'Vohann' planted behind 'Little Streaker' or 'Spanish Masquerade'. If possible choose daylilies with evergreen foliage, which will provide winter interest.

APPLE COURT DISPLAY GARDEN

Many keen collectors prefer to grow their daylilies in specially designed daylily borders, either colour-themed or

PLATE VII
RED DAYLILIES

H. 'Pirate Bride'

H. 'New Swirls'

H. 'Whooperee'

H. 'Christmas Is'

H. 'Hot Ember'

All flowers are shown at approximately ¾ size

colour-contrasted. Both have their merits and their limitations, but seem to work best where the main object is to compare daylilies of similar colours.

Our aim at Apple Court, a Display Garden for Hemerocallis Europa and a showcase for our nursery, is to introduce the best of every colour and type of daylily, mostly the newer sorts, to as many prospective growers as possible. Apple Court has a genuine garden setting, with hedges, trees, shrubs and hard landscaping surrounding the plantings.

Colour Grading

We find that subtly colour-grading the daylilies in each border and from one border to another, and providing contrast to their mainly rounded flowers with plants of spire-like or spherical outline, greatly emphasizes the sumptuousness of the daylilies. We have four daylily beds in a square, edged in tightly clipped box, in the middle of which is a raised brick bed planted with miscanthus and other grasses that start to flower as the daylilies peak. The colours of the daylilies in the four beds are: red; lemon-yellow and white; gold, orange and shades of bronze to dark brown; and melons and warm creams. The whole is surrounded by a copper beech hedge, the north side of which has two long borders of daylilies in the bluer tones, ranging from deepest purple through lavender, blue-pink and pink to rose-pink and wine-red. The purplish foliage of the beech hedge separates the hot colours from the cooler tones. Agapanthus, which contrast perfectly with all the daylilies, act as a link between all the borders; the highlight is a ravishing near-white A. 'Snowy Owl' planted next to the fire-engine-red of *Hemerocallis* 'Chicago Apache'. Height is provided by standard clipped balls of *Photinia* 'Red Robin', which do not cast unwanted shade.

THE FRAGRANT GARDEN

Many gardeners are drawn to daylilies on account of the delicious fragrance of certain species and the hybrids derived from them. However, the further away from the species the hybrid is, usually the less evident the fragrance: it is hard to name any new introductions that have the compelling fragrance of 'Dorothy McDade', 'Hyperion', 'Marion Vaughn' and 'Whichford'. I can detect virtually no scent in 'Chorus Line', 'Golden Scroll' or 'Smoky Mountain Autumn', all winners of the L. Ernest Plouf Award for fragrant diploid daylilies, though the fragrance may be more apparent in hotter climates. But the elusiveness of fragrance is one of its charms, depending as it does on temperature, humidity and still air, and it is a bonus rather than a disadvantage that the best daylilies to plant in a fragrant garden are also those of simple floral outline and soft, delicate colouring.

When designing a garden to ravish the senses with fragrance, it is best to plant in raised beds, so lifting the flowers as near to nose-level as possible, and to enclose the garden with a wall or hedge, thus creating a beneficial microclimate. A sunny terrace featuring scented daylilies in pots, would give similar pleasure, the pots brought on and off the scene as the daylilies come into flower.

Other fragrant daylilies include: the deservedly popular Lemon Lily (*H. lilioasphodelus*) and its more stately hybrid 'Queen of May'; the exquisitely scented 'Prairie Moonlight'; and 'Russian Easter', which has a powerful fragrance.

DAYLILIES IN POTS

Many daylilies can be successfully grown in pots or containers in terracotta, wood, stone or even plastic. Even when in leaf only, a daylily in a container that perfectly sets

off the proportions of the arching clump of graceful foliage, will provide a pleasing picture for many months of the year. In containers, even more than in borders, the quality of the foliage is of great importance as it will be scrutinized closely and often. On the whole the smaller daylilies work better in pots than the larger, sometimes more vigorous sorts. Not only are they in better proportion to the size and shape of a container, but they are more likely to rebloom and they are easier to handle. For pot culture we prefer daylilies with narrower, graceful, gently arching leaves, rather than wider lush foliage which, even though lowish-growing, can look clumsy and out of place in a container.

As the flowers of daylilies are so colourful it is usually

Daylilies lend themselves to planting together. At Apple Court, they are grouped according to colour and shade, resulting in a very effective display.

best to plant them in a fairly neutral or dark-coloured container set on a neutral base of gravel, and possibly echoing the colour of the flower, or the colour of its contrasting eye, in a nearby painted seat or trellis arches.

For a quieter mood, marry the colour of the container to any nearby paintwork. The plainer the container the more highly coloured and patterned the daylily can be and vice versa. The whole effect is lost if both are fighting for attention. Such details are not necessarily immediately picked up in the mind's eye but the general effect will be one of harmony. Using different coloured daylilies in pots of the same shape and colour can also be harmonious if other features in the garden are not too fussy.

There are more choices and combinations of colour when using the colour of the daylily as a foil for the container. The deep blue, khaki-greens and browns of Chinese pickle jars, not only look wonderful with yellow daylilies such as 'Crystal Cupid' or 'Happy Returns', but seem also to enhance many of the smaller Siloams of lavender-orchid and pink tint.

The container can be a singleton acting as a focal point on a terrace, or a matching pair at the side of a flight of steps or guarding a doorway, or one of a group of containers having different sorts of flower in the same colour.

Daylily containers can be planted with other perennials, such as ajugas to trail over the edge of the pot, or liriope to give another season of flower in early autumn. Foliage plants having contrasting or matching leaf shape look effective; for example, *Chlorophytum*, which will trail gracefully over the sides of the pot.

Planting Daylilies in Pots & Containers

Always choose a container of a suitable size: about ⅓ as tall as the plant. Make sure it has an adequate drainage hole, which should then be covered with crocks to assist drainage. If the container is large, a large spadeful of well-rotted farmyard manure or garden compost mixed with potting compost should be put over the crocks, followed by a layer of compost. Then carefully position the daylily so that its roots are not touching the manure and fill up with compost to the crown, firming the compost gently and making sure that on watering, the daylily does not sink more than 2.5cm (1in) below the rim of the pot.

Keep the pot out of the way of frost or hot sunshine until the daylily begins to put on new growth. Always keep containerized daylilies very well watered, as they are growing in such a limited amount of compost they will need copious amounts of moisture; feed often but with a dilute solution of fertilizer. Grooming a specimen daylily in a pot is even more important than grooming one that is growing in a border.

7
BREEDING DAYLILIES

PURELY FOR PLEASURE
EVE LYTTON

For those who enjoy growing daylilies on an amateur basis, like me, there can be few things more pleasurable than producing their very own hybrids, an activity which is not only exciting but extremely simple.

Initially, all that is required is a basic knowledge of the reproductive parts of a flower (p.13). Also necessary is a knowledge of the ploidy of the daylily chosen for parenthood, essential because diploids and tetraploids are incompatible due to their differing chromosome counts (pp.37–38).

Since the flowers of daylilies contain both male and female organs, there is some danger of self-pollination, so in hybridization programmes it is usual to emasculate the flowers (that is, on the flower chosen as the pod parent, the stamens are removed).

A certain amount of patience is also required because although it is often only nine months from seed to flower in the hottest climates, in cooler regions it takes 2–3 years, depending upon individual growing conditions; at least a further year is then needed for the daylily to mature and show its paces. After 2–3 seasons, bud count, branching and flowering may improve or change significantly.

CHOOSING YOUR PARENTS

To start with, it is tempting just to put the pollen from one pretty face on to another to see what will happen and, if you are lucky, this can work very well, but it is better to have specific aims, such as an improvement of colour or form, the development of unusual patterns or the refinement of edges. When choosing your first parent, try to select a daylily that is as near to your aim or ideal as

'Monica Mead', a sumptuous pale apricot to pink double daylily, was raised by David Kirchhoff and named for one of Australia's top daylily breeders and growers.

possible and then look for another parent to complement it, preferably with other qualities your first parent lacks, such as the ability to lift the bloom above healthy foliage on graceful scapes or well and evenly branched scapes producing many buds to give a long season of flower. Many amateur breeders, as well as the professionals, develop an eye for a good breeding plant (a bridge plant), one that will never be good enough to be introduced in its own right, but is able to pass on certain exceptional qualities.

There are also pitfalls to avoid. Two daylilies with the same weaknesses should not be crossed, however beautiful. For instance, if ruffling is wanted, 'Dance Ballerina Dance' would contribute this trait but due to its difficulty in opening fully in cooler climates, it would be unwise to use it with another daylily having the same defect. Crossing 'Dance Ballerina Dance' with a daylily that opens easily and, preferably, early in the morning, could bring about an exciting new break.

As knowledge about the pedigrees of cultivars grows, and there are now stud books to assist, one can use breeding techniques such as line-breeding, which is the crossing in succession of two parents and the resulting seedlings with each other generation by generation. Outcrossing is the crossing of seedlings with unrelated cultivars to strengthen the lines and further one's aims.

Storing Pollen

To make specific crosses it is sometimes necessary to store pollen for later use if the pod parent is not in bloom at the same time. This is not difficult. Scrape fluffy, dry pollen from the anthers of the pollen donor into a china egg cup or similar container, taking care not to add any fleshy bits as these will decay. Collecting in this manner should be done as early in the day as possible so that insects have had little chance to mix the pollen. If the pollen is only to be kept until the following day, it will be sufficient to cover the container and keep it in the fridge. If it is to be kept for a longer period say, two weeks, put it into small, well-sealed gelatin capsules, and then store in a larger uncovered container (the type of plastic tube used for pain killers or throat lozenges is ideal) and place this into a tightly covered box with some silica gel (the material used for drying flowers). This allows the pollen to be stored in the fridge without deterioration taking place. Pollen can also be frozen for a longer period, even for a year or so, as long as the same initial drying procedures are carried out. Once dried it can then be put in a sealed polythene bag, or any other suitable container, such as a contact lens case or pill box, and labelled with the cultivar name. A small square of paper towel placed under the pollen will absorb any remaining moisture. The pollen collected on the paper towel can then be applied direct to the pistil.

MAKING A CROSS

In its simplest form, cross-pollination consists of placing pollen from the anthers of one flower onto the stigma of another. The pollen should be golden-yellow, dry and fluffy (creamy-white, hard pollen is infertile). Ideally pollination should be carried out as early as possible on a cool, dry morning. This is particularly important when working with tetraploids which are more difficult; diploids can be pollinated successfully until midday or a little later.

To make the pollen transfer use an artist's small paint brush, which must be washed with soap and water to make it completely clean for each cross. Use flat-ended tweezers or fingers to hold the stamen and anther, and gently stroke the pollen on to the stigma of the pod parent. Many hobby hybridists then carefully cover the ends of the pistil with a small cap of foil to prevent further unplanned pollination, for the time necessary for fertilization to take place.

Having made the cross, mark the pod parent to help prevent the accidental removal of the flower when deadheading. Initially, a piece of coloured wool is sufficient, but once you are bitten by the hybridizing bug, it is necessary to keep records so the first step is to mark the pod parent with a small tie-on label on which are written the details of the cross number, the two parents used and the date (eg No. 1 'Sunshine' × 'Brief Shower', 10.7.98), the pod parent usually being written first. Needless to say, the details must be written with an indelible garden pen or pencil. The label is then carefully attached to the stem under the flower and each cross noted on a pad for transferral to a record book or a computer.

Do not be dismayed if some crosses do not take: pollination is not always successful and there are many hazards. Sometimes a parent is infertile, or the weather is too hot and humid causing the pollinated flower to drop off, or a seed pod may start to grow but then wither, particularly if the weather is very cool and changeable. However, if pollination is successful, the base of the pistil swells and the flower sheds, revealing the little green seed pod. Do not be tempted to try removing the withered flowers from around the emerging pods, as this can very easily snap the whole thing off. If all is well, the pod will grow and about six weeks later it will ripen, dry and crack open at the top. This is when it should be removed and the seed and label placed in small paper bags or self-seal plastic bags for storage in a container in the fridge until needed.

SOWING & GROWING ON

If heat and light are available, sowing can be done at any time during the winter but most gardeners prefer to wait until early spring, thus avoiding having vulnerable seedlings ready for planting out too early in the year. When removed from cold storage, the seeds, which will have lost moisture, may appear rather dry and wrinkled and it is a good idea to soak them for a day or two before sowing, changing the water daily. They should then be sown in open-textured compost, 5–10mm (¼–½in) deep, lightly covered and gently tamped down. Use deep trays, individual pots or special self-watering polystyrene seed trays and put them into a gently heated propagator, an airing cupboard or on a warm windowsill until germination takes place. If they are not in a covered propagating case, they will need to be covered with a polythene bag to keep the moisure in. Successful germination is apparent when strong grass-like spears begin to sprout, in about 7–10 days. The containers should then be kept in a light, frost-free place until ready to be hardened off for planting outside when all danger of frost has passed.

When planting out the seedlings, put them into a well prepared and sunny patch in the garden and plant approximately 22cm (9in) apart in rows that are 30cm (12in) apart, giving each plant room to develop over the following year or two. The seedlings should be well watered and mulched for the summer to help them develop a good root system before their first winter, after this there is not much to do other than to wait with eager anticipation for a scape to appear and to see the first flowers.

However much excitement and pleasure is obtained from the first crop of seedlings, a critical eye will be necessary as many of the seedlings may well be of indifferent quality and not worth keeping. Give them time to mature and then be as selective as possible and try to see the plant as a whole. When starting to hybridize try not to make too many crosses. Professional hybridizers produce several thousand seedlings a year but this would be far too many to handle for someone just breeding as a pleasurable hobby and a hundred or two from carefully chosen parents will probably be more than enough.

THE QUEST FOR PERFECTION
DAVID KIRCHHOFF

There is something about the magic of daylilies that causes professional men and women to abandon successful careers in midstream and turn to breeding them for a living. Without having to think too hard I can name Mort Morss, Patrick and Grace Stamile, Dr Bob Carr and myself as examples of such people.

I first grew daylilies as a child in the family's garden. I inherited my love of daylily hybridizing from my father, Ed Kirchhoff. He had had a long and succcessful career as a grower of gladioli for the cut-flower market and had observed his grandfather's hybridization of gladioli. On his retirement, with some persuasion from friends, he decided to try his hand with daylilies. His enthusiasm was boundless. Hybridizing daylilies changed my life, too: in 1971 I left a career in music and joined my father in his newfound passion.

One of my first ambitions for daylilies was to improve the doubles. An early success was 'Nagasaki' (1979), a lavender-pink blend with yellow halo and green throat. One of the first of my doubles to gain general acceptance and popularity was 'Betty Woods', a vivid Chinese yellow self with a green throat, which was also the first double to

'Betty Woods' was an early success in diploid doubles for David Kirchhoff.

win the Stout Medal. Descendants from 'Betty Woods' are many and include the popular 'Florida Sunshine' and 'Seminole Dream', as well as 'Cabbage Flower', a light yellow double, and 'Stroke of Midnight', a dark red double. Both the latter won the Ida Munson Award for doubles.

'Virginia Franklin Miller', a 16.5cm (6½in) pink self with green throat, is exceptionally vigorous and well-branched. 'Forty Second Street' is a pink double with rose-red eye. 'Monica Mead' is a delicate apricot-pink with a slight halo. 'Dancing with Pink', a 12cm (5in) light pink double and 'Schnickel Fritz', a near-white and my first dormant double, are combinations of Kirchhoff and Henry breeding. My other dormant double is 'Sandford Eyecatcher', a small double yellow with red eye. 'Jean High' (1998), a smooth, full, rose-pink double, and the, yet to be released, 'Peggy Turman', a sibling, represent my diploid doubles at their pinnacle, and complete my diploid double breeding programme.

After what seemed an eternity in hybridizing for consistently double tetraploids, I raised a chance, consistently

A vivid red with a velvety texture, 'Leonard Bernstein' performs well in Europe as well as its native Florida.

double (in Florida) daylily, 'Mother Superior' (1993). Along with seedlings from 'Double Jackpot' and 'King Alfred', this became the nucleus of my double tetraploid breeding programme. Slowly my programme progressed, with infusions of parents that had good doubling characteristics, such as 'Tet Dancing Lady', a sibling of 'Nagasaki' and 'Tet Double Decker', 'Tet Siloam Double Classic', 'Tet Stroke of Midnight', 'Tet Betty Woods' and, most recently, 'Tet Virginia Franklin Miller' and I am now convinced of the wisdom of focusing entirely on the tetraploid level.

I deliberately withheld many 'bridge plant' cultivars from the market, but released a few double tetraploids during this stage. Among the most noteworthy are 'Mango Coral', a fertile mango-orange double, 'Layers of Gold', which is golden-yellow, the melon-coloured 'Pappy's Girl', the orange-red 'Clovette Adams', 'Noble Virtue', a pastel and 'Eliza Doolittle' (1998), a pink with gold edges.

The range of colours, forms and patterns in tetraploid doubles has now overtaken the singles. The eyes and edges on doubles in all the colours are now available and the near future promises a whole new world of doubles.

Another of my early passions in hybridizing was to make improvements in the colour red. I had a preference for the type of sunfast, full, ruffled forms exemplified in 'Leonard Bernstein' and 'Crimson Wind'. After all my second ever daylily purchase was a red: Virginia Peck's 'Sir Patrick Spens'. In the 1970s and 1980s Dr Peck was a leading hybridizer of tetraploid daylilies and was renowned for her reds.

Early on in my attempts I converted an enormous seedling ('Cathay Caper' × a seedling) from another Florida hybridizer Vera McFarland. Crossed on to Virginia Peck's fabulous classic red 'Scarlock', this seedling pro-duced a group of fifteen seedlings, each one very pleasing. There was a definite improvement of form and fertility. One of them, 'Amadeus', became the genesis for most of our red lines. Crossed with John Kinnebrew's fine black-red 'Midnight Magic' it produced 'Study in Scarlet', which was used extensively – and is still being widely used – as a superior red parent. Another break of sorts was 'Kent's Favourite Two' a surprisingly large, early-morning-opening plant. A surprise was 'Magic Carpet Ride', a large, mandarin-red with a coral-orange-red watermark above a yellow to yellow-green throat. An early-morning-opener, suitable for cold, temperate and warm climates, it is outstanding when given filtered sunlight.

'Vintage Bordeaux' (1987), from 'Amadeus' × a sibling, is black-cherry, edged yellow with a chartreuse throat. The flowers are 14cm (5½in) across and the plant is evergreen, extremely vigorous and thrives in cold climates with snow cover. 'Dragon King' ('Study in Scarlet' × 'Anastasia') was a breakthrough in reds – on many levels. One of the few nocturnal reds, it is an early-morning-opener, it has a huge sunburst-yellow to green throat and is exuberantly ruffled and slightly recurved. It is an outstanding parent and has enabled a number of other breeders to break the pattern of producing reds that are slow to open. 'Seminole Blood' and 'Jay Turman' (siblings) are both early-morning-openers and perform well in the north. 'Seminole Blood' is very sunfast and its orange throat makes a good combination with the blood-red ground colour. 'Jay Turman' has a totally different look and is the most nocturnal of our reds

'Marilyn Siwik' is a striking fierce orange emphasized by a hot red eye. A red picotee edge is apparent in hot climates.

'Dragon King' is a clear mandarin-red with contrasting sunburst throat. It is early-morning-opening.

to date. 'Vino de Notte', from a cross of 'Zinfandel' × 'Midnight Magic', is a saturated wine-red, leaning towards purple, and has great scapes.

Two other daylilies that have done well in Europe are 'Farmer's Daughter', a bright medium-pink self, edged gold with yellow throat, and 'Rondure' ('Tet Sugar Cookie' × 'Tet Moonlight Mist'), a round, flat, ruffled creamy-yellow. Although yellow and gold have not been high priorities in my breeding programmes, 'Bill Norris', a flat, ruffled gold, has been a prolific parent, figuring prominently in a new generation of golds, yellows and oranges.

I do, of course, work with other colours. The foundation of my orange lines was the burnt-orange 'Bittersweet Holiday' (1982). Other successful daylilies in this colour range include 'Marilyn Siwik', a huge red-eyed orange, 'Carlee Longman', which has exceptionally well-branched scapes and produces 12cm (5in) orange flowers with darker halo, and the 1998 introduction 'Leroy', another eyed orange. There are also the crinkled, dormant full-petalled 'Paul Stout', a burnished orange, and the smooth, full, round bittersweet-orange 'Mitchell Leichert'.

In 1972 my father and I invited Mort Morss to join us in our work with daylilies. At the time Mort was working in another career in San Francisco, while studying art.

As Curt Hanson of Crintonic Gardens says: 'With the tenacity of a junk yard dog, Mort has stuck to his eyezones! From the very beginning his focus has been on the subtle patterns only vaguely suggested in the early tetraploids. With the creative imagination and the discerning eye of the artist, Mort patiently drew these patterns out through diligent hybridizing. The dramatic patterns he has given us are his unique signature in the evolution of the modern daylily. Beyond his pioneering work in creating new patterns, Mort's cultivars offer tremendous potential in the now popular field of Exotic [now Unusual Form] and Spider Variants'.

The distinctive 'Gerda Brooker' (1988), bred by Mort, is a narrow-tepalled, dramatic and Unusual-form flower. It contains much unlocked potential for Spider and Unusual Form breeding and towers above its predecessors, unencumbered by poor scapes or small plants. It is a 'must have' for the growing number of hybridizers who love the incredible eye of 'Witch Stitchery', as well as the connoisseur who fancies the grand and distinctive.

Mort's first introduction, 'Inner View' (1982), a large greyed-lavender with a wide cream pattern above the throat, is quite hardy and adaptable. His 'Mandala' and 'Gilded Mosaic' are fine examples of daylilies with lighter coloured patterns. 'Paper Butterfly', 'Witch Stitchery' and 'Weaver's Art' are all examples of eyes with patterns within them.

Mort's search for daylilies containing the elusive blue are exemplified by such cultivars as 'Jackie's Choice', 'Song of Singapore' and 'Forgotten Blues', all of which reveal hints of blue, particularly in the halo or eyezone above the throat. His fancy-edged work is seen in 'Heavenly Dragon', 'Tropical Triumph', 'Mort's Masterpiece', 'Uppermost Edge' and the upcoming 'Barbara Dittmer'.

What is being achieved today in the raising of new daylilies has only been made possible by the dedicated pioneers whose expertise and foresight have enabled a butterfly to hatch out of the chrysalis.

Gold edges, and well-spaced branches and buds are the hallmarks of sunfast, rose-eyed, 'Barbara Dittmer'.

8

SMALL-FLOWERED & MINIATURE DAYLILIES

Miniature, Small-flowered and Dwarf are official classifications of the American Hemerocallis Society, the first two referring to the flower size, the third the stature of the plant. Miniature flowers are less than 7.5cm (3in) in diameter; small-flowers are between 7.5 and 11cm (3–4½in) in diameter. The latter are often referred to as Pony.

A dwarf must be less than 30cm (12in) tall. Generally dwarf daylilies are beautifully proportioned: 'Penny's Worth' and 'Penny Earned', the tiniest, have 4cm (1½in) flowers and grass-like foliage. Their pale yellow and orange bells are borne on 25cm (10in) scapes. Just as low-growing but larger-flowered is sunny-yellow 'Eenie Weenie'.

The sizes normally cited are those given at registration; however, daylily scape height can increase or decrease to a greater extent than can flower size, depending on growing conditions.

Miniature daylilies are somewhat taller than dwarfs and flower at 30–75cm (12–30in), looking their best in natural plantings in woodland clearings or informal sunny borders. The charming 'Cherries are Ripe' has cherry-red, green-throated flowers, reminiscent of ripe berries, on wiry scapes about 70cm (28in) high, above the foliage. Darrel Apps, going against current fashion, is breeding miniature and small-flowered daylilies with tall scapes especially for their value as border plants; these include 'Fresh Air', which has scapes of 85cm (34in). He introduces only those that have a high bud count or good rebloom to avoid the possibility of tall, vacant scapes. All the progeny from 'Fresh Air', including the coffee-coloured 'Wilhelm', are well-branched and floriferous, presenting a bouquet-like effect.

Small-flowered daylilies are also generally 30–75cm (12–30in) tall, the average scape height working out at

around 45cm (18in). The shape of the flowers can vary from diminutive bells through small, round buttons to the more Unusual-form and triangular, such as 'Siloam David Kirchhoff', a soft orchid-lavender, with a thin carmine pencilled line surrounding a washed mauve eye. Even Spiders are represented in the small-flowered category, notably the curly-segmented yellow 'Rococo'. Nowadays, tetraploid small-flowered and tetraploid miniatures (mini tets) have wide, overlapping segments, but are fashioned in precise proportion to their height, perfectly in scale with their diploid kin.

Latest Trends

The range of colours in miniature and small-flowered daylilies is as wide as those of the larger sorts, encompassing the whole of the colour spectrum, from the near-white 'Absolute Zero' and 'Little Fat Cat' to the deepest red-black 'Little Fred' or 'Siloam Sambo'. In addition, there are now the subtle washed, etched and echo-eye patterned minis and small-flowered forms raised by Elizabeth Salter (p.115). These are all descended from 'Pyewacket' or 'Elf Witch' or a combination of the two, the earliest being 'Enchanter's Spell' followed by (to name the most notable) 'Jason Salter', 'Dragon Dreams', 'Patchwork Puzzle' and, most recently, 'Dark Mosaic', on which the echo-eye is a broken double ring of white pigment on a dark base. Some small daylilies with subtle and complicated patterning and colouring may require long periods of hot sun to bring out the markings; in cooler climates they may not perform so well.

Ra Hansen's smaller daylilies with huge contrasting eyes bear the hallmark of her tasteful, yet bold colour statements. The exotic 'Bug's Hug' and 'Dazzle', in shades of lavender and candy-pink, and the cherry-eyed, yellow 'Beat the Barons' are among those that seem to have settled down well in cooler English and European climates, as has her sultry Southern beauty, 'Night Beacon'. One of Hansen's several introductions given the Tuscawilla prefix,

'Absolute Zero' is a totally hardy near white to ivory-lemon of seersucker texture and performs well in most climates.

'Tuscawilla Dave Talbott', although needing winter protection in cold climates, always opens perfectly.

in honour of the nearby old native American settlement, falls into the Pony category, namely 'Tuscawilla Dave Talbott', a bold-eyed, ivory nocturnal bloomer. Many of the small-flowered doubles raised by Enman Joiner, such as 'Bubbly', and 'Baby Fresh', come in shades of soft apricot to peach and bloom for weeks on end. They open well and are hardy in a wide range of climates.

The Early Days

The diversity of these captivating plants is astounding but this was not always so. Hubert Fischer firmly believed that small was beautiful at a time when most breeders thought no one would want small-flowered daylilies. His elegant 'Golden Chimes' and paler yellow 'Corky', with their unmistakable *H. multiflora* and *H. dumortieri* influence, are still cherished by gardeners the world over and completely vindicated his faith in miniatures.

The Fischers put miniatures on the map by donating the Donn Fischer Memorial Cup. This trophy, named in honour of their son, is awarded annually by the American Hemerocallis Society to the best miniature judged during the Convention Garden Tour. The presentation of this trophy to the AHS had the dual effect of gaining miniatures official recognition and of promoting interest among hybridizers and growers. The first Donn Fischer Memorial Cup was presented in 1962, fittingly enough for 'Golden Chimes': miniatures had arrived. In 1980 'Bertie Ferris', a persimmon-orange, introduced in 1969, became the first miniature to be awarded the prestigious Stout Medal.

In 1964 the AHS created a further distinction by authorizing an award for the most outstanding small-flowered daylily. This became known as the Annie T. Giles Award named for the donor, President of the American Hemerocallis Society from 1962–3, who professed this to be her

favourite daylily flower size. The rosy-flushed orange 'McPick' was the first winner.

Small Beginnings

In spite of the popularity of Fischer's miniatures, there were, at that time, few other hybridizers specializing in this group, apart from Lucille Williamson and Lucille Warner. 'Bitsy', which was raised by Lucille Warner and introduced in 1962 is still grown in many gardens, on account of its repeat blooming quality inherited from its *H. minor* ancestry. It is the *H. minor* genes, often carried through 'Bitsy' that have produced reblooming in certain lines of miniature daylilies. Lucille Williamson is now best remembered for her Stout Medal-winning 'Green Flutter', one of the greenest daylilies, even by today's standards, and 'Little Grapette', a dusky grape-purple still treasured by gardeners everywhere.

In her time, Elna Winniford was also a well-known hybridizer of miniatures particularly with flat and symmetrically-formed flowers. Her work was overshadowed by that of her husband Ury, but it provided him with the foundation to produce such well-known daylilies as 'Bertie Ferris'.

Pauline Henry and the Siloams

Some amateur hybridizers, especially it seems, women, have a natural flair for raising beautiful daylilies, without necessarily having a scientific approach towards their breeding programmes. Pauline Henry of Siloam Springs, Arkansas is one such. Her work on smaller-flowered daylilies during the 1970s and 1980s introduced to daylily enthusiasts, especially those in colder regions, a whole range of lower-growing, less space-invading daylilies, in brilliant colour combinations and prized for their reblooming qualities. Among her best and most distinctive are 'Siloam Dream Baby', 'Siloam Merle Kent', 'Siloam Ury Winniford', 'Siloam Show Girl' and 'Siloam Gumdrop'. Every grower of Siloams will have a list of particular favourites as over 300 have been registered. Pauline Henry's last-introduced smaller daylilies are the miniatures 'Siloam Queen Bee' and 'Siloam Elfin Jewel', in 1993, and the small-flowered 'Siloam Rose Silk'.

Mrs Henry worked solely with diploids, the majority also being dormant. The starting point of her breeding programme was Lucille Williamson's miniatures 'Little Celena', winner of the Donn Fischer Memorial Cup (in 1980), and 'Little Showoff'.

In western Germany Werner Reinerman has used Siloam breeding lines in his 'Petit Nobel', 'Shakabully', and 'Sweet Tanja' and in the larger-flowered 'Ars Vivendi', 'Erika Ekstein', 'Tango Noturno' and 'Tante Ju'; these daylilies are suitable for even the coldest continental climates.

Tetraploid Conversions

American Dan Trimmer, a great converter of diploids into tetraploids, has also been at work with the Siloams, in particular 'Siloam Gumdrop', a red-eyed pink that sets seed easily. His first introduction from crossing this with Patrick Stamile's superb near-white 'Arctic Snow' produced 'Watermill Blush'.

Many of the other enduringly popular and well-known smaller daylilies have now been converted from diploid to tetraploid. Darrel Apps has converted his cranberry-red 'Pardon Me'; his 'Sugar Cookie' was converted by Jeff Salter and has been much used by his wife (see below).

Elizabeth Salter & Grace Stamile

Both Elizabeth Salter and Grace Stamile have ongoing programmes for tetraploid minis. Salter's small-flowered, ivory-yellow 'Moon Witch' and 'Guiniver's Gift', and palest cream-ivory 'Lady of Fortune', all introduced in the early 1990s, have the typical tetraploid heavy substance and smooth, leathery texture, owing their ancestry of shapely, round, full appearance to 'Tet Sugar Cookie'.

'Pardon Me' is a floriferous and vigorous classic, cranberry-red miniature with perfect proportions.

Salter's vibrant 'Bibbity Bobbity Boo', in shades of lavender-grape and deep purple, is reminiscent of Ra Hansen's huge-eyed introductions, and is now much used in breeding mini tetraploids, and her large-eyed 'Mary Ethel Anderson' was a well-deserved Florida Sunshine Cup winner in 1997.

Miniature tetraploids from Grace Stamile include her Broadway Series, of which she deemed 'Broadway Valentine', raised from [(('Gato' × 'Midnight Magic') × 'Dominic') × 'Tet Siloam Red Toy'], the most suitable so far for cooler climates.

'Tet Siloam Red Toy', converted by Oscie Whatley, well-known for his work on tetraploid conversion, is a much brighter and clearer red than the diploid version. 'Tiger Kitten', which is bright orange with a red eye, was one of her first small-flowered tetraploids, and is now used as a parent in her ongoing breeding programme.

Grace Stamile has joined Elizabeth Salter in the quest for blue-flowered smaller daylilies and her minis 'Baby Blues' and 'Pastilline' are lavender-blue and lavender-grey respectively, both with subtle eye patterns. In spite of blue being unnatural in daylilies, these two little near blues are reportedly excellent performers in many climates.

Leo Sharp, Ben Hager & Clarence Crochet

Leo Sharp has introduced a vast array of smaller-flowered daylilies. Many are raised specifically for northern and cooler regions and others, trialled in Apopka, Florida, as well as Indiana, will perform equally well in sub-tropical as in cooler gardens. His 'Brookwood Orange Drop' is as vibrant an orange as any on the market, and 'Brookwood Sympatico' is reminiscent of melon-apricot 'Naomi Ruth', but with the addition of boldly contrasting black anthers.

Ben Hager's delightful 'Cherries are Ripe', 'Coming up Roses' and 'Daily Dollar' are destined to become classic garden plants as well as daylilies worthy of a place in any collection. It is hard to believe how far his daylilies have progressed since the introduction of his 'Daily Bread', which flowers almost continuously throughout summer. Developed in California in 1973, it is still widely grown in Europe.

Like Ben Hager, Clarence Crochet is probably best known for his smaller daylilies. On the whole he has used soft, subtler colour combinations than Pauline Henry, although his 'Jason Mark', a pastel cream-buff with a contrasting dark purple eye, is up there with the brightest. His 'Little Red Warbler' is one of the best smaller reds available, opening well and flowering for long periods in a wide range of climates. Crochet's 'Yellow Lollipop', blooming several times a season, winner of the Florida Sunshine Cup and the Donn Fischer Memorial Award, is the nearest rival to 'Stella de Oro', the best-known miniature daylily ever raised.

9

SPIDER & UNUSUAL DAYLILIES

Marc King

The Classic Spiders and their close relatives the Spider Variants are modern categories of large daylily flower forms that possess open-faced blossoms and very long, slender floral segments. Many open nocturnally and have varying degrees of fragrance. The history of Spider forms dates back to the advent of *Hemerocallis* breeding.

The elegant, spider-like, long and narrow tepals of the fragrant nocturnal species *H. altissima* and *H. citrina* attracted the attention of early daylily enthusiasts. Around the beginning of the twentieth century, countless crosses were made using these two soft yellow, branched and floriferous daylilies with different diurnal species of the tawny-orange *H. fulva* group. Tens of thousands of seedlings were raised, and within just a few seedling generations, large and slender star and trumpet shapes, as well as wide-tepalled, fuller flower forms were being selected and registered.

Many of these early hybrids possessed a blend of flower characteristics that was, at that time, entirely new: namely early-morning-opening, inherited from the nocturnals, with the ability to remain open all day, inherited from the diurnals. Some hybrids also displayed the added quality of very extended blossom life, a characteristic then only present in the Lemon Daylily, *H. lilioasphodelus*, during cool weather conditions. Many of the first 'Classic' or 'True' Spider daylilies display extended bloom, nocturnally opening traits and varying degrees of fragrance. However, the hybridization of these two specie groups often resulted in more complex reproduction requirements: pod fertility the evening or night before the flowers opened, and pollen fertility during the following day. The ploidy of these first hybrids also presented numerous problems for early breeders, with many incompatible diploid, spontaneous tetraploid and anueploid types in the melting pot. (Flow-

ers with the combined nocturnal-diurnal type of fertility cycle are best pollinated by opening the swollen buds the night before they are due to open and placing dried pollen on the stigma tip.) Some of the most beautiful modern Spiders present the same difficulties to the hybridist as these near-species hybrids.

HEMEROCALLIS ALTISSIMA

An early clone of the very productive species seed parent *H. altissima* had large, unusually long and slender floral segments and was approximately 2m (6ft) tall. This clone, which was used in some of the original Spiders, is now lost to cultivation and exists only in the germplasm of some of the registrations of Dr Stout, who used it in numerous crosses. All clones of this species that I am familiar with today have much smaller flowers, ranging from 6–7.5cm (2½–3in) in diameter and approximately 10cm (4in) long, and they are only 1.2–1.4m (4–4½) feet tall.

Both *H. altissima* and *H. citrina* set seed readily and pass on very robust well-branched and fragrant seedlings with slender, spider-like flower forms and a very long period of bloom. The very thin substance of their flowers is also often predominant among their seedlings, of which 'Hyperion' is an example. This early hybrid (Mead 1924), with exceptionally long and slender tepals, has in its parentage *H. citrina*, *H. thunbergii* and a double dose of the then spectacularly large and showy, albeit slightly tender, evergreen, *H. aurantiaca* 'Major'. 'Dream Light', now lost to cultivation, was a very tall, refined Classic Spider out of *H. altissima* × 'Hyperion'. Although figuring importantly in the ancestry of some of the early Spiders, 'Hyperion' itself produces flowers that are too closed to allow it be considered as a member of the Spider-form class.

THE 'KINDLY LIGHT' STORY

Introduced by Wilds of Missouri in 1951, 'Kindly Light's (Bechtold 1950) large, soft yellow flowers and long,

'Cleopatra' has a wide, deep violet, chevron eye on petals and sepals, a vivid contrast to the melon ground colour.

ribbon-like segments – despite being on the slenderest scapes, liable to bend with the flower's weight – caused quite a stir among daylily enthusiasts as it represented the ultimate Spider ideal. 'Kindly Light' is the most historically important Spider ever introduced and to it is attributed two distinct waves of interest in the Spider forms. No parentages were recorded for many of the exquisitely refined Spiders of the late 1940s and early 1950s from Lemoine Bechtold, so that one can only guess their specific genetic makeup. It is apparent, however, from the soft salmon blush in the eyezone of 'Kindly Light' that the, then newly discovered, very slender-tepalled, rose-eyed *H. fulva* 'Rosea' had been involved. This is also evident from the fact that 'Kindly Light' breeds this 'Rosea'-influenced eye rather dominantly. 'Hyperion' is also a very likely part of the ancestry of 'Kindly Light'.

At least five 'Kindly Light' clones were introduced into cultivation, each displaying extremely long and graceful segments, and three showing some 'Rosea' pigmentation in the throat area. However, the five vary greatly in pod and pollen fertility. I grow two of these clones, both of which are top-branched; one is very pod fertile, the other virtually sterile. The true 'Kindly Light' seems a soft yellow self at first but displays a faint pinkish-salmon-blush eye in cooler weather. It has quite fertile pollen but is pod sterile. It is believed that Bechtold released a small group of very similar Classic Spiders over the first few years of 'Kindly Light's popularity. One particular clone, widely distributed in the New England area, has been both pod and pollen fertile but is slightly smaller than the cultivar released at introduction.

CONSERVATIONISTS & THE SPIDER RULING
Classic Spiders are extremely difficult to hybridize; daylilies of extremely refined Classic Spider proportions, with the linear elegance of 'Kindly Light', are a rare commodity, and a few Spiders whose measurements fall just within the definition (see below) in most gardens have wider segments in others, especially in cooler climates.

In the mid-1980s a conservation group, part of the American Hemerocallis Society's Spider Round Robin, began an extensive research project to collect and categorize the different forms and proportions of Spider and spider-like daylilies. The group was headed by Rosemary Whitacre of Columbia, Missouri, perhaps the most significant person of this conservation initiative. Willie Belle Wilson, Nell Crandall, Betty Roberts, Geraldine Courturier, Ned Roberts and Lois Burns formed the rest of the nucleus involved in this historic project.

Harris Olson, a wealthy benefactor, agreed to sponsor an award specifically for Spiders, and this led to the group

'Golligwog' is a large, opulent crispate Unusual Form – always elegant.

determining the ratios and qualities that define Classic Spider form, which in turn led in 1994 to the American Hemerocallis Society ruling that slender forms with a petal length to petal width ratio of 5.0:1 and higher would be called Classic Spiders and those with a ratio of 4.0:1 to 4.9:1 would be called Spider Variants; and these two categories would be eligible for the Olson Award. Spiders and Spider Variants must also have flat-open (rather than trumpet) shape flowers and a small heart (the point where the petals and sepals meet at the perianth tube).

To the gardener seeking an elegant, Unusual-form, hardy daylily these ratios and measurements are perhaps of little interest, but once one has seen numerous slender-formed daylilies, the Classic Spider stands apart through its sheer linear elegance: colour often being a secondary consideration.

The Spider Variants, being fuller in form, display more colour surface. Most 'modern' cultivars registered today are actually the first and second generation children of Spiders developed during the first period of their popularity.

Classic Spider and Spider Variant daylilies must comply with the criteria above at their recognized shows. However, many breeders and nurserymen, not understanding the distinction between these forms, have given the name Spider or Spider Variant to more commonplace, long-petalled trumpet and lily forms. In the 1990s a new wave of interest thrust the Spiders into the limelight. But when I first began my search for these almost forgotten daylilies in 1985, very few were listed and long waiting lists were common.

UNUSUAL FORM DAYLILIES

In researching and categorizing hundreds of Spider forms, many non-compliant but very exotically formed daylilies were rediscovered. Their base forms range from large, sharply pointed stars to round-tipped, strap-shaped near Spider Variants. Tepal shapes can vary from long and slender to wide-tipped and spatulate, as well as somewhat full willow-leaf forms, but they possess characteristics placing them apart from the popular round form and the Spiders.

In proposals made to the American Hemerocallis Society at the 1998 Midwinter Symposium for the inclusion of this new category into their judged Shows, Bob Schwarz, Chairman of the Exotics/Unusual Forms Subcommittee, presented a definition that we, of the committee, formulated simply: The Exotics/Unusual Forms must display 'distinctive petal and/or sepal shapes (Crispation, see below) and/or have distinctly spatulate-form tepals. The spatulate forms possess floral segments that are slender at

the bases and much wider at the tips, as in 'Cerulean Star' and 'Moonlit Summerbird'. In May 1998, the American Hermerocallis Society Board decided that the term Unusual Form should be used to describe those daylilies that have hitherto been known as Exotics or Exotic Form, as well as Unusual Form daylilies.

The distinctive tepal shapes also include an exciting category known as 'Crispata'. Among daylily enthusiasts, this refers to a sculptural twirling, quilling, twisting, curling, and/or pinching of the floral segments. These arise from unequal tensions in the floral segments: the surface tissues expanding faster than those of the backs of the flowers, or irregular tensions along the tepal edges, and so on. The effect is that the faster-expanding cell layers compensate by rolling or twisting back onto the flower. These crispate patterns render greater sculptural depth and movement within the form. Weather conditions play a role in the expression of these crispation patterns. Sudden cool weather in a warm

UNUSUAL FLOWER FORMS

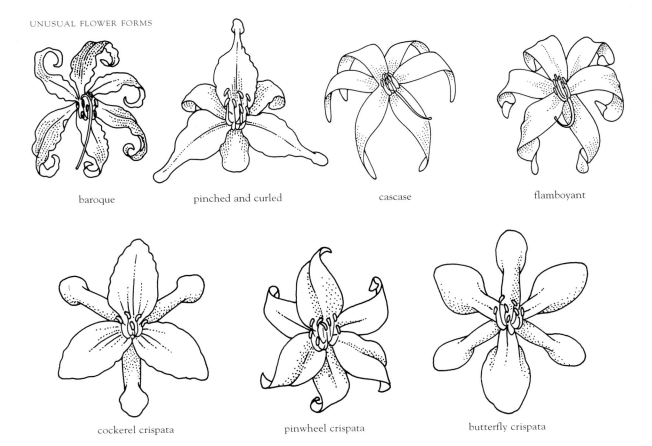

baroque

pinched and curled

cascase

flamboyant

cockerel crispata

pinwheel crispata

butterfly crispata

'Hurricane Bob', whose name was suggested by its swirling baroque form.

spell can inhibit the irregular tension development, creating a more or less smooth flower. Warm weather usually enhances the inherent crispate tendencies, sometimes adding extra bounce and swing to the curls and twirls.

Variable Crispatas, those with changing expression of crispation, are the commonest crispate forms. Consistent crispation patterns have been rare occurrences, but a few stable crispate forms I have observed in my collection of Spiders and Unusual Form daylilies are Cockerels, Pinwheels, Butterflies, Pinched and Curled Crispatas, Baroques, Flamboyants and Cascades.

Cockerel crispata has sepals that are quilled, and petals that lie out more or less flat. An excellent example of this is Lenington's 'My Pink' pictured on the front cover of the Summer 1990 AHS Journal. Another example is the rose-red tetraploid 'Bimini Twist' (Schwarz).

Pinwheel crispata has segments that twirl playfully or fold in the outer half of their length, an example being the full-formed star 'Peach Pinwheel'.

Butterfly crispata is often a combination of form and quilling: the base form has wide, spatulate segments narrowing distinctly towards the heart, with quilling only of the sepal base. The effect is an open-hearted blossom with wide, wing-like flower segments. The well-branched, soft peach 'Golliwog' is an excellent example of this rare form. The newer 'Asterisk' also often displays the Butterfly type of crispation pattern; my own soft lilac 'Dancing Summerbird', is a true Butterfly form.

Pinched and Curled crispata pattern displays curled back and pinched tips. The late Richard Webster created a number of beautiful examples, including 'Fuchsia Fashion'.

Baroque has been used often with reference to the Unusual Forms but applies mainly to Spiders and Spider Variants, their slender tepals curling and twisting, evoking images of decorative baroque ornamentation. A beautiful example is the new tetraploid 'Hurricane Bob' (Schwarz).

Flamboyant pattern refers to a stable crispation of back curling and twirling, like a cascade of ringlet locks of hair in a Victorian wig. Excellent examples are the salmon-pink and near-white blend 'Lola Branham', the chevron-eyed mauve 'Kirstin's Corsage' and the salmon 'Medusa's Glance'.

Cascade is an open-form pattern. Somewhat slender and without crispation, the flower is relaxed and wide open, as in 'Orchid Corsage'.

WHAT THE FUTURE HOLDS

The race is on for the development of the Classic Spider and Spider Variant as well as Unusual Forms on the diploid and tetraploid levels. For many years, the work of the late Richard Webster of Arab, Alabama, was perhaps the most significant in the field of Unusual Form tetraploids. More recent tetraploid work has begun to incorporate converted tetraploids from the older, Classic Spider gene pool and 'Miracle Worker' (Dickerson 1995) out of 'Tet Kevin Michael Coyne', a grandchild of 'Kindly Light', and 'Boney Maroney' (also 1995), produced the forerunners of a new age of breeding for Spiders on the tetraploid level.

American breeders Bob Schwarz, Ken Durio, Dan Trimmer, Patrick Stamile, Mort Morss and others on both sides of the Atlantic are working with converted Spider Variants such as 'Cat's Cradle', 'Red Thrill', 'Spider Miracle', 'Fol De Rol', 'Wildest Dreams', 'Black Plush', 'Garden Portrait', 'Spindazzle', 'Parfait' and 'De Colores'. The results of their work will soon be available. Many of us who are working with tetraploid Spiders also hope to incorporate patterns and the vibrancy of colours only found in the tetraploids, such as gold and picotee edges, white and buff fimbriation, and purples and reds with watermarks. Extremely tall-scaped Spiders are also in the pipeline, with both diploid and converted tetraploid *H. altissima* germplasm figuring in the parentages.

Current breeding is producing clearer pinks, lavenders and rich purples as well as ivories and near-whites, far surpassing the present predominantly yellow, orange and red hues. Further dimensions in the future will include double Spiders and new Unusual Forms.

GARDEN USES OF SPIDER & UNUSUAL DAYLILIES

The Classic Spider has a slender, ribbon-like flower that lends itself not only to traditional border schemes, settings in which a great variety of colour and shape are required in a kind of floral art gallery, but also in borders with predominantly sub-tropical focus as well as in simplistic, Japanese-influenced garden settings. The True Spiders are an excellent foil to some of the more visually compact plants in the traditional border, their thin and wispy flowers relaxing the display. The following are successful combinations I have had at Casa Rocca.

In red I have planted 'Black Plush' (blackish-red), 'Stoplight' (light medium red), 'Red Ribbons' (bright medium red), dwarf red-flowering, near species cannas, *Imperata cylindrica* 'Red Baron' and *Crocosmia* 'Lucifer'. 'Marse Connell', a very thin, large flower, and 'Red Rain', a smaller, green-throated flower, are also excellent bright red Spiders and have been planted above blue veronicas and salvias.

In yellow and golden hues the selection available is larger. Classic Spiders include 'Cat's Cradle', 'Lacy Marionette', 'Garden Portrait', 'Lines Of Splendor', 'Kindly Light' and 'Lady Fingers'. And there is the heavy-blooming, soft russet-eyed, golden Spider Variant 'Divertissment' or, perhaps, the well-matched, out-facing deep yellow 'Spider Miracle', another Variant. These command attention in front of a slender, fountaining *Miscanthus sinensis* selection such as 'Malepartus' or 'Silberfeder', combined with *Kniphofia* 'Little Maid', with wavy-edged, solid green-leafed *Hosta* 'Invincible', and *H.* 'Sea Octopus' or *H.* 'Green Fountain', tucked into shadier postions. The visual impact is a study in subtle lines and gentle movement.

For rich purple effects, the maroon-violet to deep plum eyes of cultivars like the slightly tender 'De Colores', 'Mountain Top Experience', or the hardy 'Persian Pattern', 'Parade of Peacocks', 'Marked By Lydia', and the sometimes tender 'Cleopatra', match the so-called 'horticultural purple' of purple-leafed cannas, *Plantago major* 'Rubrifolia', *Rheum palmatum* 'Rubrum', and *Heuchera* 'Palace Purple'.

Associated with these companion plants, the Spiders and the Unusual Form daylilies seem to dance quietly to inaudible music. In this choreographed setting of bold and subtle leaf forms, these hardy daylilies transcend their temperate origins, giving the impression of rare terrestrial orchids collected from remote parts of the globe.

10

DAYLILY COLLECTIONS

Some daylilies perform well in cold and temperate climates, while others do better in hotter, sub-tropical regions: in recognition of this, the American Hemerocallis Society has a long-established system of display gardens in each of its regions, thus gardeners living in the vicinity can see which daylilies do best in garden conditions similar to their own. Plainly, in order to build up a representative collection of those daylilies that do best in any one area, a number of others have to be trialled and discarded and so, since this is an on-going situation, there will always be a number of plants being tested for suitability, a few of which may turn out in the end to be unsuitable.

A similar system of display gardens is currently being established throughout Europe by Hemerocallis Europa (see p.135). These gardens are again intended to reveal which daylilies do well in which parts of Europe, but they go further in that each collection is unique in the range of daylilies it grows.

Our collection at Apple Court is planted to display modern hybrid daylilies in a colour-themed, formal garden setting, not only to enhance the garden but to give visitors a living catalogue of what is now available. Apple Court particularly concentrates on the Guidry and Kirchhoff introductions that have proved so satisfactory in a mild, temperate climate. Further south, at Little Hermitage, on a windy hill top on the Isle of Wight, Jan Wyers has a collection of Small-Flowered and Miniature daylilies (p.127) and Andy Wyers has just been awarded National Collection status for his post-1960, large-flowered hybrids. Also on the Isle of Wight, at Ventnor Botanic Gardens, with its even milder climate, a collection of Spiders, Spider Variants and Unusual Forms is being gathered and will prove a useful way of testing the hardiness of some of these forms. Eve Lytton's collection, also in southern Hampshire,

concentrates on modern daylilies in pinks, mauves and purple, with an emphasis on daylilies introduced by Bill Munson, Steve Moldovan and Patrick Stamile. Derek Carver's collection in Surrey is an eclectic selection of modern hybrids interspersed with plantings of irises and a wide range of companion plants.

Gerald Sinclair, a former schoolmaster, who runs The Nursery Further Afield in Oxfordshire, has a collection of English and European daylily cultivars, majoring on the daylilies raised in Essex by the late Robert Coe. Out of some 180 cultivars introduced by Coe, Gerald Sinclair has located over fifty. Information gained from studying daylilies growing in his comparatively harsh (by British standards) climate will help to pinpoint those that are suitable for some of Britain's less than ideal conditions. This collection is also expected to form one of the National Reference Collections. Leeds Parks Department, already a National Reference Collection holder, will shortly also become a Hemerocallis Europa Display Garden since the Yorkshire climate equates well to some parts of the European mainland.

In Europe itself, particularly in Germany, there are a number of Hemerocallis Europa Display Gardens in the making. In Schoeppingen, near Munster, Germany, Werner Reinerman runs the Schoeppinger Irisgarten. He has an extensive collection of the newest American daylilies, as well as a great number of his own introductions that were bred under European conditions for European gardens. In Hofheim, near Frankfurt, Harald Jahr has started a comprehensive collection of very new American cultivars in his Taunusgarten. These are planted with some of his own very successful introductions. Hemerocallis Europa has one of its oldest display gardens, Fubkenrech Botanical Garden, near Dirmingen, in the Saarland. This garden attracts over 20,000 visitors each year and the hemerocallis bed there displays a choice of older to modern daylilies in all colours and forms.

The copper, bronze and orange daylily border at Apple Court. Beds are tightly corseted with box hedging.

On the foot of the southern Black Forest in Waldshut-Tiengen, Anja and Matthias Thomsen-Stork have designed a daylily display garden planted with older, newer and newest daylilies, both American and European, with all sorts of companion plants. The Homburger Staudengarten also includes a selection of Spider-type daylilies and a special collection of more than twenty *Hemerocallis* species.

In Switzerland there is the wonderful Schafberg Garden of Rolf Hegi and Peter Aerne in Menznau near Lucerne. This garden has a very large collection of daylilies, from the older sorts to the very latest, with the accent on spider forms. It includes the most comprehensive collection of daylilies raised by Dr John Lambert in Europe.

And at Rocca D'Arazzo in the Piedmont region of Italy, Marc King has built up a very big collection of around 1000 different older to very modern cultivars in the Casa Rocca garden. A speciality in this garden are the Spiders and Spider-types, together with a number of Marc King's own introductions.

Both Cor Govaerts and Francois Verhaert have comprehensive Hemerocallis Europa display gardens in Belgium.

All these display gardens are open to the public either on advertised dates or on application to the owner. Full details are given in 'Where To See Daylilies' appendix.

NATIONAL REFERENCE COLLECTIONS OF HEMEROCALLIS

Hemerocallis feature prominently in the work of Britain's National Council for the Conservation of Plants and Gardens (NCCPG), the patron of which is His Royal Highness, The Prince of Wales. One of the aims of the NCCPG is to establish, through their National Collections Scheme, living museums of genera extant in the British Isles.

With over 40,000 daylilies now registered, it is very unlikely that one single garden, however large, would be able to house a complete and comprehensive reference collection. Fortunately *Hemerocallis* sub-divide easily into several different categories, which has allowed a fairly wide and representative range to be amassed in different gardens by a diversity of individual gardeners and organizations.

Leeds Parks Department

Since 1985, Leeds Parks Department (part of Leeds Leisure Services) has, as part of their now excellent and varied National Hemerocallis Reference Collection, been gathering cultivars raised by Robert Coe, the best-known and most prolific of the few post-war British hybridizers. Robert Coe's work with daylilies took place during the years 1963–73.

Robert Coe, already a noted breeder of *Kniphofia* and *Iris*, received *Hemerocallis* seed and plants from the well-known plantsman and *Hemerocallis* and *Iris* breeder Hubert Fischer of Illinois in the late 1950s and early 1960s. He began a programme of hybridizing using both diploids and latterly tetraploids, which he thought would be suitable for British and European climates. Members of the British Hosta and Hemerocallis Society are liaising with Leeds Parks Department in an endeavour to save as many Coe daylilies as possible from extinction and redistribute them to the nursery trade. ('Elaine Strutt', the first British pink-flowered tetraploid, and other Coe varieties, are being grown in my garden at Apple Court and it is encouraging to know that the tall-scaped, apricot-melon 'Michele Coe', one of the most popular daylilies in our garden, is being used by Eve Lytton (pp.107–8) in her current hybridizing programme.)

Also displaying collections of daylilies contributed by The Savill Garden and the Royal Horticultural Society's garden at Wisley, the Leeds Hemerocallis Collection is at The Hollies Park on the outskirts of the city in south-west Yorkshire. The Hollies Park is a typical Victorian garden with display beds, lawns and a tennis court, and the daylilies are growing in beds with *Philadelphus*, another National Reference Collection. The daylily collection was started by the then Curator, Gordon Cooper. Recently retired, he still takes an interest in his project, now under the control of Martin Walker.

Anthony House

The late Lady Carew Pole was chatelaine of the historic Georgian stone manor house and grounds, Antony House, situated in an idyllic setting close to Torpoint on the south coast of Cornwall, near Plymouth. One of the most renowned English daylily collectors of the post-war era, she had a keen interest in American daylilies, lecturing widely there and attending American Hemerocallis Society Conventions. She initially obtained her daylilies from Elizabeth Nesmith of Missouri and Dr McEwen of Maine. Latterly her plants came from Frank Childs, Ophelia Taylor, Gilbert Wild, Ezra Kraus and W.B. Flory. She also acquired daylilies from the late Harry Randall of Beaconsfield who, in the 1960s, raised some worthwhile hybrids.

Most of Lady Carew Pole's daylilies are in the softer shades of pink, yellow, mauve and polychrome. They are now planted in narrow beds at the foot of the ancient south-facing stone walls found in many parts of the garden although at one time she had over six hundred varieties planted in rows in the Walled Garden and The Garden Field. She raised a few hybrids herself and these were named after members of her family and, although few have ever been widely distributed, her namesake, the beautiful deep red 'Cynthia Mary' is still available in the trade.

When she died in 1982 the gardens and part of the grounds were made over to the National Trust and her daylilies subsequently offered to the NCCPG as a possible National Reference Collection. The Collection was formally instituted in 1985 and it was agreed that it would remain as Lady Carew Pole left it with daylilies neither added nor removed. Any surplus stock would be sold off.

Little Hermitage

Jan and Andy Wyers have gathered their collection of daylilies on a wooded hilltop, some 100m (350ft) above sea level, on St Catherine's Down near the southern tip of the Isle of Wight. The parameters of Jan's collection follow the American Hemerocallis Society's definitions of Small-flowered and Miniature (p.113). There are at present two borders of these colourful little daylilies amounting to about 250 named varieties.

The site is windswept – exposed to the southerly gales and cold north-easterly winds. The soil is clay and the pH veers towards alkaline over most of the garden. The only

help the daylilies receive is an occasional mulch and a twice-yearly heavy watering when wide cracks appear in the soil: Jan Wyers believes in allowing the daylilies to prove themselves hardy enough to withstand any neglect future growers might inflict upon them.

Jan and Andy Wyers have done much to raise the profile of daylilies in Britain and have exhibited their daylilies on three occasions in the Garden Heritage Marquee at the Royal Horticultural Society's Summer Flower Show at Hampton Court which, by good fortune, occurs in July, peak-blooming time for daylilies.

Epsom & Ewell Parks Departments

Epsom & Ewell Borough Council, Surrey, although not at present meeting some of the criteria demanded of a National Reference Collection, have amassed a large collection of older cultivars at Shadbolt Park in the borough. It is planned that eventually these plants will be propagated for future sale and the money raised will go to the acquisition of more modern stock. This collection consists mostly of traditional trumpet-shaped sorts but Spiders and Unusual Forms are well-represented. Derek Carver is liaising with the Borough Council, which is in his locality, and can arrange viewing of the Collection.

Part of the daylily garden at Little Hermitage, Isle of Wight, home of the National Reference Collection of Small-flowered and Miniature daylilies.

11

DAYLILIES IN NORTH AMERICA

Kevin P. Walek

Over the last hundred years the popularity of daylilies in America has grown immensely. At the beginning of the twentieth century, the daylilies in cultivation were predominantly species or, for those who could afford them, cultivars acquired from early British hybridizers. However, after 1910, with the first efforts of Arlow B Stout, hybrids started to become more popular, and by the 1970s daylilies were the bestselling perennial in America: today they are still right up at the top.

AMERICAN HEMEROCALLIS SOCIETY

The United States can rightly claim to have transformed the daylily. Breeders from Dr Stout onwards, strove to raise plants with ever broader floral segments, in a wider range of clearer colours, from the small number of species and limited colour range at their disposal. The daylilies we grow in our gardens today carry in their genes the hard won advances wrought by men and women such as Lemoine Bechtold, Frank Childs, Elmer Claar, Orville Fay, Hubert Fischer, David Hall, John Lambert, W.B. MacMillan, James Marsh, Virginia Peck, Edna and Elsie Spalding, Alan Wild, Lucille Williamson and many others. However, hybridizers alone could not have created the impact that the daylily has had on American gardens: they were responding to the demands of their customers.

In 1943, under the auspices of the *Flower Grower* magazine, the first exclusively Hemerocallis Round Robin was formed. Subsequently in 1946, the 'Flower Lady', Helen Field Fischer (so-called as hostess of the radio program, *The Garden Club of the Air*), arranged a Round Robin Party in Shenandoah, Iowa. As an immediate result of this meeting, 556 attendees became charter members of the Midwest Hemerocallis Society and by the end of the year the membership had grown to 757. Today the membership exceeds 10,000.

'Janice Brown', one of the most popular daylilies ever raised, is much used for breeding as it passes on striking eye patterns.

In 1948, along with the production of its first simple constitution, the society was renamed The Hemerocallis Society. This name was to last only two years, and in 1950 the society adopted new bylaws and a new name: American Hemerocallis Society (AHS).

When the AHS adopted its constitution in 1948, 10 regions were formed. In 1950, upon passage of bylaws, a realignment took place with the creation of two additional regions and Canadian members were asked to affiliate themselves with the regions that they adjoined. By 1959 the number of regions had grown to 15 and at that time foreign membership was designated as Region 20. (At present there are no Regions 16–19.)

The regional structure of the AHS allows for local daylily clubs, with their own newsletters, addressing the concerns of gardeners with similar growing characteristics. It also allows for the dissemination of information by distinguished daylily speakers on a variety of topics, and for garden visits and slide shows, all of which enable local gardeners to have information on the introductions that will do best in their region and the best sources of these introductions.

Can-Am – The Circle Grows Larger

On April 5th, 1997, the first annual Region 4 Can-Am Muster was held. The idea of holding a daylily meeting/symposium at the Royal Botanical Gardens in Hamilton, Ontario, Canada was an idea born of Region 4's fortunate expansion into the eastern provinces of Canada, and the enthusiasm of Kathy Guest (President of the Buffalo Area Daylily Society). Regional Vice-President, Melanie Mason, gave the go ahead necessary from the US side as did Canadian daylily people such as Maureen Strong (Canadian e-mail liaison), and hybridizers John Peat and Ted Petit, as well as Doug Lycett and Henry Lorrain of 'We're in the Hayfield Now' daylily garden in Ontario.

Internet E-mail Robin

Beginning in 1995, a group of AHS members, who were also computer *aficionados*, began a round robin over the Internet. Unlike the standard round robin, which relies on the postal system, the Internet e-mail robin is nearly instantaneous. By this means it is possible to isolate and resolve pest problems, disseminate growing information, share hybridizing successes (and failures) and other related concerns in days rather than months.

SOUTHERN EXODUS & REGIONAL DAYLILIES

While it is possible to grow daylilies from zone 10 through to zone 2, not all will span the full range of growing zones and, consequently, great discussion is taking place over whether or not we will be seeing regionalized hybridizing.

While there are well known hybridizers in most of the regions, some well-respected northern hybridizers have moved south, most often to Florida. For example, when Patrick and Grace Stamile moved from Region 4 (which includes much of New England, plus New York) to Florida, many daylily lovers from Zone 7 northwards worried that it meant the end of Patrick's strong dormant tetraploid large flower programme and, similarly, Grace's dormant diploid small flower programme. The jury is still out on the change, but out of Patrick's 17 large flower introductions for 1997, 15 were still dormant cultivars. Leo Sharp, a hybridizer in the Midwest, has acquired a breeding site in Florida, as has Ted Petit, an up and coming hybridizer from Canada. Now, Dan Trimmer, another hybridizer from the Long Island, NY area of Region 4, has made the move to Florida.

What is the Problem with Northern Hybridizers Moving South?

The primary concern is that, when grown in the south, dormant daylilies have a tendency to look more like grass, and never achieve their optimum performance, as they need the rest period to produce the energy for the next year's flush of foliage and flowering. Without an adequate dormancy, some dormants actually get smaller until they vanish back into the ground. At the same time, some of the semi-evergreens and evergreens do not perform as well in the north as they do in the south. Some of these problems relate to the flower, and others to the longevity of the entire plant.

Winter conditions Many growers have discovered that sub-freezing temperatures without snow cover can be far worse for semi-evergreen and evergreen daylilies, than when there is snow. Even in nursery gardens of close proximity, such as those of John Benz and Curt Hanson in Ohio, snow cover has allowed cultivars to be grown in one garden when they will not survive in the other. In part this is due to 'ground heaving' during freeze/thaw cycles, and susceptible daylilies being planted too late. Many growers set a date in September as the absolute last to dig and divide, and even that is not always successful.

Some regions experience multiple freeze/thaw cycles, combined with repeated ice storms. Again, the majority of losses in these cases are semi-evergreen and evergreen daylilies, which are apparently more susceptible to the oxygen deprivation to the crown that occurs under these conditions.

Is this the Death Knell for the Northern Hybridizer?

Far from it. There are still many well established northern hybridizers, as well as good up and coming breeding programmes to fill the gaps. The conclusion is that, even if one worries about the dormant/evergreen debate, or fears whether southern daylilies are northern hardy, there are enough high quality hybridizers growing their new and exciting daylilies in all regions and locales.

Light

Another interesting north/south variation, even more evident in some British gardens, is the effect of light on the prominence of certain types of eyezone. In comparing photos of daylilies it has been noticed that in cooler or shadier conditions, the chalky watermark or negative eye, particularly if of a similar shade to the main colour, may not be visible. With a greater number of sunless daylight hours in Britain, the eyes of many daylilies never become anywhere near as pronounced as they are for most United States growers, although a site in a sheltered, sunny place goes a long way to alleviate this problem. Further, the scent of fragrant daylilies tends to diminish under cooler conditions; some northern US gardeners have experienced this.

It is usually recommended that daylilies perform best in full sun but in the searing 32–38°C (90–100°F) summer heat experienced by many North American gardeners, there are some exceptions. These are the darker reds, black-reds and shades of purple from royal purple to black-purple, all of which do better in half a day's shade, preferably in the afternoon. This prevents the pigment from bleaching inwards from the segment edges, changing colour or greasing or melting. This difficulty is easily overcome by planting the darker coloured daylilies in the filtered shade of trees such as the dogwood (*Cornus floridulus*), the Honey Locust (*Gleditsia triacanthos* var. *inermis*), *Styrax japonica* or the Japanese Scholar Tree, *Sophora japonica* thus providing the daylilies with early morning sun only. Lighter coloured daylilies thrive in extreme heat which emphasizes green throats, brings out subtleties in complicated washed and etched eye patterns, makes near-white daylilies a purer white and enhances picotee, gold-wire and braided edges.

DAYLILY COLLECTIONS

In the history of the use of daylilies in North American gardens a clear transition occurred. This can be viewed as similar to a gardener changing from a landscape scheme of Jekyllesque, mixed perennial borders to a monogenus, monoculture collector's garden.

Early in the century gardeners would place a few species daylilies, and possibly some of the early cultivars, at the back of a sunny perennial border, whereas, today, daylilies are often the predominant plant in the garden.

Not all daylily enthusiasts, however, are monoculture gardeners, preferring to set off the daylily blooms against a background of ornamental grasses or coloured-leafed shrubs or to grow them among perennials so that they are part of an integral border. Some gardeners seek to match and compliment the colours of their daylilies with perennials such as *Phlox paniculata*, *Coreopsis verticillata* 'Moonbeam', certain of the new sun-tolerant purple-leafed heucheras, ground-hugging ajugas, sedum cultivars and, of course, with roses.

It is estimated that among the 10,000 current members of the American Hemerocallis Society, the average number of daylilies exceeds 200 per garden. Among the AHS National Display Gardens, of which there are 204, it is estimated that the average is in excess of 500 different cultivars, with some gardens easily exceeding 1000 cultivars.

The AHS display garden programme was 'established to display the very best cultivars of daylilies to the general public. Its purpose is to educate the visitor about modern daylilies and how they can be used effectively in landscapes.'

The following is a list of the criteria needed to become an AHS National Display Garden:

• The garden should include registered named cultivars, containing samples of tetraploids, diploids, miniatures, small-flowered, large-flowered, doubles, Spiders, Unusual Forms, eyed, edged, and examples of hybridizing breakthroughs that have not yet been classified into a category.
• The growing conditions and culture should show daylilies to their maximum potential.
• All plants should be marked with the name of both the cultivar and the hybridizer.
• The garden should be open to the public during the growing season.

If a gardener feels that they meet this criteria they may apply to their relevant Regional Vice-President (RVP).

The garden must be inspected by the RVP of the AHS and recommended by the RVP to the Display Garden Chairperson for inclusion.

While generally it is the round (bagel), ruffled daylilies that are the most sought-after, there is a surge of interest in the species and historic forms. To this end there are now several display gardens wholly devoted to these.

See Where to See Daylilies p.154.

AWARDS & HONOURS

Awards and Honours are given for specific types of achievement either in the area of hybridizing or in individual contributions to the society. The Popularity Poll (p.131), was part of the Awards and Honours Programme until 1963 when it was removed as it was thought to be more an indicator of popular appeal.

The majority of awards relating to specific cultivars are voted on by garden judges. The term 'garden judge' is a bit of a misnomer. It is used to distinguish them from 'exhibition judges', who judge various cultivars, either on-scape or by the single flower, removed from the scape and displayed on an exhibition bench. The garden judge assesses the cultivar in the garden and is judging the complete plant, including the foliage, *in situ*. This provides a better picture of the garden value of the plant.

Each region is allowed to have up to 15 per cent of its membership as garden judges, but many regions have far below that number. In fact, the number is lowest among the northern regions, and it has been argued that the winners have thus been skewed in favour of the southern cultivars.

All of the following are within the purview of garden judge balloting.

Junior Citation (JC) Some like to refer to this award as the 'watch me get better' award. It is awarded to new and unintroduced cultivars exhibiting outstanding qualities and receiving 10 votes. This award usually results from observation in the garden of the hybridizer who is contemplating its introduction and thus does not indicate good performance outside that region. There may be multiple winners of this award.

Honorable Mention (HM) Receipt of an Honorable Mention is the AHS's first stamp of approval. An HM is awarded to a cultivar if it has received at least 12 votes from different regions in the United States. The votes are based upon observation in the garden judge's own region. As with the Junior Citation there are multiple winners in a year.

Award of Merit (AM) The Award of Merit is intended to announce that a particular cultivar is not only outstanding but is also a good grower across a broad spectrum of growing conditions. To be eligible for consideration a

'Pumpkin Kid', a beautifully round and ruffled, Southern-raised daylily with a subtle eye pattern.

cultivar must have received the HM not less than three years previously and will remain eligible for three years. This award is given to the ten cultivars that get the highest votes under a formula whereby a cultivar must receive votes from at least a half of the US regions and not more than a third of the votes may come from one region, if more than a third of the votes come from one region, the votes in excess of a third are disallowed and the results ranked accordingly.

Stout Silver Medal (SSM) This is the highest honor bestowed upon a daylily cultivar by the AHS, and is appropriately named after Arlow B. Stout. To be eligible for this award a cultivar must have received an AM not less than three years previously and will remain eligible for three years. The Stout Medal is awarded to the cultivar receiving the largest number of votes cast. In case of a tie, there will be multiple winners. Recent winners: 'Siloam Double Classic' (1993), 'Janice Brown' (1994), 'Neal Berrey' (1995), 'Wedding Band' (1996), 'Always Afternoon' (1997).

Special Awards

In addition to the system that leads to the selection of a Stout Medal winner, the garden judges also vote for a number of awards that go to cultivars of a certain type or exhibiting certain characteristics. A brief description of some of these awards and recent winners follows.

Donn Fischer Memorial (DF) This award is given to the most outstanding registered miniature flower, which must be less than 7.5cm (3in) in diameter and have previously won an HM. Recent winners: 'Jason Salter' (1993), 'Dragon's Orb' (1994), 'Patchwork Puzzle' (1995), 'After the Fall' (1996), 'Dark Avenger' (1997).

Annie T. Giles Award (AG) This award is given to the most outstanding registered small-flowered daylily, which must be greater than 7.5cm (3in) but less than 11cm (4½in) in diameter and have previously won an HM. Recent winners: 'Exotic Echo' tied with 'Little Deeke' (1993), 'Strawberry Candy' (1994), 'Siloam David Kirchhoff' (1995), 'Custard Candy' (1996), 'Dragon's Eye' (1997).

Don C. Stevens Award (DS) This award is given to the best registered and introduced, boldly eyed or banded daylily, and must have previously won an HM. No hybridizer may win in two consecutive years. Recent winners: 'Pumpkin Kid' (1992), 'Always Afternoon' (1993), 'Jason Salter' (1994), 'Strawberry Candy' (1995), 'Siloam David Kirchhoff' (1996), 'Pirate's Patch' (1997).

Ida Munson Award (IM) This award is given to the most outstanding registered double-flowered daylily, which must be consistently double and have previously won an HM. Recent winners: 'Frances Joiner' (1993), 'Ellen Christine' (1994), 'Almost Indecent' (1995), 'Vanilla Fluff' (1996), 'Almond Puff' and 'Siloam Olin Frazier' (1997).

Eugene S. Foster Award (EF) This award is given to the most outstanding late- or very late-blooming cultivar, registered as such. It must be the top selection in at least half the regions and have previously won an HM and been introduced no less than five years prior to balloting. Recent winners: 'Sandra Elizabeth' (1993), 'Sweet Shalimar' (1994), 'Ed Kirchhoff' (1995), (1996 no award made), 'Lime Frost' (1997).

Harris Olson Spider Award (HO) This award is given to the most outstanding Spider as defined in the awards ballot (currently having at least a petal length to width ratio of 4.0:1) and registered and introduced for at least two calendar years. Recent winners: 'Red Ribbons' (1992), 'Mountain Top Experience' (1993), 'Wilson Spider' (1994), 'Lois Burns' (1995), 'Green Widow' (1996), 'Yabba Dabba Doo' (1997).

L. Ernest Plouf Award (LP) This award is given to the most outstanding consistently very fragrant daylily that is registered as dormant and has previously won an HM. Recent winners: 'Vanilla Fluff' (1993), 'Lemon Lollypop' (1994), 'Gingham Maid' (1995), 'Frosted Pink Ice' (1996). 'Raspberry Candy' (1997).

Numerous other awards are given for individuals (for contributions to the society or hybridizing) and cultivars. In addition, regional awards are also made. Exhibition awards are also given at both the local and national level. These awards include: Helen Field Fischer Award, Bertrand Farr Silver Medal, Regional Service Award, Regional Newsletter Award, Lenington All-American Award (LAA), David

Hall Regional Award, President's Cup (PC), Florida Sunshine Cup (FSC), Robert Way Schlumpf Award, A.D. Roquemore Memorial Award, Region 14 Slide Sequence Award, Lazarus Memorial Award.

1997 DAYLILY POPULARITY POLL

Considering the diversity of daylilies available today it is amazing to think that it took Arlow B. Stout from 1910 until 1934 to develop what was then considered the first red daylily 'Theron'. Now there are hundreds of introductions every year with over 40,000 registered cultivars. This diversity is reflected in ever larger eyezones, multiple eyezones, watermarks of varying degree and intensity, pencil-fine gold and silver edges on the outside of colourful picotees, and white shark's teeth edging on dark red flowers.

Some of these advanced daylilies are beginning to be reflected in the popularity poll of the AHS, but many have yet to enter the marketplace in sufficient quantity to achieve their place among all daylily *aficionados*.

Listed below are the top 10 daylilies. The codes immediately following the cultivar names represent awards, above the HM level, won by the cultivar and the year received. For more detail on the cultivars see Chapter 5.

'Strawberry Candy' AM-96, AG-94, DS-95
'Barbara Mitchell' AM-90, SM-90
'Janice Brown' AM-92, SSM-94, AG-90, DS-90
'Paper Butterfly' AM-90, DS-87
'Wedding Band' AM-93, SSM-96
'Siloam Double Classic' AM-91, SSM-93, IM-88, LP-85
'Always Afternoon' AM-95, SSM-97, DS-93
'Jolyene Nichole' AM-93
'Daring Dilemma'
'Pirate's Patch'

'Old Tangiers' has an arresting flower, which is enhanced by a lighter midrib.

POLYTEPALS

As hybridizers continue to delve into new areas, they discover new shapes and forms that Arlow Stout never would have thought possible. In fact, the three petal–three sepal standard (excluding doubles, which, however, also seem to follow a triadic order) seems to have been expanded upon. Beginning with 'Towhead' in 1955 and 'I'm Different' in 1981, both of which exhibit an extra petalled trait nearly 100 per cent of the time – a new group of hybridizers has arisen.

This growth has snowballed, starting with an exchange by Dr Erling Grovenstein where he put in print the term 'polytepal'. The Unusual Form Group is working to clear up the definition of polytepal and someday hope to have a separate category for them in daylily exhibitions.

PESTS & DISEASES

The few daylily maladies, such as thrips, spider mites and slugs, are well known and the remedies are everyday fare at garden club gatherings. More troubling on the east coast of North America is that the white-tailed or Virginian deer has taken a strong liking to the tender daylily buds; as few as three deer can denude over 300 plants in an evening. Current solutions range from elaborate electronic fences, to the use of organic materials such as human hair spread throughout the garden or, a new fad, spraying coyote urine around the perimeter of the daylily garden.

Other known pests and problems include crown rot, 'spring sickness', and most recently 'leaf streak diseases' and bulb mites. It is generally felt that crown rot is an inherent breeding problem and that daylilies exhibiting this tendency should not be placed in commerce. What initially was thought to be the Northern version of crown rot, and labelled by most as 'spring sickness' is often easily treated by the use of a fungicide, as is leaf streak. Not much is known yet regarding bulb mites and there is a great debate over whether it is a primary pest or an adventitious 'carrion' feeding on damaged plants. But rest assured the 'experts' are aware of these problems which, to date, do not seem rampant, and solutions are likely to follow soon.

The Author

Kevin P. Walek is President of the National Capital Daylily Club, an AHS Garden and Exhibition Judge, editor of *The Hosta Journal*, a publication of the American Hosta Society, and advises on daylily, hosta, and sedum plantings in both public and private gardens, all in addition to his profession as a managing attorney. He and his wife Margaret maintain their garden, Hummingbird Way, Fairfax Station, Virginia, which is both an American Hemerocallis Society and American Hosta Society national display garden.

12

DAYLILIES IN EUROPE

Matthias Thomsen-Stork, President of Hemerocallis Europa

Reading through current European perennial plant catalogues one is struck by the wide variety of daylily cultivars offered. This was not always the case and is the result of the work of some dedicated pioneers such as the late Countess von Zeppelin in Bavaria, Germany. The Countess started collecting, testing and offering the best of the newer American daylilies in her well-known catalogue, in 1965, long before the general gardening public were aware of daylilies other than the ubiquitous *Hemerocallis fulva* 'Europa', *H. lilioasphodelus* and possibly some older varieties like 'Maikonigin' ('Queen of May'), a very widely grown popular early blooming *H. lilioasphodelus* type.

In Germany, the slow but steady rise in popularity of the daylily had already begun when Hubert Fischer of Chicago, Illinois agreed to send over specimen plants for the International Garden Show in Hamburg in 1963. This was the first time that modern American daylilies had been seen by amateur gardeners in Europe and they created a great impact. Some of the best known daylilies on display were the dark melon 'George Cunningham', which, with its deeply saturated colour and perfect flower presentation, is still, in the opinion of many growers, unsurpassed, and the lemon-yellow 'Corky' and darker yellow 'Golden Chimes', both raised by Hubert Fischer and both very popular throughout Europe ever since.

Some European gardeners started hybridizing their own daylilies. In the 1950s and 1960s, these included Max Steiger in Germany who introduced 'Feuervogel', 'Margarite' and 'Stern von Rio'. Later came Robert Coe, Leonard Brummitt and Lady Carew Pole in England, and Dr Fritz Kohlein and Dr Thomas Tamberg, who started breeding daylilies in 1970.

The graceful, gently ruffled and twisting Unusual Form 'Brenda Newbold' was recently introduced by Marc King, and is a beautiful shade of palest pure pink.

MODERN DAYLILY BREEDERS

There are around twenty serious daylily breeders in Europe creating distinctive new hybrids especially suited to the European climate: that is they are fully hardy and have the ability to open perfectly, preferably from early in the morning.

In Belgium, daylilies are being bred by Cor Govaerts, Francois Verhaert and Alfons van Mulders, while in England Jan and Andy Wyers, Chris Searle and Eve Lytton are breeding for a narrow temperature band that includes fairly cool summers. In the Piedmont region of Italy Marc King is breeding Spider and Unusual Form daylilies that will tolerate hot and dry summers and freezing winters. He has just introduced, among others, 'Roger Grounds', a Spider in burgundy-wine, 'Dancing Summerbird', an Open Unusual Form in soft lilac-lavender, and 'Brenda Newbold', a gently curving pure pale pink Crispata Unusual Form. In Switzerland Liselotte Hirsbrunner, living at an altitude of 1200m (4000ft), is endeavouring to create daylilies that grow and bloom well at higher elevations, and the nurseryman Urs Baltensperger is working with smaller varieties to obtain non-yellow Miniature sorts.

However, it is Germany that has the largest number of *Hemerocallis* breeders: Ronald Albert is breeding for better eyed cultivars; Norbert Graue in Hamburg is trying to create daylilies suitable for the rough climate of the North Sea; and Wolfgang Heuss produces hundreds of beautiful seedlings each year. Harald Juhr has already created a whole palette of superb new varieties, some of which are Spiders and others round and ruffled; all are registered with his Taunus prefix. Juliane Kraut in Bavaria is already working with her own blood lines and has registered 'Welfo White Diamond', a small-flowered near-white, while Werner Reinermann has been one of the most successful German breeders with 65 introductions raised between 1983 and 1996. Most popular among members of Hemerocallis Europa (see below) is his apricot 'Maggie Fynboe'. Dr

'Helle Berlineren' is a wonderful performer in European gardens, increasing rapidly and forming attractive, floriferous clumps.

Tomas Tamberg has introduced 40 daylilies since 1970 including 'Berlin Red', 'Berlin Tallboy' and 'Helle Berlinerin'. I am concentrating on taller, very well branched Spider daylilies in southern Germany.

DAYLILY SOCIETIES

Today many hundreds of gardeners in Europe collect or trade daylilies and specialist daylily societies have sprung up in several European countries like the 'Vlaamse Irisvereinging' in Belgium, led by Cor Govaerts from Antwerp, which has one of its main focuses on daylilies; the British Hosta and Hemerocallis Society, now over 15 years old, is at last placing more emphasis on daylilies due to popular demand; and the 'Fachgruppe Hemerocallis', part of the German Hardy Plant Society, is a thriving organization.

The German Hardy Plant Society (Gesellschaft der Staudenfreunde) has always encouraged daylily breeding activities through a system of trials and awards which, until a few years ago, had its centre in the famous Frankfurter Palmengarten, where the late Bruno Muller, the German daylily specialist of the 1970s and 1980s, had built up a state-of-the-art collection which is still seen by hundreds of thousands of people each year. This collection includes many European introductions.

On our first visit to this garden, my wife and I were overwhelmed by Robert Coe's pure neon-pink 'Elaine Strutt' and Tamburg's ivory-melon 'Helle Berlinerin'. These beautiful daylilies were perfectly integrated into the mixed borders. Our visits to the collection of Countess Zeppelin in the same year finally convinced us of the merits of growing daylilies and since then we have been seriously hooked, collecting, testing and breeding what is now our favourite perennial plant.

It was a fortunate coincidence that, in the late 1980s, Roswitha Waterman, the International Secretary of the American Hemerocallis Society, started a series of regular yearly slide talks featuring modern American daylilies in Bad Schwalbach near Frankfurt. I remember the excitement and the 'aahs' and 'oohs' when she presented her pictures of the newest and best varieties to a rather small, but mesmerized audience of gardeners from all over Germany. We even saw slides of the newest seedlings, including an outstanding eyed variety by Patrick Stamile that later became the well-known 'Strawberry Candy', now one of the best and most popular daylilies on both sides of the Atlantic. Indeed, it was Roswitha Waterman who really gave daylilies the last, and I think decisive, push, to become one of the most beautiful and versatile hardy perennials for European gardens.

In April 1993 the international daylily society, Hemerocallis Europa, was founded in Aarau, Switzerland, by a group of European daylily enthusiasts. It now has over 70 members from 11 different European countries, as well as members in Canada and the USA, and its main aims are to promote awareness of the beauty and garden value of the daylily, as well as to further its general dissemination throughout Europe. The society operates a system of recognized international display gardens; it organizes public exhibitions, information sessions and lectures and has a yearbook in two languages. European daylily breeding programmes are actively supported and named varieties as well as new seedlings are evaluated for their garden merit and their suitability for growing in the wide variety of European climatic regions.

PURCHASING DAYLILIES

Buying daylilies from reputable European nurseries or from knowledgeable private growers should normally cause no great problems. The plants will have been tested for their suitability for European conditions. It can be a different story, though, if less knowledgeable gardeners import new or untested daylilies from America, because not all the daylilies that thrive in Florida or other very hot or sub-tropical climates will do well in European climates. Problems encountered include: flowers not opening properly or being distorted, colours not being the same as they are in America, and plants not being fully hardy. It should also be mentioned that some American breeders and gardeners like their daylilies low-growing or even very low-growing. This often means that the blooms appear only just above the foliage or are actually in it, which may not be to European taste. To the European eye flowers that hover gracefully are preferable to those which hide in the foliage. But serious collectors of daylilies, who grow them in monotypic display beds for the sake of the flowers alone, may not necessarily share this view.

However, there plainly would not be so many daylily enthusiasts in Europe were it not that a wide variety of daylilies have performed superbly well even under unfavourable conditions for many years. The following daylilies have scored very high in the Popularity Polls carried out by different daylily groups and societies in Europe: 'Arctic Snow', 'Barbara Mitchell', 'Chicago Apache', 'China Bride', 'Court Magician', 'Janice Brown', 'Joan Senior', 'Maggie Fynboe', 'Rose Emily', 'Samba Do Brasil', 'Smoky Mountain Autumn', 'Strawberry Candy', 'Timeless Fire' and 'Wedding Band'.

Among our own favourites out of 400 daylilies in our garden in southern Germany are: 'Beauty to Behold', 'Betty Woods', 'Butterpat', 'Cameroons', 'Crimson Pirate', 'Daily Bread', 'Ferris Wheel', 'Fooled Me', 'Forsyth Bonanza', 'Lauren Leah', 'Limited Edition', 'Macmillian Memorial', 'Netzuke', 'Night Raider', 'Nosferatu', 'Ruffled Ballet', 'Siloam Paul Watts', 'Silver Run', 'Spanish Serenade', 'Spindazzle', 'Sun Star', 'Welfo White Diamond' and 'Yellow Mammoth'.

I hope that within the next few years more and more gardeners in Europe will discover for themselves the excellent qualities of daylilies and will try growing them in their own gardens.

A path winds its way through a massed planting of daylilies at West Parc, Munich.

13

DAYLILIES IN AUSTRALIA

Scott Alexander

In Australia in the 1960s and 1970s many gardeners were introduced to daylilies in much the same manner that I was, that is they were given the two commonest species, *Hemerocallis flava* (correctly *H. lilioasphodelus*) and *Hemerocallis fulva* 'Kwanso', by a neighbour or gardening friend. These species were probably introduced into Australia very early in the twentieth century by Russell Prichard, grandfather of Barry Blythe who established Tempo Two in 1972, one of the first daylily mail-order nurseries in Australia.

Nurseryman Fred Danks of Victoria may have been the first person to import daylilies from the USA in 1947, but these early imports created little interest. From 1959 to 1970, the late Bryan Tonkin, a bulb and perennial nursery-man, also in Victoria, did his best to educate the Aus-tralian gardening public with daylilies from Gilbert Wild & Sons of Sarcoxie, Missouri, USA, but he found it diffi-cult to enthuse enough gardeners to make it worthwhile. There are a couple of reasons for this comparative unpop-ularity: daylilies were considered very expensive by Aus-tralian standards – at the time at around $AUS25.00 per plant – and it may have been that many were dormants and therefore unsuitable for any but the coldest areas of Aus-tralia. However, Bryan's efforts did create an interest among many gardeners and, from the mid-1960s onwards, daylilies became more and more popular.

Jim Hipathite, a Queenslander, also began importing daylilies in the 1960s. His came from Ophelia Taylor in Florida and included many evergreen cultivars, such as 'Salmon Sheen', 'Gypsy King', 'Playboy', 'Capri'. 'Easter Anthem' and 'Gay Lark'. These were much more suitable for growing in tropical and sub-tropical gardens than dormants and thrived in a climate that was similar in many ways to that of Florida.

'Booroobin Magic', a good example of a picotee-edged daylily raised by Scott Alexander of Queensland, Australia.

The 1970s saw the emergence of an even greater interest in daylilies. Many gardeners became fanatical collectors (the writer included), joining the American Hemerocallis Society and sending to the USA for seed and later, for plants. Barry Blythe in Victoria began importing the best of the American hybrids, many of which became the basis of his own hybridizing programme. The Munson and Kirch-hoff introductions that he brought in were found to be suit-able in practically every climatic zone in Australia.

In Queensland, the Daylily Display Centre, under the aegis of sisters Maureen Flanders and Monica Mead, did much to promote interest. The sisters also began their own hybridizing programme and 'Acacia Glenn', 'Brisbane Belle', 'Kolan Bubbles', 'Kolan Dee Jay' and 'Double Rosedale' are proof of their success. In 1981, Rainbow Ridge Nursery, in the hills west of Sydney, added daylilies to their well-known iris mail-order business. Proprietors Graeme and Helen Grosvenor and John Taylor quickly became another supplier of quality imported daylilies.

In 1984 I established Mountain View Daylily Gardens in the small township of Maleny, 95km (60 miles) north-west of Brisbane. The 600m (200ft) elevation, deep vol-canic soils and high rainfall was a perfect environment for growing daylilies. I imported the best daylilies from lead-ing Louisiana and Florida hybridizers and began a small hybridizing programme. My recent introductions 'Maleny Debutante', a pastel peach-pink with a bright rose star-shaped eye, and 'In Excess', a very fragrant, canteloupe-coloured double, have proved to be very popular both in Australia and overseas. One of my newest creations, 'Booroobin Magic', a mustard-yellow with maroon eye and edge, has attracted much interest from local collectors.

And so, nearly fifty years after the first hybrids were imported into Australia, daylilies, which are capable of surviving summer temperatures of up to 45°C (113°F) and winter night time lows of −10°C (14°F), and still flower for many months of the year.

'Maleny Debutante', raised by Scott Alexander, is now popular in the United States.

DAYLILY SOCIETIES

In 1996 a group of daylily collectors and nursery owners were instrumental in creating two daylily organizations: The Brisbane Daylily Club, in Queensland, and the Hemerocallis Society of Australia. Both produce quarterly journals and encourage their members to keep in touch with each other via round robins. The Brisbane Club organizes regular meetings and each November has a big display of flowers on and off scape for the public to view. A fund-raising plant auction by mail is a regular event and enables members to obtain newer plants for very little expense. Two other small clubs have been established in Bundaberg and Toowoomba, both also stage annual shows.

In 1988, both the main organizations were fortunate in acquiring the services of the highly qualified AHS members and leading hybridizers David Kirchhoff and Mort Morss to train keen collectors on how to become Junior daylily Judges.

Several Australian daylily growers, including myself, are members of the American Hemerocallis Society's E-Mail Robin, enabling them to participate in the dissemination of up-to-date information by the fastest means possible.

GROWING DAYLILIES

In Australia daylilies can be grown in just about any location, provided there is a short period of winter chill. Some of the older cultivars will flower occasionally in tropical locations, such as Cairns. Although daylilies have a reputation for hardiness, there is a greater chance of crown rot when they are grown in coastal and the hinterland areas that are affected by very high summer humidity.

Soil & Site

Daylilies readily adapt to the different soil types from the heavy clays to the almost sandy conditions prevailing in Australia, and from the very acid soils of pH 5 to the very alkaline soils of pH 8.5.

Heavy mulching has been found to be the most important cultural practice among the successful growers of daylilies, protecting the soil from the harsh summer sun and providing a cool root-run. In rural areas most growers have access to inexpensive sources of hay or animal manures, while in the cities, garden centres stock pine bark and sugar cane, which are excellent for this purpose, and for the organic matter they will eventually add to the soil.

Many gardeners experiment with siting their daylilies. Some find that they thrive in dappled shade throughout the day, while others give them all morning sun or all afternoon sun. However, most gardeners along the coastal strip plant them in full sun, accepting that many of the blooms may be slightly damaged by afternoon sun.

Australian growers are finding that they achieve excellent results with animal manures and the organic fertilizers created from them: blood, bone and seaweed. The over-use of chemical fertilizers has been known to cause overly lush foliage, very few flowers, and a susceptibility to disease.

Pests & Diseases

Despite rigorous quarantine regulations, the American daylily aphid found its way into Australia in 1985 and has quickly spread throughout the country. This little creature, which lives and multiplies deep down in the foliage, created havoc among daylilies. Often the plant was reduced to a mess of dead leaves and sticky aphid residue. Those gardeners who resisted the desire to spray with toxic chemicals were eventually rewarded with very inexpensive controllers, such as ladybirds, praying mantis and hoverflies, which quickly reduced the aphid numbers. Many gardeners these days prefer to let nature take its course and not use chemical sprays. Thrips are a much bigger problem now than in the past and white streaks on the petals in spring indicate their presence, particularly in the reds and purples.

Another relatively new pest in some areas is the white curl grub, the larvae of members of the beetle family. These

C-shaped grubs can cause considerable damage to daylily roots, particularly from February to May and hybridizers need to be very vigilant at this time. A single curl grub can devour the roots of many newly planted seedlings overnight. Unfortunately, in this case, chemicals have to be used to drench the soil and eradicate this pest.

Crown rot is unknown in southern parts of Australia but is of real concern to some growers in Brisbane and further north and west. It would seem that excessive heat and humidity trigger this disease as losses generally occur from February to April.

A good way to combat problems is through soil fertility. Australian soils are deficient in potash, the mineral that strengthens and thickens the plant cell walls and therefore gives it resistance to disease. The addition of sulphate of potash and also liquid seaweed fertilizers could prove to be an easy remedy for the problem. Some growers have taken to cutting all their daylily foliage back by about two-thirds in late autumn and this seems to reduce pest populations to a point where they cannot recover in sufficient numbers to damage the next spring–summer growth and blooms.

GARDENING WITH DAYLILIES

Being a very keen gardener with a preference for cottage garden effects, and also an avid collector of perennial plants, my daylily gardens tend to be slightly overcrowded with the large number of perennials, bulbs, groundcovers and shrubs that I grow. My aim is to show how good the daylilies look when grown with a wide variety of other plants.

For early season colour before the daylilies reach peak bloom, I make a lot of use of freesias, Louisiana and Dutch irises, hippeastrums, Oriental lilies and calla lilies. As the daylilies reach peak bloom in early November, kniphofias, alstroemerias and agapanthus are also reaching their best.

For fill-in plants, which I allow to roam, I use the silver foliage artemisias (of which 'Valerie Finnis' is a favourite), verbenas, achilleas, asters in a variety of colours, perennial phlox, penstemons, ajugas, bergenias and Australia's own brachycomes, which are always in flower. Good old impatiens is allowed to spread into vacant spaces until it threatens to overwhelm smaller plants. I have a definite liking for the New Zealand hybrid phormiums, with their variegated foliage, and these are planted throughout the garden.

Colour Schemes

In several beds I have aimed for certain colour schemes. One such has a blue and white effect with near-white and cream daylilies, such as 'Mosel' and 'Vivaldi', combined with the taller cultivars such as 'Snow Ballerina', 'Wedding Band' and 'Journey's End', and interplanted with blue and white agapanthus of different heights, white

hydrangea, buddleja and lilies. In another bed I have a variety of yellow daylilies with the Australian-bred *Lavendula pinnata* 'Sidonnie' as the complementary colour, as well as miniature blue buddleja.

One of the most outstanding effects of blue and yellow was planted beside a 30m (100ft) driveway. The alternate plantings of clumps of the tall dark blue *Agapanthus orientalis* 'Wavy Navy' and the daffodil-coloured 'In Maxine's Honour' has provided quite an attraction. Another dramatic massed planting of daylilies was on a 25m (80ft) long embankment, where I grew a sweeping drift of the old golden-yellow 'Reverend Traub'. I have been pleased to see that this type of landscaping feature is now being used far more often by landscape architects in Australia.

WHAT OF THE FUTURE?

I am convinced that the potential of daylilies has hardly been tapped and that they have a great future in Australia. Councils are setting a very good example in this way: daylilies are now appearing in parks and along the city streets and landscape architects are incorporating them into many of their projects as an alternative to agapanthus and phormiums.

Meanwhile hybridizers are working towards the perfect daylily: that is a hardy, drought-resistant plant with clear, sunfast colours, excellent branching and bud count, attractive year-round foliage and a long bloom season. Few gardeners will be able to resist them.

The Author

Scott Alexander, a retired school teacher, is a well-known hybridizer and nurseryman. He has developed the largest daylily nursery outside the USA and exports worldwide.

Raised in Australia, 'In Excess' is a sumptuous, double-flowered daylily.

14

DAYLILIES IN NEW ZEALAND

Ian Gear

There is, unfortunately, no record of how and when daylilies were first brought to New Zealand, but it is possible that during the 1800s Chinese immigrants, who arrived in Otago and the West Coast of the South Island as gold diggers, may have brought plants with them – daylilies being natives of China – or, perhaps, daylilies were brought back to New Zealand by these early settlers following their return to China to marry.

While no documented evidence is available, it is highly likely that the apothecaries who practised Chinese medicine would have had access to daylilies. However, very few of the modern daylilies now being grown in New Zealand are likely to be direct descendants of the early plants, the majority having been raised in America and, to a lesser extent, Australia.

New Zealand, like North America and Australia, covers a wide range of climatic variation. This is because it is a long mass of land stretched out over several degrees of latitude. Because it is also a very thin country, embraced by oceans on both sides, the diurnal temperature range is usually quite small, a mere 8°C (14°F) in the North Island. Since not all daylilies will perform equally well across the whole range of New Zealand's climates, the secret of success is to grow those raised by hybridizers whose climate pretty well matches one's own, although there are exceptions.

However, a high percentage of American hybridizers operate only in Florida and the Deep South where the average winter lows are not below 10°C (50°F) and the winter highs are above 21°C (70°F), with only occasional light early morning frosts lasting no more than four hours. Other hybridizers operate in areas like Indiana where the ground freezes solid in winter but the summer temperatures can be above 38°C (100°F). Some hybridizers operate in the cooler Pacific North West, in England, where climate differentials are much narrower, and in Germany, which has much colder winters, although summer temperatures can often be above 27°C (80°F). So far as I know, only one American hybridizer, Leo Sharp, has breeding sites at both ends of the climatic range, with the result that many of his daylilies will flourish in most parts of New Zealand.

The temperatures needed for daylilies to flower well are 18.5°C (65°F) by day, and five consecutive nights at over 18.5°C (65°F). In New Zealand, these requirements can generally be met but local conditions vary and unseasonable weather may produce imperfect flowers. Recent trials have indicated that plants from some breeders perform much better than others; we are getting good results from many of the breeding lines of David Kirchhoff in Florida and particularly encouraging results from those of Leo Sharp, mentioned earlier.

GROWING DAYLILIES

Daylilies thrive in virtually all the different types of soil New Zealand has to offer, except in those that are cold, wet and poorly drained. The only demand they make is that their growing medium is well aerated, otherwise they can fall prey to root rots. While these rots are not widely encountered they are present in New Zealand. Daylilies perform best on soils of pH 7.0–6.5.

Daylily growers find that fertilizer applications of a blend containing an N:P:K ratio of 5:10:5 applied around the plant in early spring, just as growth recommences, and again in early summer, is the most beneficial. This should be followed with a further application in early autumn with a blend of 5:10:10 as the higher levels of phosphate and potassium will help harden the plants for winter. Excess use of nitrogen should be avoided as, with our high rainfall, it will promote unnecessarily lush foliage at the expense of blooms.

Many parts of New Zealand have ample and fairly

'Green Flutter', a Stout Silver Medal Winner, is still one of the greenest daylilies. It is very floriferous and looks wonderful when grown with scarlet 'Christmas Is'.

'Quick Results' is a high performance daylily in many different climatic regions.

constant supplies of rain with an annual rainfall between 90–120cm (36–48in) but in much of the country there can be a deficit from mid- to late October, continuing until the rains in March and April. While irregular rainfalls occur during summer, supplementary irrigation helps to produce the luxuriant blooms of which the daylily is capable. Liberal applications of mulch and compost decrease water loss and enhance flowering.

New Zealand's narrow areas of land mass are beset by winds for much of the year, the prevailing winds being from the south and south-west. However, provided they are well-nourished and healthy, daylilies will stand up to severe buffeting, even along the coastal strips where salt winds damage or inhibit the growth of many other plants.

Pests and Diseases

As elsewhere, daylilies suffer from few pest and disease problems. Aphids are occasionally a problem and Two Spotted Spider Mite (*Tetranychus urticae*) may attack the undersides of the leaves of some cultivars. The mites characteristically form webbing on the underside of leaves. A slight silvering may also be evident where the pest has damaged the leaf tissue. Where daylilies are well fed, mulched and watered suf-

ficiently this pest is seldom a nuisance. Thrips may be found on the flowers and, as in the United States, the lighter-coloured flowers are the first to be attacked and serve as good indicators of growing thrip infestations. Slugs and snails are partial to the soft young foliage in the spring.

DAYLILIES IN THE GARDEN

Daylilies lend themselves to planting in the border in a variety of ways in association with other perennials, roses or shrubs. The persistent foliage of evergreen daylilies provides a luxuriant effect throughout the year in warmer regions and enthusiasts growing evergreens in colder regions also report good results.

The glorious blue-green leaves of deciduous cultivars, such as 'Song of Spring' (Carpenter), as they rise and grow following their winter rest, is delightful. The soft olive-green-foliaged forms with green-influenced yellow flowers look particularly good when grown in association with *Buxus*, used either as clipped low formal hedging or as billowing free-form shrubs or small trees. This tonal effect also works well with hydrangeas and hellebores, using such cultivars as 'Beauty to Behold', 'Green Flutter' and 'Quick Results'.

Daylilies are perfect, not only for growing in association with roses and the other well-known perennial plants, but also for enhancing gardens in association with native phormiums and Cape Reinga Lily (*Arthropodium*).

NURSERIES & DISPLAY GARDENS

The first New Zealand nurseryman to offer daylilies in significant numbers was Richmond Harrison in Palmerston North. During the years following the 1950s Harrison supplied dormant crowns to the garden shop trade. Now a handful of dedicated growers supply daylilies by mail-order to gardeners in both islands.

We are working with Graeme Grosvenor of Australia and Leo Sharp in the USA to introduce new cultivars to the New Zealand market. In selecting promising material we are seeking daylilies that give a long flowering period, preferably with repeat blooming over the summer. Fragrant sorts are, of course, also popular.

Access to display beds and gardens is encouraged by many of the growers. Details are in Where to See Daylilies p.154. Increasingly daylilies are found in public gardens and amenity plantings.

THE FUTURE

Daylilies have a bright future in New Zealand gardens. Plants originating in America, Europe and Australia present us with exciting opportunities and these are already providing the foundation of breeding lines for our own hybridizers. Suppliers all have their favourites and some of those currently receiving accolades include Leo Sharp's 'Brookwood Winner's Circle', the appropriately named 'Eighteen Carat' (E. Brown), Jeff Salter's 'Spanish Glow' and Lee Gates' 'Scarlet Orbit' all do exceptionally well and Stout Medal-winning 'Wedding Band' (Stamile) has its champions in both Australia and New Zealand, especially now that good results are being reported by breeders seeking gold edges for their seedlings. The improvements made over the last fifteen years have provided a range of plants of great merit and they are worthy of inclusion in any planting scheme.

The Author

Ian and Helen Gear run Heritage Roses in Hamilton and are now selling daylilies.

A stunning planting of 'Ed Murray', forming part of the daylily planting at Manurewa Botanic Garden, Auckland, New Zealand.

15

CULTIVATION

PROPAGATION AND PESTS & DISEASES

Daylilies are among the easiest of perennials to grow, provided their few essential requirements are met. However, difficulties may be experienced with some of the more inbred cultivars, especially those with complicated colour patterns and heavy edge embellishments, if they are grown in climates very different from the ones in which they were bred. That said, most daylilies will fit seamlessly into the average garden provided they are given a place in the sun and a fertile soil.

SOIL

Daylilies grow best in well-drained, but moist, rich, friable loam, cultivated to a depth of about 45–60cm (18–24in). Best with a pH of about 6, they can also be grown successfully in soils well to either side of neutral, and will tolerate chalk, heavy clay or loose, sandy conditions, provided that generous supplies of organic material are incorporated into the soil and used as a mulch.

Heavy clay is the soil daylilies least like as it is usually very badly drained which could cause rotting. Drainage can be improved by adding copious amounts of coarse grit and organic manure, preferably in equal quantities by volume. In severely heavy soils land drains may be needed. An alternative strategy, used by many growers, is to plant daylilies in raised beds filled with imported top soil or compost.

Once loosened and rendered free-draining, a clay soil can be the ideal medium for daylilies since it is usually high in nutrients. Sandy soils are free-draining but the nutrients will quickly leach out. Like clay, sandy soils improve vastly with the addition of generous amounts of organic matter which helps to make it more water retentive. Regular mulching and extra nutrients are necessary, augmented by foliar feeds in early spring and as the buds are forming.

Well-spaced, rich rose-red flowers and a very long blooming season make 'Whooperee' a superb plant in most regions.

PLANTING

Daylilies can be planted at almost any time of the year, provided the ground is open, but local conditions may make a particular season preferable. Many growers recommend spring planting, especially in cold-winter areas since the plants will then have the summer weather during which to become established, making good roots before winter. Most growers in areas with severe winters keep autumn-delivered daylilies in a greenhouse through winter. By late spring, when they are planted in the garden, they will already have produced flowers, seeds and scape increases and will often rebloom. Cultivation in the high temperatures of a greenhouse may produce uncharacteristic doubling of some daylilies, such as 'Elizabeth Salter'.

Other growers prefer autumn planting since the soil, having been heated by the sun all summer, will be warm, enabling the plants to make more rapid root growth. Most roots grow in soil temperatures of 2–18°C (35°F–65°F) and stop after 18°C (65°F). Generally speaking roots are happy at 8°C (15°F) less than the above ground parts of the plant. However, the roots of newly planted daylilies grow faster if their water requirements are met.

Autumn planting should be carried out at least six weeks before the predicted onset of frosts. Those daylilies that were in summer dormancy will make a spurt of growth in late summer and early autumn provided they have moisture, but it is not a good idea to plant evergreens recently received from hotter climates in the autumn. They should be potted until warmer weather returns. In the hottest regions, planting can be delayed until mid-autumn as there will be no fear of heavy frosts.

Planting is not recommended on hot summer days, but if unavoidable, the newly planted daylilies should be shielded from the direct rays of the sun.

A spacing of 60–90cm (2–3ft) is ideal if the daylilies are to remain in the same position for a number of years. If an immediate display of colour is required plant about 45cm (18in) apart: daylilies planted this close will require earlier division.

The planting hole should be at least twice as large as the roots to be planted and never less than 45cm (18in) across by 23cm (9in) deep. The soil should be dug out and the bottom of the planting hole thoroughly broken up. Plenty of garden compost or farmyard manure should be incorporated into the soil before it is returned to the hole. This will provide all the immediate nitrogen (N) requirements. A fertilizer high in phosphorus and potassium (P, K) should also be added and will be taken up slowly by the daylily. Nitrogen moves through the soil more quickly so needs to be added more frequently.

The roots of most daylilies grow outwards and downwards leaving an area without roots immediately below the crown, so a small mound of soil should be left in the centre of the planting hole, to fill up this rootless space. Having positioned the daylily on the mound, firm the soil around the roots. If the daylily has become pot bound, its roots will need teasing out so that they are free to spread out over the mound of soil. Remove any dead or damaged roots at this time. The crown should be planted at the same level as that from whence it came, just deep enough to cover the non-green portion of the fan, not deeper than 2.5cm (1in) in areas that have snow cover, or it may not bloom. Refill the hole with garden soil mixed with a potting mix. Make sure the soil mound is well tamped down before planting because if the crown sinks too low it may die.

If plants arrive with newly forming scapes, these should be cut off so that all the plant's energy goes into production of a healthy and vigorous root system. If new scapes appear about 2 months after planting keep just one so that the identity of the plant can be verified. Daylilies that are transplanted during reproductive or bloom periods may need some time before resuming active growth, but if transplanted just before or during their growing season, they will not take so long to establish. In any case it can take up to three years before plants exhibit their full potential.

CARE OF DAYLILIES

Mulching and Feeding
Mulching can supply daylilies with extra nutrients but far more important is the mulch's ability to hold moisture, thus moderating the extremes of wetness and dryness in the soil. Moreover, as the mulch decays it turns to humus, which vastly improves the soil structure. The best types of mulch are garden compost, farmyard manure or mushroom compost but other materials such as shredded bark, pine straw or leaves can also be used.

Well-rotted manures and garden compost are best applied after the foliage of dormant daylilies has died down and in time for autumn rains to water it into the ground. Dehydrated manures can be applied in autumn or spring as they are quicker acting. They are also easier to handle, are quite safe to use directly from the packet or container, but are highly concentrated and should be applied sparingly. Organic material from a garden compost heap can never be applied too often as it helps to build up the structure of the soil on a permanent basis in the way that artificial fertilizers never can.

A mulch for permanent cover and soil enrichment should be applied in a layer approximately 5–7cm (2–3in) thick. If it is for protecting somewhat tender evergreens in cold-winter areas, it needs to be anything up to 30cm (12in) deep and must be removed in spring to prevent the emerging shoots from being smothered. The use of leaf mould, however beneficial to the friability of the soil, has the disadvantage of significantly increasing the slug population. In some parts of the United States leaf mould can also encourage southern stem blight (*Sclerotium rolfsii*).

Feeding is necessary not only to produce the best flowers but also to nourish the root system, thus enabling the plant to increase well and remain in the best of health. Before applying nutrients other than garden compost or farmyard manure, it is advisable to have the soil checked for deficiencies. There might be only one element lacking, but to grow daylilies successfully a combination of many ingredients is necessary, so having the soil tested is well worth the time and expense. Soils differ widely so one type of balanced food is not necessarily the best for all soils, though generally it will be adequate.

For a temporary boost, apply high-potash fertilizer as a foliar feed, including a few drops of soap to act as a surfactant. This can help to keep a daylily flowering at its maximum potential and also benefits the foliage, although overdoing it could eventually poison the soil. At Apple Court we start applications of foliar feed in late spring as the new foliage is emerging, continuing once every three weeks until the buds start to form. Tomato foods also help to boost daylily flower production. High-nitrogen fertilizer, which can improve the foliage early in the season, should not be applied after midsummer since it can make new growth soft and more susceptible to insect damage.

Other soil ameliorants such as alfalfa pellets, which contain enzymes that help to unlock the nutrients in fertilizers, are much used in the United States. Many growers in the United States, including some leading hybridizers, also add sewage sludge. This contains magnesium which helps to enhance the near-blue effect in flower colours and gives the foliage a good colour. Epsom Salts (magnesium sulphate) has the same effect. It can be used at the rate of 3 tablespoons of crystals per gallon of water and must be applied in solution only. Its overuse over a prolonged period may make the soil too acid for daylilies and can also lead to a build-up of salt. Lime can help remedy acidity.

Watering

Water is even more important to the health of daylilies than feeding, since without adequate water the nutrients cannot be taken up. Some growers water only at planting time or in times of severe drought, the theory being that daylilies are only worth having if they can adapt themselves to the prevailing conditions. However, without sufficient water the plant looks limp, the foliage is a poor colour, the flowers are sparser, poorer and of thinner substance, the length of the bloom period is affected and there is less or no rebloom in areas where there is a reblooming potential. While it is true that excessive overwatering can cause daylilies to rot or die, they do require an abundant supply of water and will repay the grower with bigger, better and more colourful flowers and more and taller scapes with a higher bud count.

The best method of watering is either by leaky hoses, woven discreetly around the daylilies on the ground or by leaving a slowly trickling hose on the ground and moving it to a different area from time to time. As a general guide daylilies need 2.5cm (1in) of water per week during summer (the equivalent of 18 litres/4 gals per sq m/yd). Daylilies growing in containers in full sun need watering twice a day. Most nurseries with large display gardens water with overhead spray lines, but this can adversely affect the following day's individual blooms, especially in daylilies having an abundance of buds that virtually touch each other. The spent blooms become soggy and, if resting against other buds, can destroy many future flowers unless individually removed by hand.

Positioning

Daylilies usually require about 6–7 hours of sun per day. In milder climates they should not be planted in shade; in very hot climates the darker shades of red, red-black, purple and purple-black are best planted to receive morning sun but afternoon shade, otherwise the top layer of pigment can melt, producing an unsightly greasy effect on the surface of the bloom. In hot climates the darker shades can also change colour somewhat over the length of a day, but adequate watering gives them a better chance to overcome this problem.

Daylilies can tolerate windy conditions, making them ideal for coastal and for windswept areas. Newly planted daylilies in such conditions need some protection in the form of a windbreak until they are properly established.

Daylilies do best in conditions of high humidity with overcast skies which tend to make the colours richer; the colours are even richer in cooler climates but less flowers are produced. However, in cool climates, a sheltered place within a warm microclimate can help to ensure maximum flowering potential, particularly with tetraploids of heavy substance bred in hotter regions. All night street lighting within a proximity of 1.2m (4ft) will accelerate the bloom season. If possible plant on the sunny side of the house.

GROOMING AFTER BLOOMING

Nothing spoils a floriferous clump of daylilies more than the presence of dead and dying blooms. Breeders are trying to produce self-cleaning daylilies, but have not yet been successful, so the removal of spent blooms by hand is still often necessary. Some people remove the spent blooms early each morning and this keeps them in touch with how the daylilies are performing; an even greater council of perfection is to deadhead them late in the evening, before the deadheads have liquified into a sticky mess. This also means that one is less likely to knock off those blooms in the process of opening.

Once a scape has finished flowering it looks unsightly, so unless the pods are to be set for hybridizing purposes, it should be removed, cutting it near the ground.

When flowering is finally over for the season, evergreen or semi-evergreen daylilies will just need to be tidied up until new foliage comes up in spring, when some of the old leaves can safely be removed. Decaying dormant foliage should be removed as soon as possible in order to leave the garden tidy for winter and prevent slugs and snails overwintering in it.

Staining Sap exuding from spent flowers can stain hands and clothing during the deadheading process. These stains can be removed from clothing by immediately soaking it in a strong detergent and rinsing well. It may take several attempts to remove the stain completely. Hands should be washed in any proprietary heavy-duty cleaner.

GREENHOUSE CULTURE

Daylilies can be grown in greenhouses, conservatories or buildings facing the sun. However, such buildings invariably reduce the length of time that light reaches the plants and many will go dormant sooner than they would in the open. As the days grow shorter, daylilies produce a hormone inducing dormancy, but if they receive artificial light this hormone is absorbed and does not affect the plant. Warm white or daylight fluorescent tubes, about 10cm (4in) above the top of the plant, should be left on for approximately twenty minutes a day to prevent precocious dormancy.

DIVIDING DAYLILY CLUMPS

Sooner or later most daylilies need dividing, either because they have grown too large for the space available and the quality of the bloom has started to decline or because divisions are required for nursery sales.

A good rule of thumb is to divide after approximately 5 years in cooler regions and after 2–3 years in hotter regions where the growth rate is faster. This also depends on the rate of growth: some daylilies are slower growing, eg 'Admiral's Braid' and others are fast, eg 'Siloam Baby Talk'. In garden situations the best advice is not to divide a clump until the blooms dwindle in quantity and possibly size and never to leave a clump in the ground until it is too large to handle easily.

It is better to resist dividing a daylily too quickly or too often. Never evaluate a one-year-old plant. At times you will get beautiful flowers the first year but generally during

'Admiral's Braid', a near-white, is prized for its gold edge which is apparent in most climates. The contrasting black anthers are an attractive feature.

the second and third years it will have become established and be producing its optimum performance. (See p.151 for how to divide daylilies.)

BARE-ROOT MAIL-ORDER DIVISIONS

Mail-order nurseries often send out daylilies as bare-root divisions, with the leaves greatly reduced. These can suffer if they are in the mail for several days. They should be unpacked immediately on arrival to allow air to get to the crown and roots. Single fans without much crown or root system are the most vulnerable.

Following transplantation the plant continues to transpire, albeit at a slower rate than normal, reducing the osmotic pressure within the plant's cells, thus the plant responds by wilting. Placing the daylily roots in water can allow diffusion of water inward to the plant cells causing greater cell turgidity. Most daylily growers recommend soaking the roots on arrival, either in water or water supplemented by a weak solution of plant food. Usually 24 hours is sufficient – however, they can stay in water for several days until the weather or ground is suitable for

planting, provided that the water is changed daily.

Some daylily growers are of the opinion that it is quite unnecessary to soak daylilies on arrival since the fine hair feeder roots, which are only one cell thick, will have been destroyed during digging; but having personally seen dessicated daylilies plump up in water before my eyes, I am convinced that soaking before planting can only be beneficial.

PROPAGATION

Daylilies can be propagated vegetatively or by seed. Seeds should only be used to increase true species, grown in isolation, or for breeding programmes. Vegetative methods should always be used for increasing hybrid daylilies. Four vegetative methods are used: division, tissue culture, proliferations and the Lanolin-BAP-IAA method.

Division

Division is the simplest and most reliable method, provided that the daylilies are not divided down to single fans, though this can be done successfully with practice. Dig the clump out of the ground then, resting it on the ground or on a hard surface, such as concrete, insert two garden forks, back to back, right in its middle. Slowly pull the handles of the forks together, making the tines act as levers thus separating the clump into two lesser clumps. The forks may then need to be forced outwards and downwards to completely separate the two new clumps. The process can be repeated, dividing lesser clumps into still smaller clumps, and so on. Final divisions should consist of not less than two fans. The last few fans can be separated by hand, following the natural separation lines as closely as possible, or cut apart using a sharp freezer or plant propagator's knife. The whole operation is generally made easier if the foliage is first cut down to 2–5cm (1–2in) above the crown.

After division, roots should be trimmed back to about half their length, again using a sharp knife. This will encourage the divisions to sprout strong new roots from just above the cuts rather than trying to reactivate old roots.

The divisions can then be either returned to the ground or potted up. If they are to be returned to the ground, they should not be replanted in the same place that they were growing in originally, unless the soil in the planting hole has been renewed or re-invigorated with organic manures and fertilizer. If the plants are to be potted this is best done into a proprietary growing mix. As a rule of thumb the pot should be large enough to contain at least twice the quantity of roots visible at potting time. Plants should be watered in thoroughly, shaded from strong sun and sheltered from severe winds until established – a matter of just a few weeks. They should also be clearly labelled.

Daylilies can be divided in the spring or the autumn, but one must be aware of local weather conditions and avoid dividing when it is too rainy, too hot or too cold. The optimum time, when there will be least disruption to the growth of the plant, is directly after the second burst of growth, that is immediately after bloom. That, however, is a counsel of perfection and many daylilies, being the tough and easy plants that they are, will accept division in most conditions other than intense heat or heavy frost, as long as the foliage and flower scapes are cut down so that the energy goes into building up a healthy new root system.

Proliferations

Proliferations are small fans of leaves occurring on the scapes, usually where there is a node or bract just below the point where the scape branches. On some daylilies these proliferations can develop into baby plants with leaves of 5–7cm (2–3in) and roots of about 1cm (½in). In theory, if the rooting part of the proliferation can be brought into contact with soil or a growing medium, the proliferation will devlop into a fully fledged daylily genetically identical to the parent plant.

The practice is to sever the proliferation from the parent scape, making cuts about 2.5cm (1in) above and below. The section of stem, with the proliferation still attached, is then pushed into soil or a potting mix, the right way up, until the rooting part of the proliferation is firmly bedded in. Some people prefer to root them in vermiculite, perlite or sharp sand. After planting, the proliferations should be kept warm and in good light until established, which is usually a matter of weeks. If they have good roots while still on the scape, they may not need pampering, but if no roots are showing, new plants will develop more quickly and certainly if they are grown on under glass or in a propagator with bottom heat. Some growers recommend keeping the proliferations moist and warm by placing them under clear polythene but such close conditions may encourage rotting. The use of fungicides may avert this. Once they are established the young plants can be treated just like other daylilies.

Tissue Culture

Tissue culture is the process whereby whole plants are produced from single cells under laboratory conditions. It is a method that is really only suitable for nurserymen who want to reproduce particular daylilies in vast quantities.

At the present time, hundreds of thousands of daylilies are being produced by this method in many different countries, but with mixed success. A few, such as 'Joan Senior' and 'Gentle Shepherd', are known to come true to type, but many others do not. Most specialist daylily nurseries will know which do come true, and will not sell the unreliable varieties. If in doubt, make sure you see tissue-cultured daylilies in flower before buying.

Lanolin-BPA-IAA Method

It has been found that if the meristem or growing point of a daylily fan is damaged or removed, several fans will develop instead of just the one; although the more usual experience is that the whole fan dies. This can be done with Lanolin-BPA-IAA paste.

The lanolin-BPA-IAA paste along with full details of how to use it can be obtained from Ken Durio, Route 7, Box 43, Opelousas, LA 70570, USA.

Advocates of this method claim that it is possible to get up to six new shoots in three to four weeks, and that with repeated applications one can get as many as 20 new shoots where originally there was only one fan. Others find that the method has no advantage over normal division and may even damage what would otherwise have been perfectly good fans. It is likely to be most successful in hot climates.

Seed

The seed of daylilies may occasionally germinate by chance in the garden, but when seedlings are being raised deliberately much more care needs to be taken. In general, seed is best sown under glass where the circumstances surrounding them can be carefully controlled. Failing that they can be sown in a propagating case or raised in a conservatory or even on a well-lit windowsill (p.108).

Broadly speaking, seed should be sown in early to mid-winter, so long as the minimum temperature of 5°C (41°F) for germination can be maintained. Seedlings should be kept growing by potting them on as needed. In mid-spring they can be hardened off for planting out in late spring. If this regimen is followed plants should grow away strongly and most will flower in their second year.

Seed is normally sown in pots or seed trays, in a proprietary seed mix. The seed should be covered with its own depth of seed mix, or with silver or sharp sand. In close conditions a fungicide should be used against damping-off.

PROBLEMS

Early-morning-opening In colder regions, or temperate regions with a mild summer climate, daylilies with nocturnal ancestry seem to have a better chance of opening well early in the morning. Optimum performance is achieved in climates where there is an even night and day temperature, even if it is not necessarily a high temperature, although daylilies generally do best where the night temperatures are not less than 18°C (65°F). Some growers claim that the temperature on the previous three or four days and nights can affect the opening ability of a daylily flower.

For gardeners living in areas where the evenings and nights are significantly cooler than the days, it is best to choose daylilies that bloom in the M, ML and L periods (see p.34) so that the temperature has a chance to improve before the daylily season begins.

Now that daylilies are increasing in popularity it is hoped that more breeders will take up the challenge of producing more cultivars carrying the early-morning-opening gene. The criterion for early-morning-opening is that the blooms should be open by 6am True Solar Time. I know of two Southern-bred daylilies that are not fully hardy without protection in cold-winter regions, but which are worth cossetting because they open perfectly, early in the morning: they are 'Beat the Barons' and 'Tuscawilla Dave Talbott', showing that the genes for hardiness and early-morning-opening do not necessarily go together.

Petal Boating This is the term given to petals that have a folded or canoe-like appearance. It occurs after cool nights, especially in cultivars without early-morning-opening genes, usually tetraploids of heavy substance with picotee or gold-wire edges and most often those with a prominent petal appearing, tongue-like, above the others petals in alignment.

Green Sepals These are sepal reverses that are still green when the flower opens. This is because the pigments have not matured fully, especially at the tip and is due to the bloom season coinciding with a succession of cold nights. 'Eenie Weenie' often has green sepal reverses, which are always more noticeable on paler flowers.

Scape Blasting The scapes appear to have spontaneously broken off horizontally or to have, quite literally, exploded. The blasting does not necessarily sever the head completely and it may continue to flower provided it is still attached by the cambium layer. Scape blasting is thought to be due to irregular moisture availability or overwatering, or an excess of nitrogen, and is more prevalent in tetraploids although breeders are now aiming to eliminate this negative trait.

Scape Cracking This is vertical cracking or breaking of the scapes, often caused by overuse of unbalanced fertilizers. It can help to splint the scape with a stick if one is intending to use the bloom for the current year's breeding. It was a severe problem in early tetraploid daylilies.

Grassing An overabundance of grass-like shoots growing closely together occurs in clumps of dormant daylilies that have been raised in a cold climate, trying to adapt to hot weather conditions (for example, many of the Siloams). The shoots need to be pulled apart and replanted separately. It is not the same as a soft crown, which can regenerate by producing little fans around the rotted crown.

Yellowing Leaf Tips This condition can appear because the plant has split at the base due to expansion of the crown during frost damage, and is starting to discard the damaged leaves. If the yellowish-brown colour on the tips starts to creep down the leaves and some of the leaves split, this could be caused by spider mites.

Yellowing of Basal Leaves Yellowing or browning of the lower leaves may be the plant's natural response to unsuitable temperatures. These leaves should not be removed as they may provide a natural defence.

PESTS

Many daylily growers, breeders and display garden owners now find that as long as they practise good husbandry, in the long run their daylilies are better off not being bombarded with pesticides. Overuse of chemicals does not allow a plant to build up a natural resistance to pests and diseases, and also discourages natural predators. However, in times of serious infestation or disease some remedies are essential for the well-being of the plant.

Aphids (*Myzus hemerocallis*) This pest usually feeds on the growing buds causing a wart-like appearance. Infested plants usually start late into growth with the new foliage being yellowed, giving the appearance of a nitrogen deficiency. These aphids are not yet found in the British Isles.

Bulb Mite (*Rhizoglyphus* spp.) These tiny insects can only be seen under a powerful microscope as they are only 0.3 to 0.5mm long. They feed from fungi on damaged bulbs or roots. There is no chemical control as yet but healthy plants are less likely to succumb to an invasion.

Earwigs Earwigs eat the base of the anthers and style rendering the flower useless for hybridizing. They also eat large areas of the epidermis thus spoiling the appearance of the flower. They can be removed by pulling them out of the flowers with fine tweezers. Earwigs tend to congregate in large families so some chemicals may be necessary if the infestation is serious.

Hemerocallis Gall Midge (*Contarinia quinquenotata*) This tiny white insect places its eggs into the newly formed daylily buds and the growing larvae feed from within the developing flower bud. The damage is manifested mainly

A daylily bud showing the symptoms of *Hemerocallis* Gall Midge.

in daylilies flowering during early midsummer (EM); they show distorted and discoloured tulip-shaped buds which usually start to rot before an actual flower is produced. If opened, small white insects can be seen with a hand lens or microscope. If this midge is suspected or if plants come to you from a garden that it has invaded, then it is advisable to place the plants in a quarantine area. They should remain there for a season with the basal areas dressed with Chlorophos, which should destroy the emerging pupae. Scapes with deformed buds should be cut off at the base and burned. Infestations are worse if there is an abundance of rain in late spring or early summer. In the British Isles the Gall Midge seems to be most prevalent in the south-east of England but is radiating further afield. It has apparently spread from Europe.

Hemerocallis Thrips (*Frankliniella hemerocallis*) This is the most common of the five species of thrips found on daylilies. At its worst it can cause shrivelling and death of the undeveloped flower. Paler coloured daylilies are most often attacked. A useful biological control is *Orius insidious*, a member of the stinkbug family. When all the thrips are devoured this control will then start on mites and other insects. In some climates Hemerocallis Thrips can overwinter in the fan where the inner leaves join the crown.

Slugs and Snails These affect the leaves rather than the flowers, sheltering over winter in the foliage of evergreens and damaging the new soft shoots as they emerge in early spring. They congregate in the middle of mature clumps and are often only discovered when the clump is dug up for division. The populations can be kept down with careful garden hygiene, the use of chemical deterrents or natural predators.

Spider Mite Two-spotted Spider Mites (*Tetranychus urticae*), which are present wherever there is vegetation, suck the chlorophyll from the daylily foliage causing it to turn a dull brown and possibly die. This mite is much more of a problem in hot day climates and where plants are not watered thoroughly. The barely visible insects sometimes cover the leaf surface with a fine webbing. Treatment with a miticide may be necessary.

Tarnished Plant Bug (*Lygus rugulipennis*) The oval adult bugs, which move very quickly, are mottled light green to coppery-brown and 5mm (¼in) long. Their forewings have black-tipped, yellow triangles and from the side the body slants downward to the rear portion of the wings. Nymphs, which are yellow-green with five black dots on the body, look like adults but are wingless. Adults and nymphs pierce leaves and buds and suck plant juices; nymphs are the most damaging. The saliva is toxic and makes buds and pods drop and distorts leaves and shoots. Plants wilt or are stunted and branch tops blacken and die back. Natural predators are minute pirate bugs or damsel bugs when available. If necessary spray with Rotenone or Sabadilla. Spraying soap and oil in the nymph stage while the pest cannot fly is also effective. This bug is prevalent throughout North America.

DISEASES

Bacterial Soft Rot Often called crown rot, this results from damage to the roots or crown, possibly from nematodes, so that bacteria such as *Pythium*, *Phytophthora*, *Rhizoctonia* and *Fusarium*, present in many soils, can penetrate the plant tissue. The foliage, crown and roots are rapidly infected and the plant becomes a mushy, foul-smelling mess. It is difficult to cure once the infection has taken hold but treatment with Streptomycin may help. The rot usually attacks newly planted or freshly divided plants so it is a wise precaution to see that wounds are fully dry before replanting, allowing a new epidermis to form. The rot is also more likely to occur in high heat, humidity and very moist soil and is probably gene-related since it comes down through fairly narrow, but distinct breeding lines. It is far less of a problem in colder and cooler climates unless it has already taken hold of a plant received from a nursery in a hot climate. It is strongly recommended that recipients of daylilies from southern United States nurseries or breeders soak the plants in a 10% bleach solution before planting.

Granular Fungal Rot Not usually a problem in European gardens, *Cercospora hemerocallis* tends to attack daylilies that are under stress or possibly do not have genetic resistance to fungi. Starting with a yellow-streaked leaf, mature clumps can suddenly develop a layer of tiny, brownish-black spore sacs. The fungus produces a white, thread-like network that quickly spreads over the crown and the leaves. At the first sign of it, dig up the plant and remove any affected parts, treating the portion remaining in a 10% solution of bleach and sterilize all the surrounding soil.

Leaf Spot This is caused by types of *Botrytis or Colletotrichum* which causes the leaves to turn yellow. Affected leaves should be removed and the daylily sprayed with a fungicide effective against downy mildew.

Leaf Streak Disease (*Aureobasidium microstictum*) This is a fungal infection and widespread wherever daylilies are grown. It is often overlooked or attributed to leaf senescence or poor nutrition. It enters the leaf at a point of damage and is first seen as slightly darker green translucent spots which gradually become necrotic, then chlorotic and, finally radiate out as streaks all over the leaves. There are no controls but attention to garden hygiene and good cultivation, helps to make the daylilies more resistant.

Iris Leaf Spot (*Mycosphaerella macrospora*) This fungus overwinters on leaf debris and infects the new season's foliage growth. It becomes apparent first as brown lesions which develop greyish centres. These increase in size until the leaf withers. If unchecked, the vigour of the plant soon deteriorates. To combat this fungus, remove leaf debris at the beginning of winter and apply a copper fungicide spray when the new season's growth is 20–30cm (8–12in) high. Repeat dosage at fortnightly intervals is advisable.

Spring Sickness No one knows with any certainty what causes the problems collectively called 'spring sickness'. It can manifest itself as a twisted or pleated effect on the inner leaves. In a mild case, these may straighten and grow properly rather than turn brown and die, and scapes will appear during the current summer. But if the daylily is severely affected there will be no bloom scapes in the current year since the scape tips cannot push their way through the mushy, rotted leaves and the plant ceases to grow. Spring sickness usually occurs in regions in which there are several cycles of spring freeze/thaw conditions. A similar effect can be caused by insect larvae eating the new spring growth inside the crown rather than bacterial invasion. The new growth emerges light green with yellower edges that can be jagged, twisted or kinked.

APPENDIX I

GLOSSARY

Anther The part of the flower at the top of the stamen containing the pollen.

Anthesis The action or period of opening of a flower.

Aneuploidy The condition of having abnormal, missing or extra chromosomes.

Attenuate Long, drawn out.

Bridge Plants Seedling daylilies with qualities desired in breeding but not themselves worthy of introduction. Also called Breeder's Plants.

Cambium The plant cell layer through which the sap is conducted.

Chimaera A plant in which two separate kinds of tissue exist or, in daylilies, a daylily consisting of mixed diploid and tetraploid tissue.

Chromosomes Microscopic, rod-like structures found in the nucleus of all living cells. They contain the numerous genes that control the development and appearance of the plant.

Cultivar Named variety of a plant that is different from the species and usually an improvement on it. Cultivars of daylilies, as with most other plants, do not come true from seed so propagation by asexual means is necessary.

Distal The point furthest from the centre of the flower or from the axis of a leaf (eg the petal or leaf tip).

Distichous Disposed in two vertical rows, particularly leaves.

Diurnal In daylilies, a plant that produces flowers that open in the morning or during the day.

Dominant In hybridizing, characteristics from dominant genes are more likely to be reproduced in a new hybrid than those from recessive genes.

Epidermis The outer layer of cells.

Established In daylilies, after replanting, when a new set of feeder roots has developed so that it can take up the necessary nutrients.

Gametes Sex cells.

Meristem Growing point.

Monocotyledon A plant whose seedlings have a single cotyledon or seed leaf, usually like the adult leaf in contrast with the pair of leaves produced by dicotyledons, which are usually not like that adult leaves.

Nucleus Each living cell has usually one nucleus. This contains the chromosomes.

Nocturnal In daylilies, a plant whose flowers open during the late afternoon, early evening or night and, depending on when they open, close between late morning and early afternoon the next day.

Pistil The female reproductive organ of a flower.

Papillae Glands or protuberances on the surface of a plant.

Periclinal Cell walls that run in the same direction as the circumference of the shoot at a growing point.

Perianth The external envelope of a flower.

Photo tropic Curving growth towards the light.

Ramet A daylily fan.

Recessive In hybridizing, recessive genes are subordinate to dominant genes. However, characteristics from recessive genes often reappear in the next generation.

Selfing or **Self Pollination** The act of artificially fertilizing a plant with its own pollen.

Self-incompatible A plant that is unable to produce seeds with its own pollen.

Senescence The ageing process.

Stamen The male, pollen-producing part of the flower.

Stigma The sticky top of the pistil that receives the pollen.

Stomata On the green parts of plants, pores that 'breath'.

Tissue Culture Asexual propagation or cloning of plants by rapidly increasing cell growth under sterile laboratory conditions.

Vacuoles Liquid-filled spaces between the cells in the epidermis.

Viability The ability of a seed to germinate.

APPENDIX II

READING ABOUT DAYLILIES

American Hemerocallis Society, *Beginners Handbooks, Checklists* and *Journals*

British Hosta & Hemerocallis Society, *Bulletins*

Davis, B.A., *Daylilies and How to Grow Them* (Tupper and Love, 1954)

Eddison, Sydney, *A Passion for Daylilies* (Harpur Collins, 1992)

Erhardt, W., *Hemerocallis Daylilies* (Batsford, 1992, a translation of *Hemerocallis Taglilien* Eugen Ulmer, 1988)

Gatlin, Frances, ed. *Daylilies – A Fifty Year Affair* (American Hemerocallis Society, 1995)

Genders, R., *Scented Flora of the World* (Robert Hale, 1977)

Gregory, Ken & Kay, *Eureka Daylily Reference Guide* (published annually)

Hansen, Ra, *Lady Bug Daylilies* (1977/8)

Hansen, Richard & Stahl, Friedrich, *Perennials and Their Garden Habitats* (Cambridge University Press, 4th ed., 1993)

Hill, Lewis & Nancy, *Daylilies, The Perfect Perennial* (1991)

Kitchingman, R.M., *Some Species and Cultivars of Hemerocallis* (The Plantsman, Vol. 7, Part 2, 1985)

Lacey, Stephen, *The Startling Jungle* (Viking, 1986)

Munson, R.W. Jr., *Hemerocallis, The Daylily* (Timber Press, 1989)

Perry, Amos, *Amos Perry's Diary 1894-1945* (The Hardy Plant Farm, 1946)

Stout, A.M., *Daylilies* (Macmillan, New York, 1934, reprinted 1986)

Thomas, G.S., *The Art of Planting* (Dent, 1984)

Thomas, G.S., *Perennial Plants* (Dent, 3rd ed., 1990)

Track, Norman S., *Daylilies* (Hawkeye, 1996)

APPENDIX III

DAYLILY SOCIETIES

THE BRITISH HOSTA AND HEMEROCALLIS SOCIETY
Lynda Hinton,
Hon. Membership Secretary,
Toft Monks, The Hythe,
Rodborough, Stroud Common,
Gloucestershire, GL5 5BN.

THE AMERICAN HEMEROCALLIS SOCIETY
Pat Mercer, Executive Secretary,
PO Box 10, Dexter, GA31019.

THE HEMEROCALLIS SOCIETY OF AUSTRALIA
Helen Reid, 16 Farnsworth Street,
Sunshine, Victoria 3020.

HEMEROCALLIS EUROPA
Elke Brettschneider, General Secretary
and Treasurer, Schlomerweg 22, 41352
Korschenbroich, Germany.

FACHGRUPPE HEMEROCALLIS
Gesellschaft der Staudenfreunde,
Norbert Graue, Stockflethweg 208,
22417 Hamburg, Germany.

APPENDIX IV

WHERE TO SEE DAYLILIES

UNITED KINGDOM
Antony House National Trust,
Torpoint, Cornwall, PL11 2QA.
Apple Court (Diana Grenfell & Roger
Grounds), Hordle Lane, Hordle,
Lymington, Hampshire, SO41 0HU.
Susan Beck, 25 Bowling Green Road,
Cirencester, Gloucestershire,
GL7 2HD. Tel. 01285 6533778.
Bressingham Gardens (The Dell
Garden), Diss, Norfolk, IP22 2AB.
Derek & Brenda Carver,
2 Bird's Hill Rise, Oxshott, Surrey.
Tel. 01372 842448. By appointment.
Epsom & Ewell Parks Department,
Borough of Epsom & Ewell, Surrey.
(Older varieties). Contact Derek
Carver for an appointment.
Golden Acre Park, Leeds Leisure
Services, Bramhope, Leeds, Yorkshire.
(Older varieties).
Little Hermitage (Jan & Andy Wyers),
St. Catherine's Down, Ventnor,
Isle of Wight, PO38 2PU.
Tel. 01983 730512. By telephone
or written appointment.
Longstock Park Gardens
Stockbridge, Hampshire
(Check 'Yellow Book' for open days)
The Nursery Further Afield
(Gerald Sinclair), Evenly Road,
Mixbury, Brackley, Northamptonshire,
NN13 5YR. Tel. 01280 848808.
(Mainly older varieties).
**The Royal Horticultural Society's
Garden**, Wisley, Woking, Surrey.
Sherborne Gardens (John &

Pamela Southwell), Litton, Bath,
Avon, BA3 4PP.
Tel. 01761 241220.
Ventnor Botanic Garden,
Undercliff Drive, Ventnor, Isle of
Wight, PO38 1UL. Tel. 01983 55397.

AUSTRALIA
Daylily Display Centre (John & Kim
Spandley), Bundaberg, Gin Gin Road,
Maroondan via Gin Gin, Queensland
4671. Tel. 071 574353.
Greta's Garden, 12 Bruce Road, Wattle
Grove, Perth, Western Australia.
Kiwarrak Nursery (Raelie Douglas),
Carey's Road, Hillville, New South
Wales 2430.
Mead's Daylily Gardens (Neil, Debbie
& Monica Mead), 264 Learoyd Road,
Acacia Ridge, Queensland 4110.
Tel. 07 3273 8559.
Mountain View Gardens, Policeman's
Spur Road, Maleny, Queensland 4552.
Tel. 07 54 94 2346.
Rainbow Ridge Nursery (Graeme &
Helen Grosvenor, John Taylor), 8
Taylor's Road, Dural, New South
Wales 2158. Tel. 02 9651 2857.
Tempo Two (Barry & Leslie Blyth), PO
Box 60A, Pearcedale, Victoria 3912.
Tel. 059 786980.

BELGIUM
Cor Govaerts, Broechemsesteenweg
330, B-2560 Nijlen.
Tel. 32 34 81 78 13. By appointment.
Francois Verhaert, Fatimalaan 14,

B-2243 Zandhoven. Tel. 03 484 5086.
By appointment.

CANADA
Erikson's Daylilies (Pam Erikson),
24642-51 Avenue, Langley, BC,
V2Z 1H9. Garden open June and July.
Flowering Perennials (Nancy Oakes),
Iona, Prince Edward Island.
Les Jardins Osiris, 818 Rue Monique,
c.p. 489, St-Thomas, Quebec, JOK 3O1.
Strong's Daylilies (Maureen Strong),
Box 11041, Stoney Creek,
Ontario, L8E 5C7.
**We're In The Hayfield Now Daylily
Garden** (Henry Lorrain & Doug
Lycett), 4704 Pollard Road, Orono,
Ontario, LOB 1MO.

GERMANY
Botanischer Garten, Finkenrech,
Tholeyer Strasse, D-66571,
Eppelborn-Dirmingen.
Homburger Staudengarten (Anja
& Matthias Thomsen-Stork),
Homberger 14, Waldshut-Tiengen,
D-7976.
Schoeppinger Irisgarten (Werner
Reinerman), Buergerweg 8, D-48624.
Schoeppingen Taunusgarten
(Harald Juhr), Am Rheingauer Weg 7,
D-65719, Hofheim/Walau.

ITALY
Casa Rocca (Marc King) 14030 Rocca
d'Arazzo. Tel. 39 141 40 8591.

NEW ZEALAND

Bay Bloom Nurseries, PO Box 502, Tauranga. Tel. 07 578 9902.

Daylily Magic, RD8, Hookville Road, Waimate, South Canterbury. Tel. 03 689 5807.

Manurewa Botanic Garden, Manurewa, Auckland.

Puketapu Iris Gardens, 226 Corbett Road, RD3, New Plymouth. Tel. 06 755 2900.

Kathy Rae, 62 Tuapiro Road, RD1, Katikaki. Tel. 07 578 9902.

Summergarden, PO Box 890, Whangerei. Tel. 09 435 1759.

Taunton Gardens, Allandale, RD1, Lyttleton, Christchurch. Tel. 03 329 9746.

Tikitere Gardens, PO Box 819, Rotorua. Tel. 07 345 5036.

SWITZERLAND

Baumschulen/Staudengartnerei (Hansuli Friedrich), CH-8476, Stammheim.

Rolf Hegi & Peter Aerne, Schafberg, CH-6122, Menznau.

UNITED STATES OF AMERICA

There are far more good daylily gardens in the United States than space permits me to include. Full details from the American Hemerocallis Society.

Belvoir Gardens (Bobbie & Pat Bennett), 7910 Manor House Drive, Fairfax Station, Virginia 22039. Tel. 703 321-1456.

The Betty Jernigan Memorial Historical Daylily Garden, Fayetteville Botanical Gardens, 536 North Eastern Boulevard, Fayetteville, North Carolina 28305. Tel. 910 486-0221. (Collection of Stout Medal Winners, historical daylilies dating from the late 1800s, modern hybrids).

Brooklyn Botanical Gardens (Michael A. Ruggiero), Propagation Range, Bronx New York 10458-5126. Tel. 718 817-8047. (Collection of Arlow B. Stout's daylilies).

Countryside Daylilies (Ottis Houston & Eddy Scott), 6800 NE 65th Street, High Springs, Florida 32643. Tel. 904 752-4654.

Covered Bridge Gardens (Harry L. & Betty Harwood), 1821 Honey Run Road, Chico, California 95928-8850. Tel. 916 342-6661.

Crochet Daylily Garden (Clarence & Beth Crochet), PO Box 425, Prairieville, Louisiana 70769. Tel. 504 673-8491.

Denver Botanic Garden (David Freeman), 909 York Street, Denver, Colorado 80206. Tel. 303 331-1000. (Heritage Daylilies).

Four Seasons Daylily Garden (Johnny & Linda Daniel), 187 College Street, Yatesville, Georgia 31097. Tel. 706 472-3124.

Grace Gardens (Tom & Cathy Rood), 1064 Angus Road, PennYan, New York 14527. Tel. 315 536-2556.

The John Lambert Memorial Garden, Pullen Park, Raleigh, North Carolina.

Richard & Gail Korn, Route 1, Box 164, Wayne, Nebraska 68787. Tel. 402 375-3615.

Mauna Kea Daylily Gardens (Guy & April Pearce), 7 & E (Hawaiian Acres), Kurtistown, Hawaii 96760. Tel. 808 966-6693.

Oakes Daylilies (William, Stewart & Ken Oakes), 8204 Monday Road, Corryton, Tennessee 37721. Tel. 423 687-3770.

Pine Branch Daylily Garden (Bobby & Aileen Castlebury), Route 1, Box 93, Brookston, Texas 75421. Tel. 903 883-5351.

Sandhills Horticultural Gardens, Sandhills Community College, Pinehurst, North Carolina. (Open during daylight hours throughout the year).

Karen & Glen Schultz, 15643 E 35th Place, Aurora, Colorado 80011-1323. Tel. 303 366-9689.

Singing Oaks Garden (James & Peggy Jeffcoat), PO Box 56, 1019 Abell Road, Blythewood, South Carolina 29016-0056. Tel. 803 786-1351.

Soules Gardens (Clarence & Marjorie Soules), 5809 Rahke Road, Indianapolis, Indiana 46217-3677. Tel. 317 786-7839.

Sunnyridge Gardens (John & Geraldine Courturier), 1724 Drinnen Road, Knoxville, Tennessee 37914. Tel. 904 752-4654.

Suburban Gardens (Earl & Barbara Watts), 60 Serene Meadows Drive, Hattiesburg, Mississippi, 39402. Tel. 601 268-3884.

Valley of the Daylilies (Dan & Jackie Bachman), 3507 Glen Gary Lane, Cincinatti, Ohio 45236. Tel. 513 984-0124.

APPENDIX V

WHERE TO BUY DAYLILIES

Some of the daylilies described in this book are new and may still only be available in their country of origin. However, many of the nurseries listed can export daylilies anywhere in the world. They have all been inspected by the relevant authorities and they will send a phytosanitary certificate with all plants ordered. However, on top of a charge for this certificate, there will be postage and upon receipt by the customer, VAT and Customs Duty will also have to be paid.

UNITED KINGDOM

A'la Carte Daylilies, Little Hermitage, St Catherine's Down, near Ventnor, Isle of Wight, PO38 2PU.

Apple Court, Hordle Lane, Hordle, Lymington, Hampshire, SO41 0HU.

Bressingham Gardens (The Plant Centre), Diss, Norfolk, IP22 2AB.

David Austin Roses Ltd., Bowling Green Lane, Albrighton, Wolverhampton, West Midlands, WV7 3HB.

Glebe Garden Nursery, Kidnapper's Lane, Leckhampton, Cheltenham, Gloucestershire, GL5 30NR.

Goldbrook Plants, Hoxne, Eye, Suffolk, IP21 5AN.

Kelways Ltd., Langport, Somerset, TA10 9EZ.

The Nursery Further Afield, Evenly Road, Mixbury, Brackley, Northamptonshire, NN13 5YR.

Rosewood Nurseries, 70 Deansway Avenue, Sturry, near Canterbury,

Kent CT2 0NN. Tel. 01227 711071.
By appointment.

ARGENTINA

RMD (Margaret Deane), Avda, 562 7A (1120), Buenos Aires.

AUSTRALIA

Daylily Display Centre (John & Kim Spandley), Bundaberg, Gin Gin Road, Maroondan via Gin Gin, Queensland 4671. Tel. 071 574353.

Greta's Garden, 12 Bruce Road, Wattle Grove, Perth, Western Australia.

Kiwarrak Nursery (Raelie Douglas), Carey's Road, Hillville, New South Wales 2430.

Mead's Daylily Gardens (Neil, Debbie & Monica Mead), 264 Learoyd Road, Acacia Ridge, Queensland 4110. Tel. 07 3273 8559.

Mountain View Gardens (Scott Alexander), Policeman's Spur Road, Maleny, Queensland 4552. Tel. 07 54 94 2346.

Rainbow Ridge Nursery (Graeme & Helen Grosvenor, John Taylor), 8 Taylor's Road, Dural, New South Wales 2158. Tel. 02 9651 2857.

Tempo Two (Barry & Leslie Blyth), PO Box 60A, Pearcedale, Victoria 3912. Tel. 059 786980.

AUSTRIA

Staudengartnerei Feldweber, Ort im Innkreis 139, A-4974.

Staudengartnerei und Baumschulen (Ing. Gerhild Mattuschka), Emmersdorfer Strasse 86, A-9061 Wolfnitz bei Klagenfurt.

BELGIUM

Cor Govaerts, Broechemsesteenweg 330, B-2560 Nijlen. Tel. 32 34 81 78 13. By appointment.

Francois Verhaert, Fatimalaan 14, Belgium, B-2243 Zandhoven. Tel. 03-484 5086. By appointment.

Gilbert Verswijver, Hoge Weg 111, B-2940m Hoevenen.

CANADA

Erikson's Daylily Gardens, 24642-51 Ave, Langley, BC, V2Z 1H9.

Flowering Perennials, Iona, Prince Edward Island (no export yet).

Les Jardins Osiris, 818 Rue Monique, c.p. 489, St-Thomas, Quebec, JOK 3lO.

Kilmalu Farms Daylily Nursery, 624 Kilmalu Road, RR No 2, Mill Bay, BC.

Strong's Daylilies, Box 11041, Stony Creek, Ontario, L8E 5C7.

We're In The Hayfield Now Daylily Garden, 4704 Pollard Road, Orono, Ontario, LOB 1MO.

FRANCE

GAEC de Champagne (Michael Bourdillon et Fils), Soings en Sologne, F-41230.

Iris en Provence, Route de l'Appie, B.P. 53, F-83402 Hyeres. Tel. 04 94 65 98 30. Not open to the public.

GERMANY

Bambus Willumeit Gartenbau GmbH, Nussbaumalle, D-64297 Darmstadt. Tel. 06151-538008. By appointment.

Manfred Beer, Bielasstrasse 27, D-04430 Bohlitz-Ehrenberg. Tel. 0341-4411312. By appointment.

Friesland Staudengarten Uwe Knopnadel, Husumer Weg 16, D-26441 Jever-Rahrdrum.

Schoeppinger Irisgarten (Werner Reinermann), Burgerweg 8, D-48624.

Staudengartnerei Grafin von Zeppelin (Aglaja von Rumohr), D-79295 Sulzburg-Laufen.

Tomas Tamberg, Zimmerstrasse 3, D-12207 Berlin.

NETHERLANDS

M. Joosten, Ruttensepad 7/2, 8313 PM Rutten.

Kwekerij De Border, Oude Benteloseweg 21, NL-7491 EW Delden.

NEW ZEALAND

Bay Bloom Nurseries, PO Box 502, Tauranga.

Daylily Magic, RD8, Hookville Road, Waimate, South Canterbury.

Heritage Horticulture, 124 Woolrich Road, RD8, Hamilton.

Puketapu Iris Gardens, 226 Corbett Road, RD3, New Plymouth.

Kathy Rae, 62 Tuapiro Road, RD1, Katikati.

Summergarden, PO Box 890, Whangerei.

Taunton Gardens, Allandale, RD1, Lyttelton, Christchurch.

Tikitere Gardens, PO Box 819, Rotorua.

SWITZERLAND

Baumschulen/Staudengartnerei (Hansuli Friedrich), CH-8476, Stammheim.

UNITED STATES OF AMERICA

Belvoir Gardens (Bobbie & Pat Bennett), 7910 Manor House Drive, Fairfax Station, Virginia 22039. (General listing).

John & Janet Benz, 12195 6th Avenue, Cincinnati, Ohio 45249. (Own introductions, general listing).

Big Tree Daylily Garden (Kathy Chenet), 777 General Hutchison Parkway, Longwood, Florida 32750-3705. (Own introductions, general listing).

Brookwood Gardens (Leo Sharp), 303 Fir Street, Michigan City, Indiana 46360. (Own introductions, general listing).

Camelot Gardens (Bob Clary), 13900 Bermuda Orchard Lane, Chester, Virginia 23831-5738. (Specializes in Siloams).

Chattanooga Daylily Gardens (Lee & Jean Pickles), 1736 Eagle Drive, Hixon, Tennessee 37343. (Own introductions, general listing).

Coburg Planting Fields (Phillip Brockington & Howard Reeve Jnr.), 573 East 600 North, Valparaiso, Indiana 46383-9727. (Own introductions, general listing).

Cordon Bleu Farms (Steve Brigham), PO Box 2033, San Marcos, California 92079. (General listing).

Countryside Daylilies (Ottis Houston & Eddy Scott), 6800 NE 65th Street, High Springs, Florida 32643.

Covered Bridge Gardens (Harry L. & Betty Harwood), 1821 Honey Run Road, Chico, California 95928-8850. (General listing).

Crintonic Gardens, (Curt Hanson) 11721 County Line Road, Gates Mills, Ohio 44040.

Crochet Daylily Garden (Clarence & Beth Crochet), PO Box 425, Prairieville, Louisiana 70769. (Own introductions, general listing).

Daylily World, (David Kirchhoff & Mort Morss), PO Box 1612, Sanford, Florida 32772. (Own introductions, general listing).

Enterprise Gardens (Dan & Jane Trimmer), 1280 Osteen Road, Enterprise, Florida 32725-9401. (Own introductions, general listing).

Floyd Cove Nursery (Patrick & Grace Stamile), 1050 Enterprise-Osteen Road, Enterprise, Florida 32725-9355. (Own introductions, general listing).

Garden Path Daylilies (Jean Duncan), PO Box 8524, Clearwater,

Florida 34618.

Graceland Gardens (Larry & Cindy Grace), 12860 West US Highway 84, Newton, Alabama 36352. (Own introductions, general listing).

Irongate Gardens (Van Sellers & Vic Santa Lucia), 2271 Country Line Road, King's Mountain, North Carolina 28086. (Own introductions, many Siloams).

Joiner Gardens (Enman & Jan Joiner), 9630 Whitfield Avenue, Savannah, Georgia 31406. (Own introductions, general listing).

Klehm Nursery, 4210 North Duncan Road, Champaign, Ilinois 61821. (Own introductions, general listing).

Ladybug Daylilies (Dan Hansen), 1852 E SR 46, Geneva, Florida 32732. (Ra Hansen's introductions, general listing).

Le Petit Jardin (Ted & Susan Petit), 7185 NW County Road 320, PO Box 55, McIntosh, Florida 32664-0055. (Own introductions, general listing).

The Lily Farm (Jack Carpenter), Route 4, Box 1465, Center, Texas 75935. (Own introductions, general listing).

Marietta Gardens (John, Faye & Elizabeth Shooter), Box 70, Marietta, North Carolina 28362. (Own introductions, general listing).

Mauna Kea Daylily Gardens (Guy & April Pearce), 7 & E (Hawaiian Acres), Kurtistown, Hawaii 96760.

Mercer's Garden (Roger Mercer), 6215 Maude Street, Fayetteville, North Carolina 28306. (Own introductions, general listing).

McRae Hill Top Garden (Benny McRae), 574 McRae Road, Hamilton, Alabama 35570. (Own introductions, general listing).

Oakes Daylilies (William, Stewart & Ken Oakes), 8204 Monday Road, Corryton, Tennessee 37721. (Own introductions, general listing, including spider daylilies).

Pine Branch Daylily Garden (Bobbie & Aileen Castlebury), Route 1, Box 93, Brookston, Texas 75421. (Own introductions, general listing).

Rollingwood Gardens (Jeff & Elizabeth Salter), 21234 Rollingwood Trail, Eustis, Florida 32726. (Own

introductions, general listing).

Roycroft Daylily Nursery, 942 Whitehall Avenue, Georgetown, South Carolina 29440. (Le Fever introductions, general listing).

Stephen's Lane Gardens (Bill & Joyce Reinke), Route 1, Box 136 H, Bells, Tennessee 38006. (Own introductions, including spiders, general listing).

Stover Mill Gardens, 6043 Stover Mill Road, Doylestown, Pennsylvania 18901.

Sunnyridge Gardens (John & Geraldine Courturier), 1724 Drinnen Road, Knoxville, Tennessee 37914. Tel. 904 752-4654.

Dave Talbott, 4038 Highway 17 S, Green Cove Springs, Florida 32043.

Walnut Hill Gardens (Barrett & Lynn Stoll), 999 310th Street, Atalissa, Iowa. (General listing).

Woodside Nursery (Darrel Apps), 327 Beebe Run Road, Bridgeton, New Jersey 08302. (Own introductions, general listing).

INDEX